NEW ZEALAND TEST CRIC

CAPTAINS

From one fine
cricketer to another
I hope you enjoy
this book.
Happy Birthday.
my good friend.
lots of love
Wilson
October 2002

NEW ZEALAND TEST CRICKET
CAPTAINS

MATTHEW APPLEBY

FOREWORDS BY WALTER HADLEE AND STEPHEN FLEMING

REED

Established in 1907, Reed Publishing (NZ) Ltd
is New Zealand's largest book publisher, with over 300 titles in print.

For details on all these books visit our website:
www.reed.co.nz

Published by Reed Books, a division of Reed Publishing (NZ) Ltd, 39 Rawene Rd, Birkenhead, Auckland.
Associated companies, branches and representatives throughout the world.

ISBN 0 7900 0836 X

Designed by Craig Violich
Cover photograph of Stephen Fleming by Andrew Cornaga,
courtesy of Photosport

First published 2002

Printed in New Zealand

CONTENTS

FOREWORDS

Walter Hadlee

I am pleased to be invited to write a foreword to Matthew Appleby's *New Zealand Test Cricket Captains*. I have read the manuscript and found it quite absorbing. It covers the history of New Zealand test cricket for over 70 years from 1930, and, as such, makes a major contribution to our cricket literature. For those interested in cricket statistics, there is a complete record of the performances of the 25 individuals who have had the honour of captaining their country.

The author has been most diligent in his research, with the result being a 'warts and all' presentation of the vastly different personalities. I am proud to have been one of them, especially to lead the 1949 team to England. That was a truly magnificent experience.

Captaining is an art, not easily acquired. For some it is easier than for others. In modern times, with added demands from the media, it can be onerous. But it is probably no more so than 50 or more years ago, when captains were often expected to address large audiences at formal dinners, especially during a tour of England.

One thing has not changed — the responsibility to ensure that all team members play, not only within the laws, but within the spirit of the game we love and cherish so much.

Walter Hadlee

Stephen Fleming

New Zealand cricket has been blessed with a line of great captains. This honourable tradition is one I have always been very conscious of when representing my country.

The earliest New Zealand test captain whom I have had the pleasure to meet is Walter Hadlee, who led the team on the famous 1949 tour of England. Walter, the oldest surviving leader featured in this book, has passed down to following generations a great sense of respect for the captaincy, such is his integrity and dignity as a cricketer and administrator.

I am fortunate to have followed outstanding individuals such as Walter, but like him I am aware of the need to take the game forward in New Zealand. To have our cricket respected worldwide is very important to me.

As a captain and leader my role is concerned with not only the way our team plays but also the style in which we play. What we look to achieve is positive cricket, with a clear emphasis on getting the results that the crowds want to see. The branding we seek to stamp on New Zealand cricket involves a more decisive way of playing, which I am certain will take us forward and make cricket in our country the most entertaining it can be.

Teams are judged by their results and as such I am responsible for the team's performance. Against Australia in 2001/02 we achieved some of the best results so far in my time as captain. However, it is in my nature to analyse, review and debate after play has ended in order to learn from what has happened on the field. So I am always striving to improve both my own and the team's performance.

Having been at the forefront of New Zealand cricket for several years now I know the job can sometimes be daunting, but being tested in different ways makes the successes all the more memorable. I constantly look for new challenges, whether it is improving my batting by playing for Middlesex, or setting new goals by moving province to Wellington. I feel these changes have kept me fresh and given me new focus to carry on taking every opportunity given.

So in a sport in which I've always wanted to achieve recognition, I would like to leave cricket in better shape than when I started, as I'm sure has been the aim of other test captains. Those who went before me did not have the luxury of drawing upon the depth that has been developed in the player base of New Zealand cricket, and there have been many changes over the years in the role of the test-match captain in New Zealand.

This book gives a valuable account recording the formidable tasks the early skippers took on, then up through the glory years of the 1980s under Geoff Howarth to the present day. As such the book forms a history of test cricket in this country and provides an important document for lovers of cricket.

PREFACE

The scope of this book encompasses New Zealand's male test match captains, beginning with Tom Lowry in 1930 and ending with the present incumbent, Stephen Fleming.

To include all New Zealand cricket captains would have quadrupled the size of the undertaking. As it is, 25 men have led New Zealand in tests.

The longest reign — almost ten years — was that of John Reid. Remarkably, Stephen Fleming may pass that record in just a few years — remarkably because of the huge increase in the number of matches played, as well as the higher expectations and the intense media coverage that has generally resulted in the tenure of New Zealand's captains becoming shorter.

In some ways their tenure has become easier, since they now have the help of managers and coaches; in other ways it is more difficult, on account of the increased pressure from the public and media in an age of professional sport.

While researching the book I interviewed most of the captains, beginning with the Christchurch triumvirate of Walter Hadlee, Lee Germon and Graham Dowling. The project began when I talked with Walter Hadlee for CricInfo, the cricket website, as suggested by CricInfo New Zealand editor Lynn McConnell. A piece on my St Andrew's College colleague Lee Germon led to meeting St Andrew's governor Graham Dowling, and the idea of a book came from there. With three men down and 22 to go I was under way.

Acknowledgements

Thanks go to all the captains I spoke to, wrote to and emailed. Also to Don Neely, Lynn McConnell, Stephen Fleming, Peter Sharp, Brian Adams and Walter Hadlee for reading the manuscript or adding information or comments.

A special thank you to TelstraClear for their promotional support.

For use of their archives I thank the National Cricket Museum, *Christchurch Star*, Macmillan Brown Library, Surrey and Somerset County Cricket libraries, and private collector Steve Gilbert.

I would also like to thank Reed Publishing, especially Peter Dowling and Eva Chan; the *Christchurch Star*, especially Nick Tolerton and Bob Cotton; CricInfo, especially Lynn McConnell and Duane Pettet; National Cricket Museum, especially Stan Cowman, Donal Duthie and Adrienne Simpson; Geoff Allott, Stephen Boock, Cran Bull, Alan Burgess, Bevan Congdon, Graham Dowling, Roddy Fulton, Lee Germon, Sam Guillen, Brian Hastings, Johnny Hayes, Jack Kerr, Rod Latham, Paul McEwan, Tony MacGibbon, Vic Pollard, Matt Poore, Mark Priest, John Ward, and John Wright.

ABBREVIATIONS

CCA	Canterbury Cricket Association
GABBA	Woolloongabba (Brisbane)
ICC	International Cricket Council (formerly the Imperial Cricket Conference)
MCC	Marylebone Cricket Club
MCG	Melbourne Cricket Ground
NZBC	New Zealand Broadcasting Corporation
ODI	One-day international
SCG	Sydney Cricket Ground
WACA	Western Australian Cricket Association Ground

1. TOM LOWRY

10 January 1930 – 18 August 1931

Born to the cricketing purple

New Zealand's first test match cricket captain died only 25 years ago. Yet he came from a largely forgotten age of amateurism, audacity, deference and charm. Tom Lowry was a lion-hearted fighter, the man who delivered the national team into the test arena back in 1930 against the might of Harold Gilligan's MCC touring team. Raymond Robertson-Glasgow, perhaps the finest scribe of the times, described Lowry as 'the single most dominant personality in New Zealand cricket between the wars', and certainly by 1930 Lowry was already a legendary figure in New Zealand sport. He was also the bridge between the English cricket establishment and the fledglings down under.

Lowry came from a well-known New Zealand family. His grandfather, also Thomas, was a pioneer settler in the Hawke's Bay area, while his father, T.H. (Thomas Henry) Lowry, owned Okawa Station in Hawke's Bay. T.H. Lowry represented Hawke's Bay in first-class matches in 1889/90. He took 118 wickets at the tiny average of 5.9 in all matches for his province.

Wanganui cricketer H.E.B. Newton, who knew Lowry better than most, recorded how young Tom was 'born to the purple'. Indeed, Lowry's comfortable family background was more reminiscent of the more privileged amateur players of England than that of the shopkeepers, insurance agents and accountants that made up most of the New Zealand team.

In his book *English Cricket*, Christopher Brookes argues that one of the reasons the aristocracy became so involved in cricket was that it gave them a chance to come into contact with a large cross-section of people employed on their estates. By their presence the ruling class were able to impose greater authority over their workers. David Lemmon, in *The Crisis of Captaincy: Servant and Master in English Cricket*, highlights Mike Brearley's view that 'Birth, breeding and superficial attractiveness are dangerous grounds on which to select a leader.' Luckily for egalitarian New Zealand, Lowry fitted the template of the English amateur leader, as well as knowing the game and being able to

T. C. Lowry,
Wellington.

An old Cambridge Blue. While still at Cambridge was selected by M.C.C. to tour Australia and New Zealand in the 1922–23 season. Captained New Zealand team during the 1927 Tour in England, scoring 1,277 runs for an average of 38.69, took 15 wickets and proved that he was still one of the finest cricketers ever produced by New Zealand. Is undoubtedly the best New Zealand captain she has ever had.

Lowry learnt his cricket at Napier High School, and when at Cambridge was captain in his last year. His batting average for Wellington (his home team) last year was 45.00.

Also captained the New Zealand Team during the visit of M.C.C. 1929–30.

T.C. Lowry — New Zealand tour of England brochure, 1931.
Collection Dr Steve Gilbert

motivate others — the main tenets of Brearley's seminal treatise *The Art of Captaincy*.

One of the young Lowry's coaches in Hawke's Bay was former England player Jack Board. Of his own unconventional start in cricket, when he was unearthed by W.G. Grace and invited to debut in a match at cricket's headquarters at the turn of the century, Board once said, 'I did not know where Lord's was. I was only a poor gardener.' As coach of Hawke's Bay from 1910/11 to 1914/15, Board was a major influence on Lowry. A wicket-keeper, Board played 124 games for Hawke's Bay between 1909 and 1914, and in 1910 one of the boys he coached, 12-year-old Tom Lowry, scored an unbeaten run for each year of his age for Board's Colts side against a Veteran's Eleven.

Following tradition Lowry was sent to boarding school, Christ's College in Christchurch, where he captained school teams in 1915 and 1916. Roger Blunt, later secretary of the Cake and Biscuit Alliance in the UK, developed his cricket skills in the teams Lowry captained, and succeeded him as captain for 1917 and 1918.

Lowry narrowly missed action in the First World War, although he trained as a bomber pilot at the end of the war. He made his debut in first-class cricket as a wicket-keeper for Auckland in January 1918, going on to a varied top-class cricketing career.

In 1919 Lowry made his English debut for Henry 'Shrimp' Leveson Gower's Scarborough festival team. In 1921, following in his father's footsteps, he went to Cambridge University, as did his brothers in their turn. In 1922 he scored 572 runs in 15 games for his adopted county, Somerset, and in 1922/23 he toured Australia and New Zealand with Archie McLaren's MCC side. He played twice for Cambridge University and ten times for Somerset, scoring 536 runs, including 81 against the light blues of Oxford University. He won his first Blue in 1923 and was university captain the next year. Lowry scored 1077 runs at

48.95 for Cambridge, Somerset and The Gentlemen that year. Suffering appendicitis prior to his captaincy year meant a slow start for Lowry, but 133 against Northants, who were to take key players Bill Merritt and Ken James from New Zealand cricket a decade later, was the turning point. The season's climax, the Varsity match, resulted in a nine-wicket triumph, Lowry scoring 68 out of 83 during his time at the crease.

Digby Jephson, a Cambridge Blue at the start of the 1890s, and later captain of Surrey, has said, 'The captaincy of Lowry was a perpetual joy to those who understand the old-time game. There was no fuss — no needless shifting of a well-placed field, no hesitation. One could feel in the pavilion the strong magnetic influence of the one man over ten.'

Lowry's eccentricity was already showing through, however. Noticing that Robertson-Glasgow, another character, was playing without socks, he made him bowl all morning.

Although Lowry was an original in many ways, it was P.R. (Randall) Johnson (1880–1959) who pioneered the route from New Zealand to Somerset, making his debut in 1901. Australian-born Sammy Woods, Somerset's captain and a former Australia and England test player, 'was never particular about some of the recruits he enlisted', according to David Foot. Johnson followed his father and uncle to Cambridge University via Eton, having been born in Wellington. On the pitch he wore a silk handkerchief around his neck and a Homburg hat on his head, akin to Lowry's predilection for wearing the Moawhango club cap. Johnson's uncanny foreshadowing of Lowry's career included a trip to Australia and New Zealand in 1902/03 as part of Lord Hawke's team. Hawke had planned to lead the first full tour to New Zealand himself, but stayed at home as his mother was ill. Pelham Warner led the team instead.

Much later, Lowry joined Johnson at Somerset, using the same ruse of pretending to have been born in Wellington, Somerset, rather than near Wellington, New Zealand. John Daniell, Somerset's captain, was keen to recruit young talent from Cambridge University, his alma mater, and Lowry was housed in his Taunton home.

After Board, who taught Lowry technique, Daniell was the next major influence on the young player. Daniell was at Cambridge at the turn of the century, captained Somerset between 1908 and 1912 and between 1919 and 1926, and was also an England rugby international captain and later president of the Rugby Football Union. It is fair to say that Lowry was heavily influenced by the dominating figure of Daniell, reprising everything from his

New Zealand's first test
series opposition at the
Basin, 24 January 1930.
Collection Dr Steve Gilbert

honest plain speaking, to his attitude to professional players, to his wearing of a Homburg hat. Lowry learnt from Daniell's unconventional style, first emulating then surpassing his achievement.

Martin Donnelly, 1937 England tourist, recalled: 'I talked with Tom about his field placing skill. He gave the credit for whatever he had picked up to his old Somerset captain John Daniell.'

In May 1922, Gloucestershire's Walter Hammond had been discovered by Lord Hawke to be Dover-born. Sammy Woods urged his county to play him against Somerset, perhaps thinking of Lowry's deceit.

Over 60 years later Peter Roebuck, an Oxford man, helped Martin Crowe settle in at Somerset in a similar way to Lowry. Crowe shared a house with Ian Botham during his early days with the county. In his history of Somerset, Roebuck described Lowry as an assertive, impossible to intimidate, self-deprecating leader in a thousand, recalling how he once, when 'in his cups', referred to someone important at Lord's as 'an old faggot'.

In December 1925 Lowry toured Australia with New Zealand under Canterbury stalwart Billy Patrick. He made his Wellington debut in December

1926, scoring 90 in 138 minutes against Otago. For six years he captained the province, winning the Plunket Shield three times during this period. He also captained the 1927 tourists to England, scoring 1277 runs at 38.69, including four centuries.

'We hope to do well, but we will not cry if we don't. We are a team, and we are going to pull together as a team,' Lowry told the Bristol *Evening Times* soon after landing in England in April 1927. 'A Cambridge Friend' wrote in the *Evening News*, 'His easy manner covers a powerful personality, and there are few men more capable of creating a contented side. If a touring XI does consistently badly it is because it is not happy, and if it is not happy, look to the captain.' This friend could have been E.W. (Ted) Dawson, H.J. (Jack) Enthoven, R.J.O. (Jack) Meyer or 'Bunny' Austin, an illustrious quartet who were Lowry's contemporaries at university.

Somerset Test Cricketers, a series of 25. Number 11, T.C. Lowry: 'He was both strong, courageous and a born leader as well as being one of the most colourful characters in the whole history of cricket.' *Somerset Cricket Club* (*artist Mike Tarr*)

But it was on 10 January 1930 that Lowry made his biggest mark on world cricket. The *Cricketer Spring Annual* of 1930 reported that: 'In the course of their travels, our cricketers, like Puck, have once again put a girdle around the earth.' For two England teams were playing the colonies that month, Frank Calthorpe's slightly stronger eleven drawing in Barbados while Harold Gilligan's far from representative national side won at Lancaster Park. Gilligan, who was to become father-in-law to future England captain Peter May, was the brother of the better-known Arthur Gilligan, another who skippered England. Arthur would have led the MCC team to New Zealand, but was replaced by Harold because of illness. A third brother, Frank, played cricket for Wanganui for a time, and died there in 1960.

England seemed as overstretched as they had been when they had last attempted to contest two test series simultaneously, in 1891/92 in Australia and South Africa. However, debutant opening bowlers 'The Two Maurices' (as they titled their classic tour book) Nichols and Allom had New Zealand virtually defeated by the end of the first day's sixteenth over. Lowry was lbw to a swinging ball at windy Christchurch for a duck, then wicket-keeper Ken James and well-travelled professional Ted Badcock completed the first part of what were to be pairs. The ignominy had begun when Allom bowled Stewie Dempster with the second ball of the over — which subsequently read: lb w . w w w — completed by the tenth hat trick in tests. 'Big' Maurice, the nickname Allom used to distinguish himself from fellow Cambridge alumni 'Little'

NEW ZEALAND TEST CRICKET CAPTAINS

Maurice Turnbull, was described in *The Two Maurices* as 'whipping the ball back appreciably from the off and making tremendous pace from the pitch'.

Nevertheless, the game was not all over. After a rained-off Saturday, Lowry changed his six bowlers with alacrity on the third day, leaving a first-innings deficit of 69. The Maurices wrote, 'Tom Lowry's captaincy earned our admiration' with 'the sheer wizardry' of his bowling changes and field settings. 'He found Roger Blunt (3/17) to be the bowler for the occasion; then he switched to Badcock and even Curly Page, both of whom took a wicket at once. One's pet shot he turned into a trap.'

The captain, despite being jeered for wearing his beloved Moawhango club cap, went in at 65/3 and gave New Zealand hope of saving the game before Nichols bowled him for 40, to leave England needing 63 in 105 minutes.

A magnificent catch to dismiss Frank Woolley was Lowry's most important contribution to the second test, held at Wellington. New Zealand's surprisingly competitive showing in the draw was followed by disappointment at Auckland when Lowry put England in after two-thirds of the game had been lost to rain.

In the last, specially arranged, match, played at the same venue, Lowry made New Zealand safe with 80, his highest test score.

So Tom Lowry led the first team to play a test wearing the silver fern, having done much of the work to bring New Zealand test status. In 1927 Lowry had imbued an attacking public school approach to the batting and, as he said, had dressed his boys 'in long trousers for the first time'. Lowry's adventurous manner combined with his hands-behind-the-back air of easy nonchalance undoubtedly appealed to the MCC hierarchy, contributing to 1927 tour manager T.D.B. Hay's belief that 'New Zealand only has to apply for test status and it would be granted for the next tour'.

'The most agreeable and pleasant lot of fellows', was how Lowry's team was described, an attitude that survived for almost another half century — when the patronising view of many writers ended as the English cricketers began to lose to the Dominion.

While 1920s England captain Percy Chapman married Lowry's sister Beet in 1925, having met her during May Week at Cambridge in 1921, Lowry married a daughter of knight of the realm and war hero Major-General Sir Andrew Russell. Lowry hit 183 in the Cambridge Freshman's match in the same month that Chapman married. The erstwhile undergraduate hell-raisers met again in an unofficial test in 1931 at Lord's. The pair were renowned for the zest of their social life together. Lowry used to keep wicket by standing behind the stumps after a particularly good night and allow the ball to hit him, after which first slip would come and pick it up and return it to the bowler. During the match at Lord's Chapman made a pair, Lowry a century. According to tour correspondent 'Budge' Hintz, the New Zealanders' greatest ever victory was down to Lowry's 'masterly' captaincy.

The contrast between the friends' fortunes was perhaps a portent for the future. Chapman became a sales rep for a whisky firm, Lowry a successful landowner and racehorse breeder on the Hawke's Bay farm his father had developed. While Chapman died 'a musclebound alcoholic' in 1961 aged 61 (the marriage was dissolved in 1942), Lowry was made of sterner stuff and died a rich man of 78 on 20 July 1978. He and his wife Margot had four children — Ann, Tom, Pat and Carol.

Lowry's other sister married Reg Bettington, the first Australian to captain Oxford University. Bettington took a record 182 wickets for the university between 1920 and 1923. Tom's brother Ralph played rugby for Cambridge, his brother Jim, tennis.

Ian Cromb, who later captained New Zealand, although not in test matches, grew to respect Lowry as 'a great person' on the 1931 tour. 'He was always at his best when the situation was tough. Against Middlesex we lost four wickets quickly and I was preparing to go into bat,' recalled Cromb. 'Tom brushed me

New Zealand in England, 1931. Left to right: H.G. Vivian, A.M. Matheson, R.O. Talbot, I.B. Cromb, J.E. Mills, G.L. Weir, J.L. Kerr. Sitting: R.C. Blunt, M.L. Page (vice-captain), T.C. Lowry (captain), C.F.W. Allcott, C.S. Dempster. Front: K.C. James, W.E. Merritt.
Surrey Cricket Club

aside and went out to do battle against Gubby Allen, whom he regarded with a certain amount of disdain, following some incident that had taken place in a University match some years previously. In his hurry to get to the crease, Tom had forgotten to wear a box and the first ball hit him where the protector should have been. In anger he threw his gear on the ground and rushed off past the startled old gentlemen in the Long Room and put on a large wicket-keeper's box. The next ball he received from Allen he played with his stomach, just like a tank, to the amusement of all those at Lord's.'

The Cricketer portrayed 'Mr Lowry' as 'a most capable and inspiring leader', whose 'experience and his equable temperament, coupled with a sly sense of humour — has marked him out for the job; he did it very well'. The Pelham Warner-edited magazine continued, 'Adopting perhaps the tactics of the old owl in the oak, he may have appeared to nod every now and again, but few caught him out. Many times he went in to stop a gap and did so.'

Lowry's tour of magnitude followed the successful template of 1927, and made £8000 compared to £3300 four years previously. Characteristically, Lowry laughed off the difficulties Depression- and earthquake-hit New Zealand had gone through in raising money for their first test-playing tour.

The weather affected many matches, and ruined the third test. The first test, at Lord's, was a triumph for Lowry's team. Winning the toss and batting, Lowry was caught for one by Walter Hammond, who was known to share Lowry's on-pitch Homburg hat wearing affectation. Halfway through the match at 230 behind, after Les Ames and Gubby Allen had added a record 246 for the seventh wicket, all looked forlorn for the New Zealand team. But Dempster, Lowry's vice-captain, his successor Curly Page and Lowry's former Christ's College schoolmate Roger Blunt batted so well that New Zealand were given two more tests as a reward for sharing the honours with their illustrious opponents.

A month later Lowry's 62 was the top score in an innings and 26-run defeat at the Oval, and two weeks later rain at Old Trafford ended his test career. He moved on to roles as three-time Plunket Shield-winning captain of Wellington, national selector (in 1935/36 and on his own in 1938/39), New Zealand Cricket President (1950/51–1952/53) and Master of the Okawa Stud. The stud closed in 1996 after a century as a mainstay in New Zealand horse racing, and Okawa reverted to cattle and sheep farming.

In its obituary *Wisden* described Lowry as 'an outstanding captain' and a man who 'aimed at winning, not drawing, insisted on absolute punctuality and abhorred waste of time'. Pre-First World War New Zealand captain Dan Reese, who also played for Essex and was another important figure in gaining New Zealand test status, wrote that Lowry was 'always chasing the batsman — he drove rather than led his side'. Arthur Carman, editor of *The Cricket Almanack of New Zealand*, acknowledged that he captained 'more by force of character than persuasion'. The 1931 baggage-man/scorer 'Fergie' Ferguson described him as 'a quiet-spoken individual who could swear like a trooper if it suited him, but very easy to get along with'. Contemporary Jack Cowie described Lowry as the best captain of his career, because he was 'a keen student of the game, he knew what he wanted and set an example. A man of strong personality.'

Named as captain in a team of New Zealand's best players by Arthur Carman, Lowry was an immense figure in the development of New Zealand cricket. The normally circumspect Carman wrote in 1974, 'I would want T.C. Lowry in my team, mainly for his aggressive, dominating captaincy which always sought to have his opponents guessing.'

There was, of course, another side to Tom Lowry. Doyen of New Zealand cricket writers the late Dick Brittenden interviewed 82-year-old Bill Cunningham in 1982, just two years before his death. The most successful bowler on the W.R. Patrick-led tour to Australia in 1925/26 (on which Lowry was wicket-keeper), Canterbury's Cunningham won selection for the ground-breaking Lowry-led tour to England in 1927. He barely played. 'The stories about a difference with Tom Lowry are correct,' Cunningham told Brittenden. 'We were the best of friends in Australia, but he turned against me. To my mind he was prejudiced against anyone from the working class. I was involved in the union movement with Bob McFarlane. Besides, my father came from Ireland and that did not seem to please Tom.' To illustrate his point Cunningham told of how Lowry spoke of Charlie Oliver, another who hardly featured on the tour, as coming from the same district as 'this fellow', waving disparagingly at the nearby Cunningham, who apparently replied, 'At least we didn't steal land from the Maoris.' Both Oliver and Cunningham were rugby players, Oliver a dual international (union and cricket), Cunningham a Canterbury league representative. Oliver attended the same Christchurch primary school (Waltham) as Walter Hadlee, test captain from 1945/46, perhaps a demonstration of how quickly egalitarianism came to New Zealand cricket after the 1939–45 war.

Partway through the June 1931 tour, 'The Sportsman' in *Pearson's Weekly* retold an illuminating tale from Lowry's farming days. 'Tom rode up to one of the hired men and, with just reason, gave him a dressing down for a certain sin of omission in connection with the sheep. Then he paused for a minute to say, "Let me see. You played in the match yesterday and bowled me out with a jolly good ball. If you can bowl that swinger three times in an over you ought to take a lot of wickets." Then he went on with his lecture, winding up with, "If you can't do your job, you'll have to go." '

So on the one hand, 'some averred he occasionally took too rigid a view of the limitations of a player. As he wouldn't suffer fools gladly, he failed to get the best out of a player because he would not humour him.' Others (such as H.E.B. Newton) have said, 'Not only was he capable of controlling the diverse group of men under him, but he was also astonishingly original.' He was 'widely admired for his extensive knowledge of opposing batsmen's strengths and weaknesses, his quickness in picking loopholes in the technique of players not previously encountered, his skilful field placing and his masterly handling of limited bowling resources'.

Jack Kerr, who toured in 1931 and 1937, recalled, 'He was a good captain and he always tried things. He was a bit unorthodox but he knew his way around as far as captaincy went. He was a good cricketer. A hard disciplinarian, he was out to win all the time. He was a biggish man, you knew he was the captain — he was on the job, a good disciplinarian too. Some of us were quite green and English cricket was at its height in those days, but he knew his way round. He was always trying something and really in the game all the time. Not talkative to any extent, but his presence indicated he was in charge. I would say he had a New Zealand accent.'

Contemporary Eric Tindill described Lowry as having 'a great capacity for placing the field when he was captain. I'd give him credit for being clever, astute. He was a bit abrupt. He made the decisions.'

Jack Cowie: 'I didn't know whether it was luck, but things seemed to happen for him.' There were no curfews in those days. 'As far as Tom was concerned we were supposed to be in a fit condition to play the next day.' In 1937 Lowry was manager ('They couldn't find anybody else,' he said) and was also standing in as wicket-keeper, when Cowie, who was bowling, noticed all his slips had moved to the leg side. Said Cowie, 'He didn't ask you; he just told you. He just did these sort of things and a lot of them came off. He had flair and was a thinker. He was a darned good skipper.'

Lindsay 'Dad' Weir agreed: 'I felt he was a captain who often made decisions instinctively and then pulled them off as often as not.'

'His knowledge of English players and conditions was profound — a special and inspiring captain,' wrote Brittenden.

Walter Hadlee recalls that Lowry was 'a big man, used to controlling the situation. I always found him a kindly, well-disposed person. But he was not a great communicator with the younger players. I think he felt that if we were

When I was asked by the authors of this booklet to write a foreword, I was more than pleased to do so—it enables me to do two things—to emphasise the immense good to cricket in the Dominion this tour will do and to wish the New Zealand team the best of good fortune on their tour.

Those stalwarts in New Zealand who control cricket over there have had many anxious moments over the sending of this team and apart from financial worries they were beset at a moment when final negotiations were taking place, with the recent terrible earthquake in Napier, which town incidentally possesses, or possessed, one of the finest wickets in New Zealand. The last M.C.C. Team to visit New Zealand, which I had the honour to captain, was received everywhere with wonderful kindness, and my wish for this team which Tom Lowry is captaining is that they enjoy their tour here as much as we enjoyed ours in (wonderful) New Zealand, and at *the same time have a most successful season.*

4.3.51

A.H.H. Gilligan, MCC tour brochure introduction.
Collection Dr Steve Gilbert

playing for New Zealand, we should know all about it. In fact, we could have done with a bit more help here and there.'

In 1937 Lowry seemed to usurp the duties of the vice-captain, Giff Vivian, by captaining the side when Curly Page was rested, although he was on tour as manager and fill-in player. In 12 matches he managed 409 runs in 1937, compared with 1277 ten years before and 1290 in 1931.

Between the wars New Zealand cricket had grown from obscurity to test match status.

As a man of his times Lowry was one of the pioneers in the internationalisation of Kiwi sport, whose methods linked inextricably to his background, just as those of his land-owning and university contemporaries were. His figurehead role in the three tours to England helped legitimise New Zealand cricket and bring test cricket to the country.

Raymond Robertson-Glasgow wrote that Lowry was 'strong, versatile, courageous, original, a leader in a thousand. His comments on the run of play, had they reached the spectators, would alone have justified the Entertainment Tax. He was a man first and a cricketer second, but it was a close finish.'

Note: The exclusive club of cricketers who have led their nation into its first test match is: Dave Gregory (Australia), James Lillywhite (England), Owen Dunell (South Africa), Karl Nunes (West Indies), Tom Lowry (New Zealand), C.K. Nayudu (India), A.H. Kardar (Pakistan), Bandula Warnapura (Sri Lanka), David Houghton (Zimbabwe) and, the latest to join, in 2000, Bangladesh's Naimur Rahman, who captained his side in a test against India.

2. CURLY PAGE

27 February 1932 – 17 August 1937

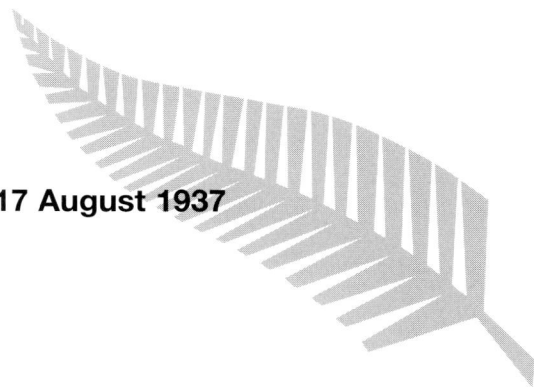

The complete sportsman

One of New Zealand's greatest sporting heroes', for almost a decade the last survivor of New Zealand's first test, the last of the 1927 tourists who laid the way for New Zealand to play tests — that was M.L. (Curly) Page, who in a lot of ways created the mould for many of his successors as their country's cricketing leader.

Yet the wire-haired Cantabrian games player in a thousand almost lost his life before his magnificent service to New Zealand sport had begun. Diagnosed with the symptoms of tuberculosis, Page was sent to the Canterbury hinterlands in the hope that the alpine air would cure his illness. It worked, and Page went on to become a double international and a yardstick for fair play among Kiwi youth for decades to come.

Page was born in Lyttelton, went to school at West Lyttelton Primary, then on to Christchurch Boys' High. He would be followed there by Ian Cromb, who captained New Zealand against Errol Holmes' 1936 tourists, and Walter Hadlee, 13 years Page's junior and an acolyte of Page's abilities and demeanour. Hadlee's sons, then Lee Germon, along with many more test players also learnt their early cricket at the Riccarton school.

At high school Page, the son of a rowing champion, excelled at cricket (captain in 1920/21), tennis, the mile, and rugby. He made his first-class cricket debut in 1921 aged just 18 years 286 days, scoring 27 against the Australians in a 'quiet but sound' manner, in the words of pioneer New Zealand cricket historian and former Canterbury player Tom Reese.

Because of the TB scare Page, the seemingly invincible teenage sporting all-rounder, virtually disappeared from 1923 to 1926. His illness was diagnosed after he collapsed at a cricket match at Sheffield, in Canterbury, and he returned just in time to be selected for the 1927 tour, under Lowry, to England. Page had made 260 runs at 43.3 in the preceding season with his characteristic leg side nudges and wristy late cuts.

M. L. Page,
Canterbury.

Was Captain of Christchurch Boys High School in 1921, has played for Canterbury and New Zealand for several seasons and is a very sound batsman. Played against M.C.C. on last Tour with an average of 37.50. Is a very keen fieldsman and can bowl a decidedly awkward ball. Captain of Canterbury Team, and has a perfect knowledge of the game. Can be depended upon to pull the game round in a crisis.

M.L. (Curly) Page, New Zealand v England, 1931.
Collection Dr Steve Gilbert

'He was somewhat frail compared to Tom Lowry,' recalled team-mate Jack Kerr. 'There wasn't too much of him one way or the other.'

Fragile-looking perhaps, but Page's characteristic determination helped him recover well enough to be a top rugby halfback and to live to the age of 84.

In 1927, on what was New Zealand's first tour to England, Page scored a maiden first-class century in just the second game, against Cambridge University. He and Lowry added 129 in 65 minutes.

In 1922/23 Page had made his Canterbury rugby union debut as a halfback. A lightweight (64 kg) but tough player, he played for the South Island in 1923 but missed selection, probably because of concerns about his health, for the 1924 Invincibles team. He was not selected for the 1925 team to Australia, and when he received a late call-up declined to go. His rugby career peaked in 1928 when he played for the All Blacks against New South Wales at Lancaster Park.

Page made his test cricket debut soon after New Year 1930 at the same venue, in New Zealand's first test, scoring one and 21, and taking the wicket of Maurice Nichols, who had Page caught and bowled in the first innings. Page had earlier hit 'with freedom' 86 in 68 minutes for Canterbury against the tourists on Christmas Day 1929. 'A real captain's innings,' cheered Reese. 'The unusual experience of batting against real fast bowling' was no bar to Page, who made a breakthrough with his first 50 against a national eleven.

The second test emphasised Page's form, with a bright knock of 67 in 103 minutes, including eight fours, and a further 32 in the second innings. In the other two drawn tests Page had just a single innings, and took one wicket, that of Cornford.

New Zealand's next test and Page's finest hour, the match Reese called 'the most famous game in the history of New Zealand cricket', was held at Lord's in

June 1931. Canterbury had won the Plunket Shield under Page and he had become a key part of the national team. In the second innings at Lord's, with New Zealand 130 behind and with eight wickets standing, Page, now Lowry's vice-captain, came in and hit 104, New Zealand's fourth test century. Page recalled that test in 1985, when he was the oldest honoured guest among the New Zealand test captains at the launch of the history of New Zealand international cricket, *Men in White*. Page told the story of how, after he had been 99 not out at lunch, Bill Voce had promised the batsman a single on the resumption, after the pair had shared a lunchtime whisky. Page missed the leg side gift, but soon reached his century anyway. Voce had earlier been practising a prototype of the 'bodyline' (England's captain was Douglas Jardine) and had been admonished for it by the MCC's Pelham Warner.

Page's innings was New Zealand's best at Lord's until 1949. Warner congratulated him, with a 'Well batted, Mr Page', but 12 and three in the next test, both times dismissed by Maurice Tate, were a representative part of a weak batting performance in an innings loss at the Oval. Page made just 990 runs at an average of 26.75 on tour, but as vice-captain he was the natural choice to continue from Lowry as leader when New Zealand played again.

Acting as captain in two matches on tour, Page won respect and admiration by recalling two batsmen on separate occasions, when there was doubt about their dismissals. 'It doesn't matter whether we win all of our games or not,' he is reported to have said. 'But what does matter is whether or not we are to be classed as sportsmen. You'll find out one of these days,' he told some of the younger players in the team, 'that people think more of a good sportsman who loses than a bad sportsman who wins.'

In 1931/32 Page made his best score, 206, to save the match for Canterbury against Wellington at the Basin, although Stewie Dempster dropped him four times before brilliantly catching him after a five-hour innings.

Page succeeded Lowry as New Zealand captain when the South Africans visited that February. At Page's home ground there was an innings loss and the tourists won the other test by eight wickets. He scored just 52 runs in his four test innings.

The English newspapers, which had championed New Zealand as 'a serious competitor, not an inferior to South Africa', were proved wrong. Although 19-year-old Giff Vivian scored a century (and 73 in the second innings) in the second test, the defections of experienced players like Bill Merritt, Roger Blunt, Stewie Dempster, Ian Cromb, Ces Dacre and Ken James to England

The New Zealand team, 1937. Left to right: T.C. Lowry (player/manager), W.N. Carson, J. Cowie, N. Gallichan, W.A. Hadlee, J.R. Lamason, J.A. Dunning, D.A.R. Moloney. W. Ferguson (scorer/baggageman). Sitting: E.W.T. Tindill, A.W. Roberts, H.G. Vivian, M.L. Page (captain), G.L. Weir, J.L. Kerr. Front: W.M. Wallace, M.P. Donnelly.
Collection Dr Steve Gilbert

were to blight New Zealand for the rest of Page's captaincy. Nearly 50 years later the financial benefits of English cricket were to lose New Zealand their captain Glenn Turner, but they were to give the Kiwi players experience that benefited the national cause.

The next summer New Zealand's inexperience as a test-playing nation showed even more. Following the Bodyline series England's Walter Hammond made 227 in the first match, which was a draw, and 336 not out, a test record, in the second. Page then retired from test cricket.

Between 1932/33 and 1935/36 Page scored just 441 runs at 22.05 for Canterbury in 13 sporadic appearances. He scored three 50s in 1936/37, but 'was rarely able to play in the old free-flowing style', according to his obituary in the *Cricket Almanack of New Zealand*. Scores of 73 and 37 against Auckland, 83 in a first-wicket partnership of 235 with Hadlee against Wellington and, most importantly, 50 out of 146 with Vivian against the MCC on his return as captain were quite modest. Yet he won a place on the second test tour to England, this time as captain. Cromb had taken over as leader of both New Zealand and Canterbury, but continuity from 1931, when Page was second in command to Lowry, seemed to swing selectors A.N.C. ('Nessie') Snedden, H.B. (Harry) Whitta, J.J.M. (Jack) McMullan and Lowry. They were possibly influenced by the martinet Lowry, who was a selector in 1935/36 and 1938/39, and more importantly managed the 1937 tourists. Whatever the reason, Page's experience won the day.

There was some bad feeling between the traditionalist Page and the unconventional 'Cranky' Cromb, and Walter Hadlee recalls rushing between their sports shops in Christchurch in an attempt to settle the differences between the pair of prospective test captains. Cromb captained Page during Page's 1936/37 comeback season for Canterbury, insisting that he open the batting, which did not suit Page's technique. Typically, Page made a success of the role, and won the competition to captain the 1937 tour. There was one condition — that Cromb was not in the touring party. After being captain against Errol Holmes' 1935/36 MCC side, Cromb never played for his country again.

Another who fell by the wayside was Canterbury leg theory in-swing bowler Ted Mulcock. That he didn't go to England was down to Page. A Cromb protégé, Mulcock wrote, 'I would probably have gone to England.' But he noted that there was a 'great animosity' between the two, and when Page was recalled to captain New Zealand, Mulcock's chance was gone.

Mulcock's Canterbury career ended when Page became sole selector in 1939/40, and a picture of a surprising ruthlessness in Page emerges. In three club matches Mulcock took a record 36 wickets. 'In spite of this Page stubbornly refused to select me for any further rep games. I am appalled by the fact that I so consistently bowled with such heart-breaking lack of real success against Page's Old Boys,' the gentle Mulcock wrote. 'Never at any time was I able to impress Curly in anything. To him I was just an upstart, a simpleton who lacked the character and skill to be a good cricketer. In my cricket career this was the rock on which I perished.'

Stewie Dempster was another who, like Page, played in New Zealand's first test. Dempster was appointed captain of Leicestershire in 1936, succeeding Ewart Astill, who broke the taboo of all-amateur captaincy for county teams. If Dempster had not gone to England to play for Julien Cahn, with a New

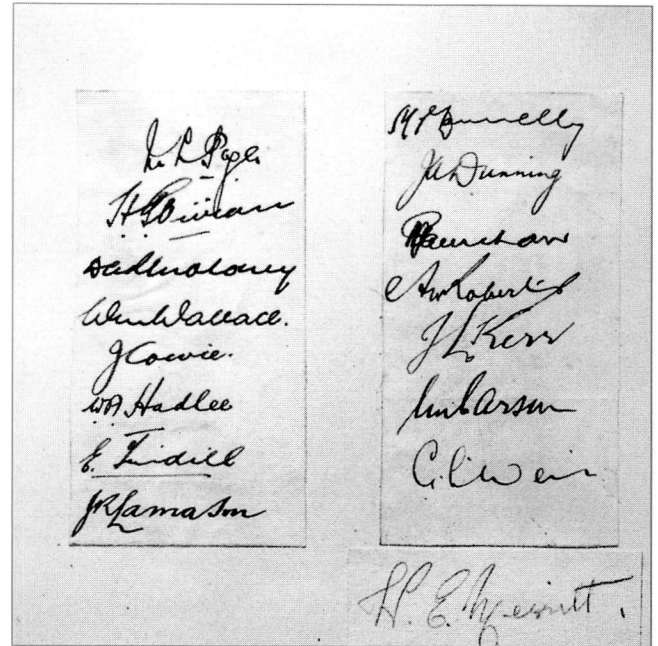

An autograph sheet from the 1937 tour of England: Curly Page, Giff Vivian, Sonny Moloney, Merv Wallace, Jack Cowie, Walter Hadlee, Eric Tindill, Jack Lamason, Martin Donnelly, Jack Dunning, Norm Gallichan, Albie Roberts, Jack Kerr, Bill Carson, Lindsay Weir and Bill Merritt.
Collection Dr Steve Gilbert

The New Zealand team in England, 1937. Left to right, back: W. Ferguson (scorer/baggageman), D.A.R. Moloney, J.A. Dunning, J.R. Lamason, W.A. Hadlee, N. Gallichan, J. Cowie, W.N. Carson, T.C. Lowry (player/manager). Seated: J.L. Kerr, G.L. Weir, M.L. Page (captain), H.G. Vivian (vice-captain), A.W. Roberts, E.W.T. Tindill. Front: M.P. Donnelly, W.M. Wallace. *Surrey Cricket Club*

Zealand record test average of 65.73 that remains intact, he may have been chosen as test captain ahead of Page.

After more than four years without a test, New Zealand had six test debutants in 1937, including future skippers Walter Hadlee and Merv Wallace. Brittenden wrote that Page 'had a hard row to hoe that summer'. It took all New Zealand's defiance to hang on for a draw at Lord's in the first test. Merv Wallace had his best test as a batsman, scoring what Jack Hobbs described as 'adventuresome' 50s in each innings, but Page scored just nine and 13, both times falling to Walter Robins.

They lost the next match at Old Trafford by 130 runs, after Jack Cowie had taken 10/140 in the match. Walter Hadlee made his best test score to date, which was to stand for ten years. New Zealand played just two tests in that time, and it was to be almost nine years before Hadlee had the chance to step into the shoes of Page.

Gloucestershire's Tom Goddard took 6/29 as New Zealand chased 265 in 245 minutes. Also in the England team were Goddard's county team-mates Walter Hammond and Charlie Barnett, who detested each other. Hammond also loathed Ces Dacre, New Zealand's Gloucestershire representative of the thirties. In contrast, the Kiwis were a harmonious group, and were to grow more so under Hadlee after the war.

The Cricketer recorded that, 'Page must be regarded as a decidedly observant and admirable captain. Therefore it is curious — and worth indicating — that he has never attempted to establish anything like a regular order of going in for his New Zealand side.' Six batsmen were moved around in the first test and three in the second. Page tinkered with the order in 18 of the 27 first-class games on tour.

The last test, at the Oval, was drawn. Page finished his test career, at the age of 35, with a 50, but pulled a muscle fielding and had to hand over the captaincy to Giff Vivian. During the tour Lowry had covered for Page when he rested, rather than Vivian, perhaps showing the power behind Page's leadership.

The right-hander had played 86 games in over a decade for the New Zealand team. A match against South Australia and, during the war, two army games ended his career.

The stalwart's last tour brought 666 runs at 22.2, and included a single century, 109 against Nottinghamshire, when he added 108 for the sixth wicket with his old leader Lowry.

After ably selecting the Canterbury side in 1938/39 Curly Page later worked in E. Reece and Company's sports shop and for ABC Cables. He and his wife Phyllis had two children.

Wisden said of Curly Page, 'He handled his bowling and conducted the general duties of captaincy in a manner that never warranted criticism. His batting however fell from grace mainly because every time he went to the wicket his side was badly placed. He was rarely able to play in his old free flowing style.'

Jack Kerr recalled, 'He was a different personality altogether to Tom [Lowry]. Not so aggressive really. He was a thoughtful captain, but he captained the side more by example, while Tom had a presence on the field. But he could hold his own when it came to talking cricket — there's no doubt about that.'

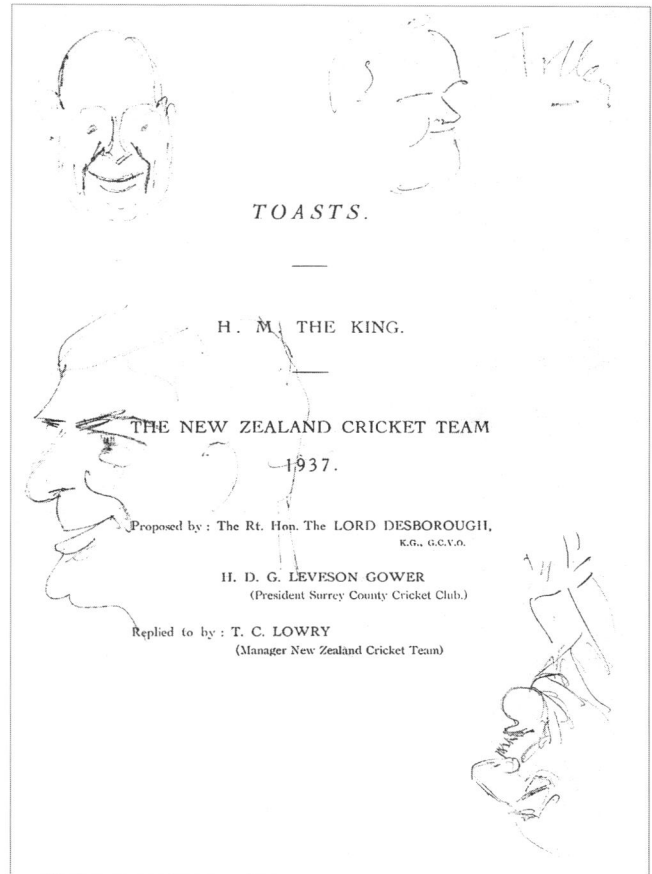

TOASTS.

H. M. THE KING.

THE NEW ZEALAND CRICKET TEAM
1937.

Proposed by : The Rt. Hon. The LORD DESBOROUGH,
K.G., G.C.V.O.

H. D. G. LEVESON GOWER
(President Surrey County Cricket Club.)

Replied to by : T. C. LOWRY
(Manager New Zealand Cricket Team)

Original sketches by Tom Webster on the occasion of the 1937 British Sportsman's Club Luncheon at the Savoy. 'We will try to play as brightly as we can, but we are not going to sacrifice any game at this level to that end,' said captain Curly Page. The cartoons include Leveson Gower and Tom Lowry.
Collection Dr Steve Gilbert

A trusted willow after an unbroken partnership of 46 years. Curly Page retired this bat in 1931 after making 104 at Lord's in the drawn first test. Page had the bat signed by every county player with whom he played on the rest of the tour. The photograph was taken for the Canterbury Cricket Association's anniversary in 1977.
Christchurch Star

'Page was a modest man, almost embarrassingly so,' Dick Brittenden wrote. 'Always a good winner, always a good loser.' An enlightening tale regarding Page's self-effacing nature relates to his greatest moment as a cricketer. After Page had scored a century at Nottingham Walter Hadlee, at the other end, marched down the wicket to shake his captain's hand in congratulation. 'A tip of the cap would have done,' said the bashful Page.

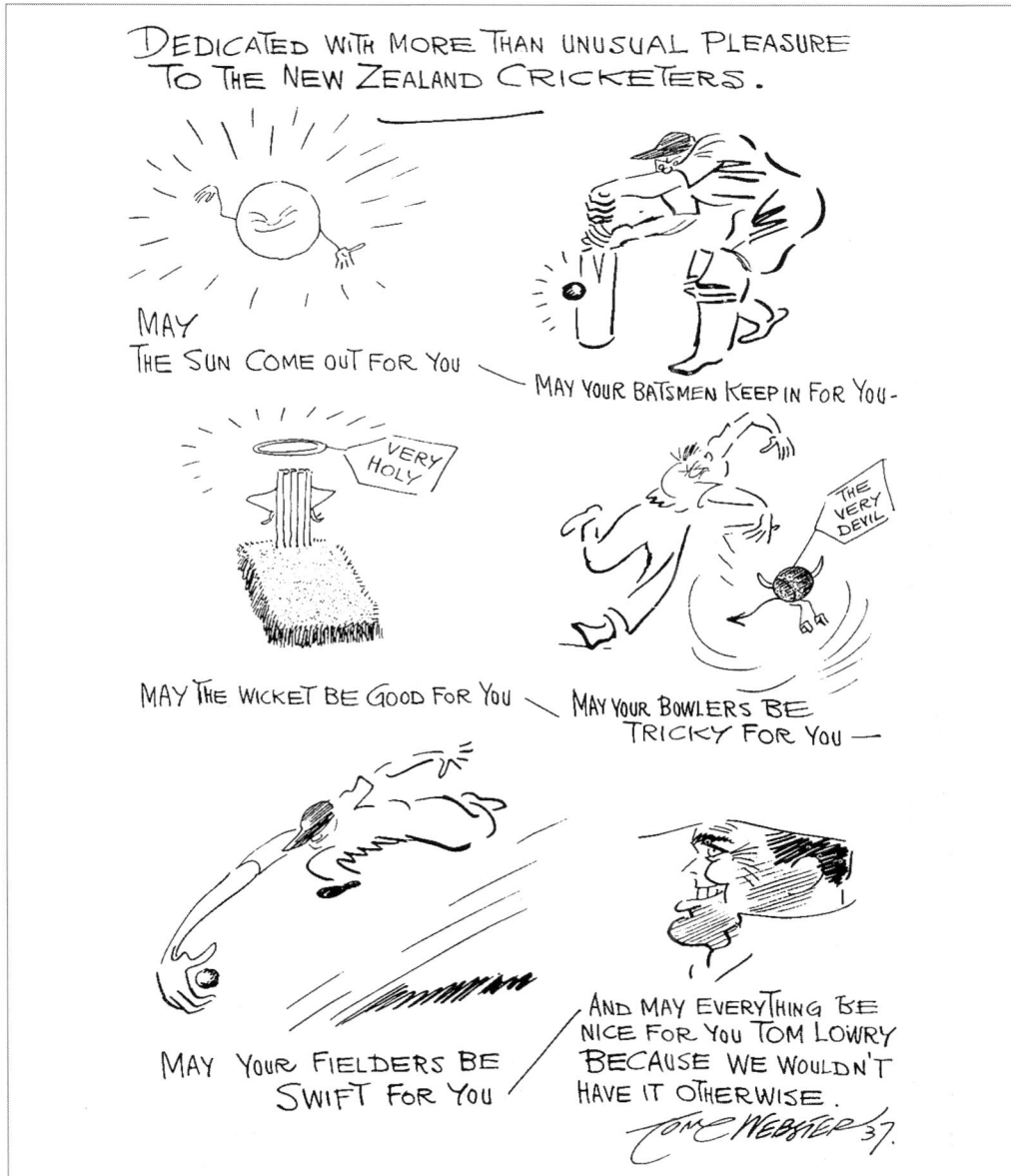

DEDICATED WITH MORE THAN UNUSUAL PLEASURE TO THE NEW ZEALAND CRICKETERS.

MAY THE SUN COME OUT FOR YOU

MAY YOUR BATSMEN KEEP IN FOR YOU-

VERY HOLY

THE VERY DEVIL

MAY THE WICKET BE GOOD FOR YOU

MAY YOUR BOWLERS BE TRICKY FOR YOU —

MAY YOUR FIELDERS BE SWIFT FOR YOU

AND MAY EVERYTHING BE NICE FOR YOU TOM LOWRY BECAUSE WE WOULDN'T HAVE IT OTHERWISE.

TOM WEBSTER 37.

Luncheon menu, 6 May 1937.
Collection Dr Steve Gilbert

Father of the post-war game

Walter Hadlee never played for a winning test team. Yet it could be said that he had more influence on the future success of New Zealand cricket than his record of six draws and two defeats as captain suggests. Record public interest after the lean war years meant that between 1945/46 and 1950/51 the nation toured and hosted England, as well as playing their first test against Australia. Hadlee not only led his country with his 'grand personality', he was also made an OBE for services to cricket. Sons Dayle, Richard and Martin were also born during this time.

Hadlee can reasonably be called the grandfather of the modern game in New Zealand, having filled most of the top roles in the game. He was awarded a CBE in 1978, his final year as chairman of the New Zealand Cricket Board of Control, while his son Richard went one better in 1990 when he received a knighthood. At the time Richard Hadlee held the world record for wicket-taking in tests, but Walter had contributed just as much in his half a century connection with New Zealand cricket.

Christchurch Boys' High School, the nurturer of many a future test player, was where young Walter Hadlee was educated. He was a keen student of the game, assiduously taking notes and listening obsessively, but a key moment in his development as a cricketer occurred when Curly Page, Ian Cromb and Bill Merritt attended school assembly before embarking on the 1931 tour to England. Hadlee later wrote, 'with pride we bade farewell to the three old boys'. He recalls this formative event with clarity even today; such was its influence on his desire to play for New Zealand.

The most notable part of Hadlee's career, particularly as a test captain, was his leadership of the 1949 tour to England. It was just the fourth tour there, and only the third on which tests were played, after Tom Lowry's 1931 team and Page's 1937 squad of 15. Lowry's team included Page, and Page's, in turn, included 21-year-old Hadlee. Thus, the national captain emerged as part of a natural progression. Lowry had been educated at Cambridge and played for Somerset, Page was his vice-captain and heir apparent, while Hadlee was the most experienced and best qualified player to captain the side after the war.

Unfortunately, the 1945/46 Australians trounced the New Zealanders, bowling them out for just 42 and 54 in the only test between the two countries up to 1973/74. Because of the war the team was inexperienced, six making their test debuts, although they didn't know it at the time as the Imperial Cricket Conference (the forerunner of the International Cricket Council, or ICC) did not ratify the match as a test until Australian pressure brought about recognition in March 1948. Thirty-year-old Hadlee was the natural choice as captain. He had made his New Zealand debut in March 1936 and was a successful Canterbury skipper, leading the province to the 1948/49 Plunket Shield during his 23 matches as provincial captain. Twelve of these were won. A week before the test, Hadlee made 198 for Otago against the Australians at Carisbrook, still the highest score by a New Zealand batsman against an Australian team.

Walter Hadlee at Eastbourne, 14 April 1949.
Collection Dr Steve Gilbert

Hadlee won the toss and batted on the damp pitch, hoping it would get worse for the Australians. The last eight New Zealand wickets fell after lunch, for just five runs. Hadlee commented simply, 'We failed and that is all there is to be said.' In the second innings, after the Australians had moved in fits and starts to 199/8 declared, Hadlee was bowled by Keith Miller for three, and the team, five of whom were not to play for New Zealand again, fell in 32 overs and two balls.

In a pre-tour guide for the 1949 New Zealanders, Peter West commented, '— from all accounts, Hadlee will be a splendid captain, thoughtful and sagacious'. One of these accounts was undoubtedly that of Joe Hardstaff senior, who had coached in Auckland. 'He is a captain with a thorough knowledge of the game. He will make an ideal skipper in England and a good

The New Zealand team in England, 1949. Left to right, back: J.H. Phillipps (manager), F.B. Smith, T.B. Burtt, C. Burke, G.F. Cresswell, G.O. Rabone, H.B. Cave, J.A. Hayes, J.R. Reid, F.L. Mooney, W.A. Watts (scorer). Front: B. Sutcliffe, V.J. Scott, W.M. Wallace (vice-captain), W.A. Hadlee (captain), J. Cowie, M.P. Donnelly.
Surrey Cricket Club

example to younger players both on and off the field.' At the time Hadlee had more centuries (13) than any other player in New Zealand, one of which had been scored in the one-off test against England in Christchurch in March 1947. This was scheduled as a three-day match, but after Hadlee and Bert Sutcliffe added 133 for the first wicket in 116 minutes to begin the match, rain washed out the last day. Even an added day, the fourth, was rained off.

Hadlee planned the tour to England meticulously. He saw a cricket match 'as a kind of balance sheet'. Hadlee's 'remarkable gift for prognostication' came into play here. 'I set us a number of team targets. Briefly they were:

1. We were to play 32 first-class matches. I wanted 16 wins.
2. 30 centuries.
3. We would play about 400 innings. Run-outs were akin to economic waste in business and must happen only in the event of: (a) a direct hit from a fieldsman; (b) a calculated risk in chasing runs to win a match. I set a limit of 2% — eight for the tour.

Our final results were: 13 wins, 29 centuries, 11 run-outs.'

Hadlee wrote, 'I rate this tour as the highlight of my playing days, not only because of the achievements on the field or the welcome profit of 17,000 pounds, but for the companionship, fun and fellowship that endures to this day.'

Even now, in old age, Hadlee recounts the targets he set for the tour with accuracy and pride, relishing his near-parody of a parsimonious, teetotal, Methodist accountant, although he stresses he enjoys the odd glass of wine these days.

Graham Dowling, another undemonstrative Christchurch accountant who captained and administered New Zealand cricket, had many similarities in approach to Hadlee. Of course, Hadlee had helped pave the way for New Zealand teams to succeed in tests by the time of Dowling's reign in the late 1960s and early 1970s. Hadlee's target-setting strategies were ahead of their time in many ways; strategies that are now formulated by coaches and other specialists, who have taken over many of the roles of the captain. Interestingly, Hadlee believes a modern day coach would not have fitted in on this tour.

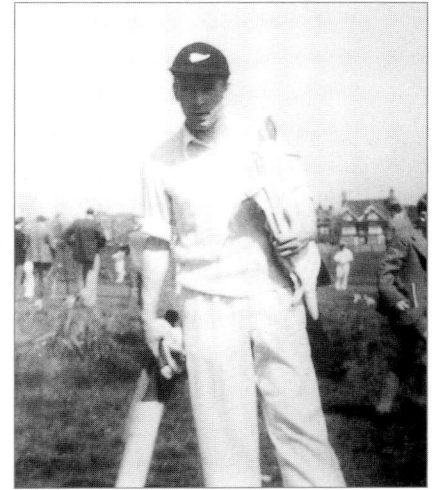

Martin Donnelly at Eastbourne, 16 April 1949.
Collection Dr Steve Gilbert

In 1965, when Hadlee managed the New Zealanders on tour, he continued his captaincy philosophy into management. 'My approach to the game was to look after my players. They were more important than I was.' On the pitch Hadlee sought to 'read and assess a game — something I enjoyed. Trying to assess the strengths and weaknesses of the opposition. Making the best of what we had.'

Hadlee aided tour captain John Reid early in his New Zealand captaincy by giving him advice on nursing and resting bowlers, field placings, and similar things. Other innovations Hadlee pioneered were looking to the minor associations for national players, such as Fen Cresswell from Marlborough and future national captain Harry Cave, from Wanganui. But it is for his cricketing knowledge and unfailing fairness that Hadlee is best remembered.

Brittenden wrote, 'Perhaps it was easier for him, than for most, to be a team man, for he has always had a very highly developed appreciation of the game as a study of tactics and strategies.

'So he knew, almost without question, what had to be done at any given moment. He usually succeeded in doing it.'

Hadlee had the umpires recall England's Cyril Washbrook in the Lancaster Park test of 1950/51, when the batsman was on his way to the pavilion after being given out lbw for 13. Hadlee felt certain Washbrook had hit the ball onto his pad, and did not hesitate to act. It was not the first time Hadlee had displayed such sportsmanship. When he was captaining a New Zealand XI in March 1944, Hadlee had seen Roy Scott of the New Zealand Services XI given out, caught by wicket-keeper Frank Mooney. Asked to resume by the doubting skipper, Scott's 36 delayed a possible innings victory and rain wiped out the final day, leaving the match drawn.

Hadlee retired from test cricket after the second test against England in 1951, which New Zealand lost by six wickets at the Basin Reserve. Bert Sutcliffe took over the national captaincy for two matches against the West Indies in February 1952, while Merv Wallace captained the team for the two tests against South Africa in New Zealand in March 1953.

'Merv Wallace would have been the logical choice to take the team to South Africa [in 1953/54] as he was vice-captain in 1949,' said Hadlee. 'Then, Merv decided he wouldn't make himself available in fairly much of a last minute decision.'

In 1953, after a meeting at Government House, 38-year-old Hadlee was asked by the president of the New Zealand Cricket Council, Tom Lowry, if he was available to captain the forthcoming tour to South Africa. 'I said I'd discuss it with my wife and my partners. All three were willing that I should take the tour of South Africa and I advised the chairman of the New Zealand council, Dave Colville, that I would be available if selected. That was the last I heard of the matter.'

Wallace's bombshell left the way open for Geoff Rabone 'to take the team and make such a good job of it, topping both the test batting and bowling averages with quite remarkable figures', in Hadlee's carefully chosen words. 'I was not disappointed because, having retired, I had not expected to be involved,' he concluded.

Writing in *The Crisis in Captaincy*, David Lemmon commented: 'Leaders fall into two categories: those who manipulate and control with intellectual clarity while not necessarily being great performers; and those who inspire by example.' While Hadlee's next effective successor, John Reid, was a prime example of the latter, Hadlee fell into the first category.

John Arlott called Hadlee 'a strategic commander of real ability', though his military-style planning was not a result of war service, as his poor eyesight had made him unfit for duty. Having to wear glasses — which Hadlee believes was the result of copying cricket scores from *Wisden* as a boy — also prevented him moving beyond playing rugby for Canterbury to higher honours.

It was on the voyage to England in 1937 that Hadlee met his wife Lilla. The couple has five sons — Barry, Dayle, Richard, Martin and Christopher — and it could be argued that teaching his sons so well on a backyard pitch is a bigger contribution than any other to New Zealand cricket.

Hadlee's stern side comes out when he is asked about his current influence on New Zealand cricket. Dayle, who played 26 tests, is now director of the BIL Cricket Academy at Lincoln near Christchurch, and a former coach of the New Zealand women's team. Sir Richard, of course, is chairman of selectors. 'He has played far more cricket than I have and should have far more knowledge,' Walter Hadlee says when asked if he offers his son (a veteran of 86 test matches) advice on selections. 'It's none of my business!'

Hadlee believes, 'For a country of our size we do well. In my own assessment I am very happy as long as we are competitive.'

Walter Hadlee had a prolific club career for High School Old Boys, playing 306 matches between 1932 and 1967, scoring a record 15,393 runs and 38 centuries. Here he is pictured during a 1960 innings.
Christchurch Star

4. BERT SUTCLIFFE 8 February 1952 – 9 February 1954

Too nice to be a captain

Great batsman that he was, Bert Sutcliffe was not an outstanding captain. Perhaps the selectors should not have given him the task of leading New Zealand after Walter Hadlee retired. Merv Wallace was unavailable for the 1951/52 tour by the West Indies, and while future captains Geoff Rabone and John Reid were in the side, the selectors took the familiar option of choosing the best batsman to lead the team.

'Bert was a lovely person and as a batsman he was an artist in whatever he did. I think that he was probably too good a player to be made captain,' concedes selector Jack Kerr.

Before play began in the first game between New Zealand and the West Indies the teams had a moment's silence in honour of the recently deceased King George VI. Sutcliffe won the toss and batted, which was a significant decision in view of his future choices.

'I had been appointed captain of the New Zealand team for the two tests against the visitors,' Sutcliffe wrote matter-of-factly in his 1962 autobiography *Between Overs*. He continued, 'I shall always remember the first game, at Christchurch, as one that produced a really keen struggle — almost to the end the game could have gone either way.'

'Spin twins' Ramadhin and Valentine, who had troubled England in 1950 by taking 59 wickets in the series, took 14 wickets between them. During Ramadhin's 74.6 overs he had Sutcliffe caught behind for 45 in the first innings and then bowled for 36 in the second, to record figures of 9/125. 'Ramadhin kept me very much on the defensive for some time,' Sutcliffe recalled.

Frank Worrell, 'looking half asleep', and Clyde Walcott, 'as big and strong as a bull', added 129 for the West Indies' fourth wicket, but the tourists, 'with seven out, were still 47 behind us'. Then, 'the exuberant Simpson Guillen', later New Zealand's wicket-keeper in their first test win, which took place against his old nation at the same venue four years later, 'flung his bat here and there' to score a career-best 54 in 78 minutes, after surviving a Johnny Hayes hat-trick ball.

'It was a very keen struggle for the runs,' Sutcliffe wrote of the 139 the West Indies needed to win. Worrell's 'lovely relaxed innings of 62 not out' saw them home in three hours in front of a crowd of 20,000, a tenth of the city's population. Frank Worrell, playing under John Goddard, hit two 50s on a wicket that was turning viciously and the West Indies won by five wickets on the final afternoon. Record takings of £5900 were established.

In Auckland Sutcliffe put in the West Indies, but rain in the first 30 minutes took the shine off the ball. The West Indies prospered in easy batting conditions and the weak New Zealand attack of Hayes, Beard, Reid, Burtt, Moir and Rabone struggled. Famously Moir allowed Rae to gain his ground in what Sutcliffe called 'an expensively quixotic gesture' when he slipped after Stollmeyer sent him back. From nine, he went on to 99, and the West Indies to 288/2 after day one, finally declaring on 546/6. As it is put in *Men In White*, 'New Zealand was fortunate that rain intervened to prevent what must surely have been a severe drubbing in this test.'

Bert Sutcliffe at Eastbourne, 14 April 1949.
Collection Dr Steve Gilbert

Sutcliffe's recollections of Auckland were 'not nearly so pleasant' as those of Christchurch. He says, 'The moment I made it [the decision to put the opposition in] light rain began to fall — it certainly left the pitch without much life at all.'

In his 1961 *Book for Boys*, Sutcliffe wrote, 'Who is the man who match after match decides the difference between his team winning and losing? The star batsman? The star bowler? They play important parts, but often the role they play, the success they have, the victory they help win, is brought about by the skill and judgement of the team captain.' He goes on to detail a captain's responsibility to 'study play with every ball bowled' in the field and while batting, as well as setting 'an example in his behaviour off the field'.

Another glorious off-drive. 'Too good a player to be made captain,' admitted selector Jack Kerr. *Christchurch Star*

As president of the New Zealand Cricket Council, Tom Lowry, the man who pioneered these characteristics in New Zealand test cricket, nominated Sutcliffe as one of New Zealand's five greatest cricketers. At the time he was the only player to be named who was still playing. But Sutcliffe and New Zealand were feeling the loss of two of Lowry's choices, Martin Donnelly and Jack Cowie, as well as the even more recently departed Hadlee and Wallace.

Sutcliffe proved his eminence as the world's top left-hander with 385 out of 500 for Otago in 1952/53, but Merv Wallace, who was now available again, was appointed captain for the visit of South Africa. From the 'almost Gilbertian situation' faced by the selection panel, which included Merv Wallace, Jack Kerr and Sutcliffe, the master left-hander was thrust to the fore again. Wallace, who was the 'natural choice', was keen to stay at home for business and family reasons. Then Geoff Rabone, who had come onto the scene 'hardly noticed at first' to fill in for Wallace, had his foot broken batting against Border. Once again the captaincy fell to Sutcliffe, who scored 196 in the match with Border. A week later he was putting in another test team, two years after his mistake at Eden Park.

'It is without much satisfaction that I report we lost by nine wickets,' Sutcliffe wrote of the fourth test, held at Johannesburg. 'We were all out for 79 on a good pitch at Ellis Park, and Tayfield, bowling straight ones, took six for 13. It was a woeful display by the batsmen against a bowler who seemed to have everyone mesmerised.'

The facts were plain. After Sutcliffe put the opposition in for the second time in three tests as captain, South Africa made 243, including 104 between Jackie McGlew and Dick Westcott for the first wicket. Sutcliffe made a duck in the first innings then scored 23 at number six in a rejigged follow-on batting order.

The South Africans made 243, to which New Zealand replied with 79 all out. Hugh Tayfield, on his 25th birthday, took 6/13 with 'subtle variation in flight and length' on a pitch 'offering minimal spin'. Sutcliffe's duck (one of five in the innings) came in three balls, the last of which was hoisted to McLean at long on. The pressure of carrying the batting and being captain may have brought the rush of blood.

The second innings, following on, took exactly twice as long as the first —

376 minutes compared to 188 minutes. Sutcliffe, batting at six, made 23 before the home side won by nine wickets.

Winning the toss and batting, Sutcliffe and company dug in during the final test at Port Elizabeth. The captain uncharacteristically took 142 minutes over 38 and New Zealand were just 11 behind on the first innings. Two sixes and four fours in a 124-minute 52 helped New Zealand set a target of 212 in 225 minutes. South Africa lost 3 for 81 in 90 minutes, but won with 40 minutes to spare. Endean hit 87 out of 107 for the fourth wicket in 94 minutes, exposing the lack of bowling depth, particularly in the spin department. The selectors had preferred Bill Bell, who had taken 11 wickets during the season, to the experienced Alex Moir and Tom Burtt. Later the *Cricket Almanack of New Zealand* of 1955 wondered 'whether Burtt and Moir would not have been most acceptable in South Africa and far better prospects than two of those chosen for their style of bowling. Selection of the best possible side could well have made all the difference.'

'If we lost the fifth test too, at least it was a better game and one in which we had a distinct chance of success. We were headed on the first innings by only eleven runs, and set them 212 to make on a pitch taking spin. When they were 81 for three, we had a real chance, but our fieldsmen could not get to the catches, and that was that.'

Not quite, though, as three matches in Australia on the way home from South Africa 'brought us considerable satisfaction'. Gordon Leggat, Rabone's replacement, who along with Tom Burtt and Alex Moir was originally overlooked for fitness reasons, made runs in each innings against Western Australia 'and reminded us again of how useful he would have been in South Africa'.

Nevertheless, Sutcliffe's best chance of a test win was gone, and although he played test cricket for 11 more years, he was never in a winning team.

South Africa marked a watershed in Sutcliffe's career. His experience there, one of the most widely reported pieces of cricket in New Zealand history, dented him badly. 'There's no doubt it affected my confidence. It shouldn't have, but it did. For the rest of my career, when a ball came through shoulder high, I instinctively walked away from it. I'd swat rather than hook. My feet were all over the place.'

Before being given the added responsibility of captaincy, Sutcliffe's

Bert Sutcliffe, smiling as ever, prior to an innings defeat at Lancaster Park in February 1959. Trueman, Tyson and Lock, plus 141 from Dexter, trounced New Zealand.
Christchurch Star

Now a veteran, and vice-captain to John Reid, Bert Sutcliffe turns Len Coldwell of Worcestershire to leg. Norman Gifford is in the background.
Christchurch Star

technique had been dissected by fast bowler Neil Adcock, and he was never to recover completely. He averaged over 50 (twice over 100) in six out of seven seasons, plus the 1949 tour of England, only falling below in 1951/52. After scoring 1155 runs at 46.20 in South Africa (305 at 38.12 in tests), plus three successive centuries, making 480 runs at 80 on the way home via Australia, he fell away, with just the 1960/61 season seeing an average over 50.

Recalling the South African tour, Sutcliffe wrote: 'I had led New Zealand against the West Indies in 1951/52, admittedly without much success, and the feeling was, I believe, that my batting was of sufficient importance to the team to demand that I should not be burdened with leadership.'

At the end of March 1954, New Zealand XI captain Harry Cave dismissed Sutcliffe for 56 in Rabone's return game, which took place in Christchurch immediately after the tourists had arrived back from South Africa. 'This cheerless match' finished on the last day of the season.

Rabone was back as captain in 1954/55 against the MCC. Sutcliffe top scored in three of four innings, but 11 in the Auckland test's second innings of 26 showed the weakness of the team. Sutcliffe 'flailed wildly' at Wardle, after seeing off 'Typhoon' Tyson.

'For a short while before he went to Northern Districts Sutty [Sutcliffe] captained us,' Otago and New Zealand pace bowler Frank Cameron recalled in the year after Sutcliffe's death. 'We had both Alabaster and Moir bowling, who were both New Zealand leg spinners, which was a great luxury. Sutty had them to use and he used them a lot. He was such a nice fellow. He was really too nice to be a captain. He was sort of — too fair. Both [Moir and Alabaster] were contesting for one [New Zealand] position and he was trying to give them equal opportunities, equal numbers of overs, a bowl at each end.

'I remember one game when I had three for 11 and they were five for 40 and I came off and the spin bowlers bowled,' Cameron recalled ruefully. 'I didn't mind when conditions were right but when the ball was moving around — we had Alan Clark and Norman Woods, and there was no need to bowl the spinners, but Bert managed to slot them in a for few overs!

'Bert was a cavalier as a player, and fellows followed him. They played for Sutty and he was quite astute and knew his game. But he probably wasn't mean enough to be an outstanding captain. Let him bat and run round in the field, but I wouldn't have burdened him with the test captaincy. I don't think he wanted to be a captain.'

After retiring from international cricket Bert Sutcliffe's major role was as a member of the Rothman's Sports Foundation. With Don Clarke, Peter Snell and Arthur Lydiard, Sutcliffe helped organise the spread of sport round the country. Martin Horton coached 2000 junior coaches and 600 seniors, with Sutcliffe employed as an expert instructor. He and his wife Norma, who had three children, lived in Auckland.

Today Sutcliffe's legacy lives on at the Bert Sutcliffe Oval at Lincoln University, which was opened shortly before his death on 20 April 2001.

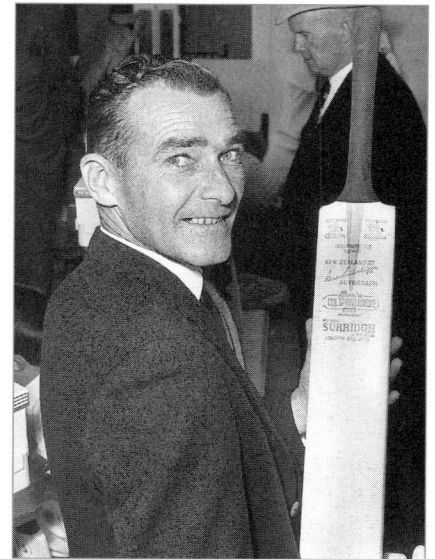

Bert Sutcliffe, at 41 the veteran of the New Zealand team, examines a bat at Surridge's sports shop in London, April 1965.
Christchurch Star

5. MERV WALLACE 6 March 1953 – 17 March 1953

A vast fund of knowledge

Best known as the coach who masterminded the defeat of the West Indies in 1955/56 that gave New Zealand its first test win, Merv Wallace was one of the most influential figures in New Zealand cricket in the postwar years.

He was Auckland captain in 23 first-class games between 1939 and 1958, and a selector for his province from 1944 to 1948 and from 1963 to 1965. Moreover, Wallace was a New Zealand selector in the years after the war up to 1950, and again from 1952 to 1954 and from 1963 to 1965. But it was as a player that Wallace delighted the cricketing public in a long career that included 67 matches, but just 13 tests, for New Zealand.

Selected for Curly Page's team to England in 1937 at the age of 20, Wallace topped the tour averages with 1641 runs at 41.02. Twelve years later, in England for the second time as vice-captain to Walter Hadlee on that happy tour, he scored 910 runs by the end of May. Wallace's test career culminated in two matches as captain against South Africa in 1952/53.

'Flip' Wallace made his debut for Auckland as a sturdy 17-year-old, and first played for New Zealand against the 1935/36 MCC tourists aged 19. He scored 19, 27 and 38 in three non-test matches under Ian Cromb's captaincy, and made his test debut in 1937, making 151 runs at 25.16, exactly the same figures as future captain Walter Hadlee. Because of the Second World War New Zealand played no tests between August 1937 and March 1946 — this was from when Wallace was aged 20 to when he was 29, and would have been in the prime of his career. One test each against Australia and England over the next two seasons brought Wallace modest scores of 10, 14 and 9, although he helped his province to its sixth Plunket Shield triumph in nine seasons in 1946/47. He scored 3409 runs at 50.13 for Auckland and with Verdun Scott led their batting in the thirties and forties.

Despite Wallace's feeling that 'I always preferred to be second in command, a bit closer to the boys', he eventually succeeded Walter Hadlee after another reluctant captain, Bert Sutcliffe, had two unsuccessful tests in 1951/52 against the West Indies, when Wallace was unavailable due to work commitments.

Wallace took charge as a result of several factors. 'Bert Sutcliffe, great batsman that he was, was not suited to the captaincy,' he says. Of the other candidates, John Reid was in his first season as Wellington skipper and 'was in the middle of a nightmarish run of low test scores — the last thing he needed was the added burden of the captaincy'. Geoff Rabone 'was doing a good job' of captaining Auckland, but his business and personal commitments meant he was unavailable for at least the first test against South Africa.

Selectors Jack Kerr, Bert Sutcliffe, Ken Uttley and Wallace decided Wallace himself was the best man for the task.

In his 2000 biography of Wallace, Joseph Romanos states: 'There is no doubt he could have been a very good New Zealand captain — his record leading Auckland supports that view. But, by 1953, he was playing first-class cricket only sporadically. It seems he agreed to lead New Zealand to help them out of a sticky position, rather than because of any desperate desire to do the job.'

Merv Wallace at Eastbourne, 14 April 1949. *Collection Dr Steve Gilbert*

Wallace himself, a modest and self-effacing man, has said, 'I wasn't particularly keen to captain New Zealand, but I didn't mind. The trouble was by the time the tests began we were all out of touch. We had so few games back then.'

Wallace lost the toss at Wellington and match-hardened South Africa made the highest score against New Zealand of 524/8 declared (Jackie McGlew made a record 255 not out). New Zealand's players, who had been on a diet of club cricket, lost by an innings and 180 runs, with Wallace making just four and two. It all could have been different, had McGlew not been put down three times off the bowling of Bob Blair, who had a spell of 3/8 before McGlew and Anton Murray added a test record 246 in 219 minutes for the seventh wicket.

The next test was a disappointingly dull draw, with South African off spinner Hugh Tayfield bowling eight consecutive maidens on the third day during his 5/62 off 46.2 overs. Wallace made 23 before Tayfield had him caught by Percy Mansell.

Wallace holds firm views regarding captaincy. 'A captain should generally field at mid-off so he can speak to his bowler between deliveries if necessary. A captain who spends all his time at slip doesn't have the same ability to communicate and tends to let the game drift more,' he says.

The man regarded by many as New Zealand's finest coach believes, 'A captain must be able to get his message through to a bowler, without making the bowler feel uptight. You want to be able to advise the bowler without him feeling like he is being put under pressure.

'All players are different. A captain must know which players need more praise and which ones need to be sat on. A captain needs to be honest and encouraging. A captain must be worth a place in the team in the first place. If not his authority will be severely undermined.'

After staying at home for the South Africa tour, Wallace next played first-class cricket in 1956/57, for Auckland against Australia. A couple more appearances led to his eventual retirement after making 29 not out and 44 for the Governor-General's XI in 1960/61, nearly 30 years after his debut.

Wallace almost ended up taking the team to South Africa in 1953/54, but 'I couldn't bring myself to give the selectors an answer. There were so many reasons not to tour. Greg [his son, born in 1950] was three. By the time I got back he'd be four and I'd have lost a year of his life. I'd already had a lot of cricket tours by then. My business had been going a few years, and I was closely involved with it.'

Geoff Rabone didn't play in the trial match in March 1953, and Wallace and Sutcliffe captained the two teams of hopefuls. 'Scotland Yard would have had problems deciding who should lead the team,' wrote Don Cameron. In the end Wallace didn't go and Rabone, initially unavailable to tour for the same reasons as Wallace, was chosen as captain.

Wallace continued to run his sports shop business, and was associated with Auckland representative cricket for 50 years from 1933 until the mid-eighties. He lives in Auckland with his wife Yvonne and has two children, Adele and Greg.

6. GEOFF RABONE

11 December 1953 – 28 March 1955

Bomber command

Geoff Rabone was captain on New Zealand's first tour of South Africa. In all, he led his country in five test matches, losing four of them. But the bald facts give no hint of Rabone's courage and fortitude at a difficult time in the development of New Zealand cricket, when the retirements of the 1949ers had left the national team weak and inexperienced.

Walter Hadlee — who Rabone, along with Sutcliffe, Wallace and Cave, followed with so little success — was the big influence on Rabone's captaincy style.

'Playing so much under Walter — particularly in 1949 — gave me ample opportunity to pick up his style of captaincy, and be impressed by it,' Rabone said later.

'I can only judge my own style of captaincy by the comments of others — some informed, some far from it. Seems I was a driver rather than a leader, but the odd scribe has added that perhaps that style was necessary in my day.'

Rabone is referring to comments made by Dick Brittenden, who accompanied the tour to South Africa, chronicling the experience in his book *Silver Fern on the Veldt*.

Brittenden described Rabone, an all-rounder, as 'taciturn and unrelenting on the field', but added, 'To his task he lent all his energy, determination and skill.'

'As a captain,' Brittenden wrote, 'Rabone won a stern reputation for his firm discipline. He tried desperately hard, and expected everyone else to do the same.' Brittenden judged that Rabone 'dearly loves a fight', but also that there are 'few more conscientious captains' in the game.

The adversity and responsibility he faced in South Africa brought out the best in Rabone, but the side went down 4-0 in the face of fearsome fast bowling from Neil Adcock. 'There were only four players who had been overseas playing cricket,' Rabone said later. 'How do you win games that way?'

Geoff Rabone.
Christchurch Star

Shortly after making his first-class debut for Wellington against Auckland at the Basin Reserve in 1940, Rabone went to war as a bomber pilot. It was not until 1949 that he made his international debut, as a useful lower middle order batsman and medium pacer, who could also spin the ball both ways. Even then he was described by one critic as 'not even average'. He later commented, 'When you get that sort of thing it strengthens your resolve to perform.'

Rabone was a success in 1949, as were so many others. He reached Hadlee's target of 1000 runs on tour in the second to last game. He also took 50 wickets, exactly meeting Hadlee's target, but he was not a success in the tests.

In describing the selections for the 1953/54 tour of South Africa, *Men in White* says: 'Some surprise was evident when Geoff Rabone was announced as the touring captain. He had previously announced himself unavailable for the tour, but had arrived at Lancaster Park to play in the trial. Wallace, one of the selectors and many people's first choice as captain, was not among the touring party. It seemed that he had accepted the captaincy after Hadlee retired on the understanding that it was his duty to lend his experience to the team. When he declined the leadership the selectors had pleaded their case to Rabone, who had eventually consented.'

Tourist John Reid wrote: 'Wallace should have been selected — his tactical leadership would have been invaluable.' But Wallace was reluctant to make himself available. Hadlee had offered to make a comeback, while Sutcliffe was seemingly not considered to be test captaincy material any more.

In his autobiography *Sword of Willow*, Reid wrote: 'Geoff Rabone gave his heart and soul to the team, a fighter of tremendous reserves. For sheer guts, some of his test innings were the greatest I have ever seen. But just as he was gaining flexibility as a captain he broke a bone in his foot and was lost to the team.'

Reflecting on his captaincy almost 50 years later, Rabone said, 'Perhaps my wartime experience did help. However, being 32 years of age and having a fair experience as provincial captain probably eased me into it, with confidence to do the job.'

But while opening against Border, just prior to the fourth test, Rabone's foot was broken by a fast full toss. Sutcliffe took over and scored 196. He captained the team for the rest of the tour.

Having a captain like Rabone was a boon to previously wayward opening bowler Tony MacGibbon. 'He helped me and he brought my confidence out. He was a great competitor and led by example. We should have got a lot more out of him in his career than we did. He had some guts. I remember one game when he was facing Adcock, who was bringing the ball back into him. Geoff took the ball on his body and must have been hit 19 or 20 times between his knee and his shoulder down one side,' MacGibbon recalled.

'I remember another occasion in Bulawayo when we dropped 12 catches, or certainly a lot of catches, in the morning session. Geoff got stuck into us during the lunch break and then the fourth ball after lunch the ball was snicked and went to him, and he dropped it. That caused a few laughs. But he would not have been out of place as a current captain. He tried to get a professional attitude into us. I remember in the third test, at Cape Town, I got the first four South African wickets to fall. I thought I was going to get a bag of five but then had to watch Geoff pick up the next six.'

MacGibbon did not doubt that New Zealand could have won the fifth test had Rabone been available and able to use his particular captaincy skills to the side's advantage. However, he concluded, 'Geoff's problem was that he was a Lancaster bomber pilot in the war and he tried to run his team in a similar way. The hard cases didn't respond too well.'

Rabone topped both the batting and bowling averages on the tour. His best performances came in the first test at Durban, when he scored 107 out of 230 and 68 out of 149 in the innings and 58-run loss. In the third test 56 and 6/68 helped New Zealand to enforce its first follow-on in a test.

'Never having led a New Zealand side to test victory,' Rabone recalled, 'I guess the highlight was leading New Zealand against South Africa at Newlands, Cape Town, in the third test in 1954.' This was when New Zealand, batting first, scored 505, made South Africa follow on in their second innings, but just failed to dismiss them a second time. 'At that stage New Zealand had never won a test match.

New Zealand Test Cricket Captains

New Zealand captain Geoff Rabone pads up for a knock at the MCG after a massage on his injured foot, 5 April 1954.
Christchurch Star

'The wickets were green and I finished black and blue after some of those test matches. I didn't even wear a thigh pad — we just didn't have them. I used to wear towels around my chest. What else could you do?'

The nadir of this barrage came at Ellis Park, Johannesburg, when Rabone lost the toss for a sixth time in nine matches, and also failed twice with the bat. This match belonged to Bob Blair and Bert Sutcliffe, who on Boxing Day 1953 provided New Zealand with its proudest moment to date.

Blair's fiancée, 19-year-old Nerrissa Love, was among the 151 people who died in the Tangiwai rail crash on Christmas Eve. Bouncers bowled by Neil Adcock had hit Sutcliffe and Lawrie Miller, but both bravely returned in front of a 25,000 crowd to try and avoid the follow-on. With the score at 154/9 Blair unexpectedly laid aside his grief and went out to join Sutcliffe, whose head was turbaned in bandages, to face the onslaught. The pair attacked bravely, adding 33 runs in ten minutes, each hitting sixes and restoring New Zealand self-respect on the tour.

Meanwhile, it was perceived that South African hospitality — the downfall of several later tours, particularly the 1994/95 tour under Ken Rutherford — was affecting the fielding. Rabone instituted early morning practices — at 6.30 a.m. — which not surprisingly proved unpopular.

'It was the first time I had ever felt rebellious towards a captain,' recalled John Reid, who with Bert Sutcliffe made his point by turning up in his pyjamas.

All was not well on the tour, in contrast to Hadlee's 49ers and the next trip to South Africa, led by John Reid in 1961/62. Two cliques had developed — one of drinkers and one of non-drinkers. Teenage batsman John Beck, a player of great potential, fell in with the more sociable tourists Frank Mooney, Bob Blair and Murray Chapple. Matt Poore, 23 at the time, recalled, 'Life was a ball.' Guy Overton remembered the tempting array of invitations, which ranged from barbecues to safaris, and admitted that as a result of all the socialising, 'Our cricket performances did suffer at times.' Most of the men had never left New Zealand before, and after the deprivations of the war years the temptation to enjoy life was too great to resist.

At Kimberley, against Griqualand West, New Zealand fielders dropped nine catches before lunch after a heavy night that resulted in Beck having to be helped onto the train to get to the game. This was not the only tour where alcohol and the temptation for young men to have a good time have proved damaging. The role of alcohol in New Zealand cricket has sometimes been significant — as far back as the 1890s Canterbury fast bowler Albert Moss joined the Salvation Army as an alcoholic, while in the 1980s Geoff Howarth's problems were well known. While Walter Hadlee, John Reid and Tony MacGibbon were teetotal, Ken Rutherford loved Speight's beer, and his rival Martin Crowe was fond of Italian wine. Other players, including future captains Stephen Fleming and Dion Nash, admitted using cannabis during the 1994/95 South African tour.

In hindsight, the players recognised that Rabone and manager Jack Kerr never had control of the whole team during that 1953/54 tour to South Africa.

The following season the MCC came to New Zealand after beating Australia 3-1 in a five-match series, and the New Zealanders had to deal with fast bowler Frank Tyson. In the first test at Dunedin, Rabone helped Sutcliffe (74) add 60 for the second wicket. He took three hours over 18, but second top scored in New Zealand's 125. They lost by eight wickets. The other test that year was at Eden Park where, infamously, New Zealand made just 26 in their second innings.

'When I captained that side that made 26, I got an lbw decision against me when I was seven. In actual fact it took the edge of the bat. Now, I'm captain and I get out when we are eight down. In that situation, the lowest score in test history, I get a decision that wasn't correct. But did I rush into print? I took it and you've got to take it,' Rabone commented later, laughing that if he had stayed New Zealand could have made 30.

Rabone was commitment personified. He used to end the day with a raging headache and sometimes vomited. 'I'd hardly eat for three days before a test match,' he told interviewer Nigel Smith in 1990. 'We were always on the damn losing side in those days and coming second hurt. I didn't like that.

'My cricket success wasn't based on natural talent, it was based on a hell of a determination to succeed. I probably proved that players don't have to have a great natural talent if they have a deep desire to make it, which counts for a hell of a lot.'

By 1955 Rabone was working in marketing for Shell and had a young family. He ended his international cricket career after the Eden Park debacle.

He was modest enough to say in later years that his 'experiences as captain, compared with most who followed, were very limited'. However, there is no doubt that Rabone's old-school, lead-from-the-front approach was representative of his era, bridging the gap between Walter Hadlee and John Reid, and making a valuable contribution to New Zealand's development and later test success.

7. HARRY CAVE

13 October 1955 – 6 February 1956

Perhaps too gentle

No New Zealand test captain was more modest than the gently spoken, warm-natured Harry Cave. The best of a large family of cricketers, Cave was another of New Zealand's captains who had a lengthy cricketing pedigree. His father and five uncles were all part of the notable cricketing Caves from Wanganui and this legacy, if nothing else, made him a good choice to be the seventh test captain.

Cave, who died at the age of 66 in 1989, would have been 80 on 10 October 2002. Although he made two first-class centuries for Central Districts, for whom he was a founder player in 1950, Cave was best known as an economical right-arm medium-fast bowler, with firm control, who was prepared to keep going until he was exhausted. He was the first bowler to captain New Zealand in tests.

G.B. Cave, Harry's grandfather, emigrated to Auckland from Sunderland in the UK in 1886, living a cricket ball throw from Eden Park where, on 13 March 1956, his grandson Harry was to be the star bowler in New Zealand's first test win. H.E.B. Newton described G.B.'s six sons as 'basically unathletic — but enthusiasm, practice, application, acquired techniques and qualities of character have taken them to the top of the cricket world as players and umpires. Their integrity and fairness are a byword.' Probably Harry's best-known relative was his Uncle Kenny, who was an umpire in all three tests in New Zealand's 1929/30 inaugural test series.

Harry was tall, slim, with a modest disposition and sincere nature. He began his test career on the 1949 tour to England and acted as a stock bowler for New Zealand throughout the fifties. He toured England again in 1958, aged 35, as vice-captain, after being presented with the Winsor Cup for being the best bowler in New Zealand in both 1956 and 1957.

Cave succeeded Geoff Rabone as captain for New Zealand's first tour of India and Pakistan in 1955/56. Although he won the appointment at a time

Harry Cave.
Collection Dr Steve Gilbert

when New Zealand cricket was at a low ebb — after 'the nadir', as John Reid aptly called it, of New Zealand's 26 all out loss against England in Auckland in March 1955 — Cave was a popular choice as captain.

The team was announced on 2 August 1955. Bert Sutcliffe, Rabone's deputy in South Africa, was allowed to concentrate on his batting and Rabone was unavailable. The 27-year-old Reid was completing his leadership apprenticeship and was made vice-captain, so Cave was asked to lead by selectors Giff Vivian, Eric Tindill, Walter Hadlee and Lankford Smith. Nine of the 15 tourists had international experience, but not on the subcontinent where, as a result of illness, attributed to the foreign conditions, 'it was eight games before we could put into the field the team selected the night before', according to Reid in *Sword of Willow*.

The team had played eight tests in less than four months by January 1956, losing four and drawing four. The tour organisers were criticised for 'making a farce of international matches', by Australian Keith Miller, due to the frequency of the tests. The itinerary and conditions stretched the players, but there were benefits to be had. Cave admitted after the second leg against India 'we were beaten by a better balanced side. I think we have now learned how to play big cricket rather than Saturday afternoon cricket.'

In the previous 25 years New Zealand had played only 33 tests, and to play eight in such a short time proved too much for the tourists. Cave himself bowled most test overs (334), but took just 13 wickets at 46.92, as New Zealand suffered from an unbalanced attack that was unsuited to Asian matting pitches. Cave's high windmill action could move the ball in the air and off the pitch, given the right conditions, at medium pace, but he was often worried by an elbow injury, which had been a problem since the war. To be harsh, it could be said that he lacked the pace to penetrate at the top level.

In the first test against Pakistan at Karachi, although Jack Alabaster and

Alex Moir both played, Alabaster did not actually get to bowl in Pakistan's only innings, which lasted for 130 overs. Alabaster was selected for the tour without any previous first-class experience, and he played in the tour opener against the Chief Commissioner's XI, bowling 19 overs without taking a wicket.

Because of illness, New Zealand found themselves with only 11 players who were fit enough to take the field. Alabaster was one of these, and thus made his test debut with one first-class match and no wickets to his name. Pakistan made 289, recovering from 144/6, but Alabaster did not get to bowl. He believes that his captain decided not to use him because of his lack of experience. The bowling was shared between Tony MacGibbon (37.1 overs), Cave (24), John Reid (30), Moir (37) and Matt Poore (2).

New Zealand lost by an innings and one run, with Zulfiqar Ahmed's off-spin taking 11/79, match figures that would stand as a record between the teams until 1990/91. Cave took 3/56 from 24 overs, but his batsmen failed to make a 50 between them on the unfamiliar matting wicket. Partly because of this, they had struggled to 145/8 on the first day. Bert Sutcliffe wrote, 'In our second match, a test — every second match was a test — we were completely at sea on matting over turf. Our scoring was achieved at a crawl in this Karachi test — our first innings lasted six and a half hours.'

The second test was closer, with Noel McGregor scoring a maiden first-class century, and Noel Harford making 93 on his debut. But from 111/6, Pakistan's Waqar Hussain (189) and wicket-keeper Imtiaz Ahmed (209) then added a record 308 for the seventh wicket. Although 86 from Reid and 64 from Harford set Pakistan 117 to win, it was not quite enough. Reid took 4/38 and Johnny Hayes 2/25, as Pakistan won by four wickets.

The third match was delayed by incessant drizzle until the third day. New Zealand struggled to 70 all out and 69/6 on wet coir matting, although Cave's bowling had the Pakistanis in trouble at 86/5, until Hanif Mohammed took over to score 103 before he became Cave's third victim.

In the first test against India, in Hyderabad, Cave bowled 41 unsuccessful overs for 59 runs, as India ran up 498/4 declared, with Polly Umrigar making 223. John Guy made 102 in New Zealand's reply and Sutcliffe 137 not out following on.

In the next test Vinoo Mankad made another 223, but no one could support Sutcliffe's innings' high scores of 73 and 37, as New Zealand lost by an innings. Cave took 3/77 from 48 overs.

In the third test against India, Sutcliffe's 230 not out was supported by Reid's 119 not out, and Cave declared at 450/2. Cave had to bowl 50 overs this time, for 68 runs, as India reached a record that was to stand until 1986/87 of 531/7 declared.

The fourth test was another draw, when Hayes, Cave, Reid and Alabaster bowled out India for the lowest total made against them — 132. Guy (91) and Reid (120) took New Zealand to 336. However, India was able to declare at 438/7 (Cave 57-26-85-2), and set New Zealand 235 in 90 minutes. They reached 75/6. Cave helped bat the game out.

The final test, in Madras, was one too many for New Zealand, with India making 537/3 declared (Cave 44 overs for 94, Vinoo Mankad 231 and Pankaj Roy 173 adding 413 for the first wicket). The tourists lost by an innings and 109 runs. Cave shared an eighth wicket second innings stand of 68 in 115 minutes with Reid to prolong the game, which ended 105 minutes before time.

Cave 'toiled with great stamina and control', according to *Men in White*. 'Under his leadership the team retained a good spirit in strange and occasionally trying circumstances.' He was 'perhaps too gentle to be a great captain. But he lost nothing because of that,' the ever-generous Dick Brittenden wrote in *New Zealand Cricketers*.

One of John Reid's 'great players', Cave 'was a man for accurate bowling, and for courage and application too'. In India and Pakistan 'he set a tremendous example in sheer guts — he slaved and toiled away and yielded 412 runs. But he yielded them most reluctantly. He bowled 254 overs in terrible heat, and often in ill-health.'

Cave was retained for the West Indies' visit and captained New Zealand for the last time less than three weeks after the tourists' return from India. He won the toss and batted, but Ramadhin and Valentine exposed the jaded batsmen, making 'good use of the unpredictable wicket' (*Men in White*). Cave took 2/47 from 26 overs in a typically valiant effort, but was still dropped from the team for the second test at Christchurch, to be replaced by John Reid as captain. That match was also lost by an innings. But after New Zealand suffered a nine-wicket defeat in the next test, played at Wellington, Cave was recalled under Reid, 'in the sort of situation which would convince many a cricketer that his dignity had been outraged'. Reid described how Cave 'struck like a snake immediately'. Brittenden described how, in 'his calm and smiling way' he scuppered the West Indies' quest for 258 to win, giving New Zealand their first test victory in 45 matches after 26 years.

'Playing for me in this match I had my old captain from the India-Pakistan tour, Harry Cave,' wrote Reid. 'Now he gave everything he had under my captaincy, just as he had never spared himself in the team cause through his years of cricket.' A worthy epitaph indeed.

Harry Cave, a farmer who later became a specialist in camellias which he grew at his home in Wanganui, took 362 wickets at 23.9 in his career, third on the New Zealand list at the time. He died in 1989, leaving his wife, Vonnie, and two sons.

8. JOHN REID
18 February 1956 – 13 July 1965

A man of a thousand words

John Reid captained his country to its first test victory, and to its first away victories. For over 30 years Reid held the record of his country's most prolific captain, as well as holding records for most appearances, runs, wickets and catches on his retirement in 1965 at the age of 37, by which time he had become New Zealand's oldest skipper.

In the words of Dick Brittenden, New Zealand's most respected cricket writer, Reid was 'a cricketing one-man band — and he was a virtuoso with each instrument'.

But despite his great skill as a player it is as a captain that Reid is best remembered today. In this area also Reid was omnipotent, unchallenged, and seldom made a false step — a man who epitomised the leader of a New Zealand test cricket team.

Reid's seniority, playing stature and forceful personality, as well of his use of 'a thousand words' to dress down his team in the dressing room, made 'Bogo' Reid one of the best of New Zealand's skippers.

The Wellington right-hander's early test experience was gained on the 1949 tour to England where, as a 21-year-old, he impressed Walter Hadlee enough to win a debut. Brun Smith missed out, although the Cantabrian had made 96 and 54 not out in the first test. Hadlee, Wallace, Scott, Donnelly and Sutcliffe were a group of outstanding players from whom Reid could learn. Innings such as 188 not out against Cambridge University, 82 in the match-winning 247/5 against Sussex and, just before the test, a double of 107 not out and 72 versus Northants prompted Hadlee to give Reid his test debut.

Neville Cardus described Reid as a 'club cricketer in excelsis', with his mixture of common sense and 'brawny blows against the bad one'. He made 50 and 25 at Old Trafford, and fielded excellently at mid-off.

Scores of five and 93, caught in the covers off Jim Laker after effectively saving the game, helped ensure Reid was to remain in the test team for life, never to be dropped or rested again. This was despite 12 subsequent test innings in which his top score was 11. To drop him would have been 'like throwing away sunglasses because there was a cloud in the sky', wrote Brittenden. Reid scored 1488 runs on the 1949 tour.

After the short-lived and unsuccessful efforts of Bert Sutcliffe, Merv Wallace, Geoff Rabone and Harry Cave, Reid was belatedly made captain in 1955/56. He had scored 1347 runs at 42.09 in South Africa in 1953/54, including a maiden test century of 135 in the drawn third test at Cape Town. He had also taken 56 wickets at 21.33, including 12 in the tests. In India and Pakistan Reid had topped the averages with 1024 runs at 53.89, and had taken 39 wickets on the arduous tour. This included 493 runs and six wickets in the five tests.

Back in New Zealand Cave was dropped after a pair and 2/47 in the innings and 71-run loss to West Indies in the first test, which began less than three weeks after the team's last match of an exhausting tour of India and Pakistan.

Reid had already captained Wellington since the end of the 1951 season, when he took over from Trevor Barber, a player he regretted was given just a single test chance, in Reid's second game in charge. Reid later sought to establish continuity in selections.

Reid had also captained Hutt Valley High School, and played under five of New Zealand's seven test captains. He was a constructive vice-captain to Harry Cave on the subcontinent. 'A vice-captain supports his captain,' says Reid, who later had Murray Chapple and Graham Dowling as his lieutenants. In England Reid had played in the Central Lancashire League for Heywood between 1952 and 1954. 'I didn't captain, but you were the pro and you actually captained anyway, telling the amateur captain what he should do.

'I was a poor captain for a start,' Reid has said. 'I didn't have the man management skills that came after. I used to say go down to third man and I'll

Reid tosses up on his fifty-sixth successive test appearance, the first test against England at Edgbaston, May 1965. Mike Smith won the toss and batted, and England won by nine wickets. *Christchurch Star*

bowl, because you've got to get the job done. You can't have a long conversation out in the middle.'

Reid certainly did not believe he should have been given the job sooner. 'I was getting on with battling through a rough spin with 12 innings without a 50. I was opening the bowling so I was worth a place in the side, but I never thought I should be captain before I was.'

Reid, at 27, presided over another innings defeat at Christchurch in the second test against the West Indies, although he top scored in the second innings with 40, as well as having the best bowling figures (3/68) and diving to catch O.G. 'Collie' Smith off MacGibbon at backward square leg. But the match had been lost when Alf Valentine bowled Reid when he was on 28 in New Zealand's innings.

Another heavy defeat followed, this time at Wellington's Basin Reserve, with Reid again leading bowler (3/85) and batsman (55 in the first innings). Don Taylor made 43 and 77, and Valentine and Ramadhin found it less easy to expose the batsmen's technique against spin.

After this some fundamental changes took place in the New Zealand camp. Merv Wallace was appointed coach, and Cave was recalled to the team, as were Don Beard and Don Taylor. Cave fitted back in as a lieutenant, as Sutcliffe had done for Rabone in South Africa in 1953/54 and Sinclair and Congdon, among others, were to do in later years.

History was made when New Zealand won the next test — its forty-fourth in 26 years — by 190 runs. Cave struck 'like a snake' to return 4/22 and 4/21. Reid made the highest score in the match and his highest test score in New Zealand to date, of 84. Ramadhin left the field with cramp at a crucial moment, perhaps showing his lack of toughness in the view of some of the men playing. In contrast, Reid wrote that Cave 'gave everything he had under my captaincy'. The captain concluded that Noel McGregor's on-side outfield catch of Everton Weekes, who scored five centuries in successive first-class innings, and three in three test innings prior to Auckland, 'was the winning of the game'. Sam Guillen, the former West Indies wicket-keeper, effected the match-winning stumping, and passed the ball on to Reid as a souvenir.

'Long before this notable success,' wrote Brittenden, 'Reid had shown that he was able, by personal example, to lift the level of performance of the team he was with.' This was the essence of his no-frills captaincy style and policy.

John Reid was the first player to win both the Redpath and Winsor cups (to be followed by Vic Pollard, and later Chris Cairns in the nineties). He was the greatest all-round cricketer to play for New Zealand until Richard Hadlee, and only Hadlee has made as great a mark on New Zealand cricket. Yet Reid's prowess as a player overshadowed his record as a captain, and it is as an all-rounder how he is primarily remembered by many.

He was selected, twice, to captain World XIs, and when he retired he had played in 58 of New Zealand's 86 tests, captaining 34; the previous record was Cave's nine. Only Sutcliffe, with 42, had as many as half the number of test appearances as Reid.

In an era when New Zealand test cricket was at its lowest ebb, Reid was unstinting in his efforts to raise the standards. To do this he led from the front. The records for highest innings and best bowling by a New Zealand test captain inevitably became his. He even made a stumping!

After the West Indies series New Zealand played no further tests until 1958, a gap of almost 27 months, after what Reid condemned as 'a very heavy burden for New Zealand cricket to bear' — 12 tests in five months between October 1955 and March 1956. Seven had been lost; four drawn; and there was the final win against the West Indies.

Australia visited in 1956/57, although their games with New Zealand were not given test status. Reid's team scored two draws before a ten-wicket defeat against the second-string opposition. After a year off, that season's Auckland captain, Geoff Rabone, and Harry Cave played under Reid, in a team 'handicapped by an inferiority complex' according to Australian captain Ian Craig.

It was over two years later that New Zealand played, and lost, their next test, during their first England tour for nine years. Before the tests the side had a tremendous 13-run win at Lord's against a strong MCC side after a generous Reid declaration.

The five-match test series was lost 4-0, with one draw. Reid's batting average was 16.33, and he took just six wickets. However, he was fourth in the national averages, and having had to face Tony Lock, Jim Laker, Frank Tyson, Brian Statham and Fred Trueman, he concluded, 'I was reasonably happy with my form.'

After being criticised for not bowling leg spinners Jack Alabaster and Alex Moir in 1958, Reid insisted on being a selector, just as he had insisted on being captain of Otago in 1956/57, when he transferred there with Shell Oil. The 'kindergarten selection' of 1958 hurt Reid who, prior to the England tour, came close to relinquishing the captaincy for the only time in his career. A falling

The New Zealand team who toured England in 1958. Standing: John Ward, Jack Alabaster, Noel Harford, Bill Playle, Tony MacGibbon, Trevor Meale, Bob Blair, John Sparling, Alex Moir. Seated: Eric Petrie, Lawrie Miller, John Hayes, Harry Cave (vice-captain), John Reid (captain), Jack Phillipps (manager), Bert Sutcliffe, Jack D'Arcy.
Collection Dr Steve Gilbert

out with one of New Zealand's better batsmen, Lawrie Miller, resulted in the Wellington left-hander never playing for the province again. In the tests Lock and Laker took 51 wickets for 427 runs as no New Zealand batsmen improved their reputations.

'I offered to stand down from the captaincy so that Wallace could be coach and captain. I got him as coach in 1956, but he became the forgotten man of New Zealand cricket — a great player,' said Reid.

The reciprocal MCC trip in 1958/59 brought an innings defeat and a rain-affected draw. The lack of experience and depth in New Zealand cricket was never more exposed. Australia's next visit in 1959/60 ended in a 1-1 draw after four non-test internationals. Finally, Reid had a good enough team to take the pressure off his batting, and he averaged 41.71, as well as taking eight wickets.

Another non-test visit, this time a full tour by the MCC in 1960/61, was won 1-0, New Zealand's first international series success. Reid's all-round contribution of 146 runs and seven wickets in the three matches was again a key.

Reid's next test success was New Zealand's first away win, against South Africa in 1961/62. At the time Lord Cobham, New Zealand's governor-general from 1957 to 1962, and president of the MCC in 1957, commented, 'It is hard to over-emphasise John Reid's part in this splendid achievement, both as captain and player.' Lord Cobham was a former Worcestershire captain, who as the Hon. C.J. Lyttelton had toured New Zealand with the MCC in 1935/36.

John Reid

In South Africa, '[Reid's] fame and fortune reached their zenith', lauded Dick Brittenden. At one down with three to go, Reid 'knew he had a side that could beat South Africa'. His overwhelming confidence in his own ability found its ideal stage in the 'superb climate, cricket and social' and the 'friendly people, not strange and more like New Zealanders'.

The contrast between 1961/62 and 1953/54, when New Zealand had last visited South Africa, was huge. This was largely due to the faith Reid's men had in him. There was just one player, John Guy, who rebelled, compared with half the team on the previous tour. Early on in the tour, in Australia, Guy was competing with Reid for runs. However, Reid rested him against Western Province to give other players a chance to stake a test claim. Reid 'buggered the averages up' by scoring 200. Guy responded badly both off and on the pitch, and lost confidence against the short fast bowling of Neil Adcock. Reid rued not bringing Barry Sinclair on the tour, but he had not scored well in the home season. Guy refused the offer of manager Gordon Leggat's ticket home. 'Form isn't always the story,' said Reid.

The New Zealand captain was only bowling when he had to, having hurt his knee fielding on the boundary in Perth on the trip out. 'I don't know what I was doing out there,' said Reid. 'Captains don't field on the boundary. I dived and ripped the cartilage and it was not diagnosed, so I was on cortisone injections that they shoved right into the knee with a nine-inch needle three times a day.

Reid hitting to leg during his 83 against the MCC at the Basin, February 1961.
Christchurch Star

I decided the remedy was worse than the complaint and quit.'

The injury was to trouble Reid for the rest of his career and, except for an occasional effort, curtail his bowling for ever.

'It was a magnificent tour for me,' Reid said of the 1961/62 series. With seven centuries in nine innings, including two in tests, Reid led his best team. He also had 'a superb manager' in Gordon Leggat. 'I had the team right behind me,' he said.

Not always was he able to have such faith in his players. 'I had some good advisers,' Reid admitted. Frank Cameron, Jack Alabaster, Murray Chapple and Gordon Leggat were the lieutenants he 'bounced decisions off, and I bulldozed some of them through, sure', he has admitted. Reid's vice-captain in 1961/62, Graham Dowling, was not one of his trusty henchmen. 'I hadn't thought about Graham that much. He didn't do much in South Africa in 1961. We had trouble finding an opening pair. With Graham it's hard to say, he's hard to classify,' said Reid, who recommended Barry Sinclair as his successor when he retired in 1965, despite his inexperience as a leader.

New Zealand lost the first test against South Africa. Chasing 197, New Zealand was all out for 166. They had never successfully chased a total in a test. 'My flu added almost as many degrees to my temperature as I did runs to my score,' wrote Reid. 'I set my heart on winning that first test — our approach to scoring 197 runs was not the right one — the tempo from the start of the innings was disappointingly blind to these requirements [to keep the scoreboard moving].' From 79.3 eight-ball overs plus 15 no balls New Zealand made just 166 runs. New Zealand drew the second, but Reid's scores of 92 and 14, plus 2/21 in the second innings, helped force a victory in the third test that put the captain in a masterful mood for the rest of the tour. The test started on New Year's Day 1962. Reid won the toss for the third time in the series and elected to bat on a plumb Newlands pitch. His batsmen did not let him down and scored 385, led by Zin Harris' 101 (his only test century) and 92 from the skipper himself in just over two hours.

The South African reply was a mournful 190, opening bowler Cameron and Alabaster accounting for nine of their opponents. Reid sent his batsmen out again and was able to declare at 212 for nine — leaving South Africa needing 408 to win in a shade under eight hours — but only because his wicket-keeper, Artie Dick, stood out on an otherwise undistinguished scorecard with an undefeated 50.

'I was criticised for not making South Africa follow on,' Reid said later. 'They batted last and myself and Jack Alabaster especially proved match winners. If they'd gone and scored 500 we'd have been struggling. I took a bit of a risk — that's me. We were able to declare because Artie Dick scored 50. That was a good bit of captaincy and I think I did the right thing.'

'Fittingly, it was Reid who broke the deadlock less than half an hour from the safety of stumps,' says Don Neely in *Men in White*.

Another loss, at Johannesburg, this time by an innings, was not in the script, but the final test at Port Elizabeth certainly was.

Reid hammering the Australian bowlers on the way to a 73 not out in 1963.
Christchurch Star

Reid didn't enforce the follow-on when New Zealand were 195 ahead, as his bowlers were not fresh. In *Sword of Willow* he gives four reasons for his decision — as always, 'very definite ones' — 'batting fourth on a wicket with a reputation for breaking up and taking spin on the fourth day — bowlers not as fresh as they might be — psychological effect — setting a total of 400 a better proposition in my book — New Zealand is not completely equipped to make runs, perhaps against the clock, to win a test match. I say this with the experience of two other wins — against the West Indies where we bowled the opposition out. Our one opportunity to win by scoring runs against the clock failed at Durban.' And who was there to argue with New Zealand's cricketing colossus?

Reid bowling for New Zealand against the MCC at Wellington in 1959. Willie Watson is the non-striker, Peter Richardson the facing batsman.
Christchurch Star

Back in Port Elizabeth and the final test, South Africa were set 314 to win. Reid, having already made 26 and 69, as well as taking 2/26 in the first innings, took 4/44 from 45 (eight-ball) overs of 'unremitting devotion to duty'. His total score of 1915 runs on the tour was twice anyone else's total.

The team's devotion to duty was shown by Zin Harris, 'who was not an opening batsman and not a good player of fast bowling', recalled Reid. Harris stayed for 40 minutes to hang on for stumps on the second day of the fifth test at Port Elizabeth, after being promoted to number three during a bouncer war.

In this game, 'It was the first time I felt I had to bowl,' said Reid. 'I took 4/44 from 45 overs and all the guys pulled their weight. It was a very satisfying win.'

So, after topping the batting and bowling averages and winning two tests in the series, Reid was a hero when he returned home. But there were to be no more successes for Reid after that tour, and by the mid-sixties New Zealand had earned a reputation for dullness in their efforts to avoid defeat. Three heavy defeats, this time in tests, on another MCC tour emphasised Reid's isolation as a quality batsman. Even 74 and 100, out of 159, were not enough to save the third test.

He achieved his highest score, 296, with a world record 15 sixes, on 15 January 1963, for Wellington against Northern Districts. He had become the 'Kiwi King of Slog' in some English minds, but sixes off Tom Puna, Don Clarke and Gren Alabaster showed it was a quality Northern Districts attack that he had to hit. Reid's attitude was a forthright (as ever) 'in general the batsman's task is to get on with it as much as possible'.

But while Reid was undoubtedly a crowd-pleaser, did he please his players?

He certainly stood up for his rights, which benefited his team-mates. Sledging from South African quick bowler Peter Heine brought a threat to 'use the bat on him'.

For the first time in his career Reid missed a match for reasons other than injury when Pakistan toured New Zealand in early 1965. 'I was strongly of the

opinion that my wife and children needed a holiday,' he wrote, and he withdrew from Wellington's game against the tourists. On the first morning, while Reid was fishing near Rotorua, the home side was all out for 53.

Frank Cameron, opening bowler from 1960 to 1965, and a player during Reid's work-related tenure at Otago from 1956 to 1958, said, 'We didn't have 11 test players at that time. We often had players who proved to be not good enough, or players who weren't getting enough cricket. We only played about three tests a season and didn't have the continuity to develop players.'

Nine tests in succession were drawn. In 1965, New Zealand played exhausting successive series against India, Pakistan and England. Reid retired after the final disappointment, a 3-0 test series loss against England. Six of the nine tests on tour were lost and Reid felt that New Zealand had 'made no material progress internationally' on the trip as he had expected.

'1965 was not a good year for me. In those days I was trying to run a business, which I left with my wife while I was away for six months. You were not as dedicated as if you had nothing else to do. It's no excuse, but with a business and a family and with cricket with no money in it, working for yourself was the only way I could have afforded to go on tour.'

On the Pakistan-India leg of the tour there were the familiar complaints about conditions and umpiring, as there had been in 1955/56 and as there

A sniper in the crowd? No, Reid has caught Pakistan batsman Mohammad Ilyas for four after a juggle. Collinge and Congdon congratulate him. Reid took a record 43 catches in New Zealand tests.
Christchurch Star

would be under Coney in 1984/85 and beyond. Reid did not shirk responsibility and took his stout leather bag, bought back in 1949, on a second visit to the subcontinent almost ten years after his first. The passage of New Zealand captaincy history later altered when incumbents such as Howarth and Wright opted out of tours to Asia.

Reid, although he worked for Shell Oil, was the only one of his era other than Sutcliffe who played the game as if it was his career.

His work took Reid to Otago in 1956/57, unpopularly usurping captain Lankford Smith. 'I got a bit tough but I had to look after myself as far as experience goes,' he said. More importantly, Reid felt he 'came of age' as a man-manager thanks to Shell. 'This was an area I was sadly lacking in my early days as captain,' Reid told Joseph Romanos, his 1999 biographer. 'I tended to grab the ball and try and do it myself.' Reid realised this was 'not the way to increase the development of team spirit', concluding that, 'The real art of captaincy is being able to get the best out of your players.'

But what sort of captain was Reid? What was it like to play under him? Artie Dick told Romanos, 'He believed in confronting the problem, discussing it and then leaving it behind.' Surprisingly, perhaps, given what Reid has described as his early 'dogmatic' attitude, Dick said, 'I always found he was happy to listen to advice.'

He had 'tremendous expectations' before games, so much so that team talks became 'rantings'. Afterwards, 'a thousand words' was Reid's early form of a rollicking, and given his seniority, playing stature and forceful personality, who could fight back?

Frank Cameron, Reid's team-mate, and later a test selector for 18 years, said, 'He was an aggressive captain. When in doubt he would always attack. He wanted the batsmen to play shots and the bowlers to take wickets. That's the way he played himself. Bogo was an impatient captain. He wanted things to happen immediately. He didn't have a great deal of time for shoddy performances and was liable to tell individuals, or more likely a team meeting so, which I thought was fair enough.'

The great all-rounder even described himself as a 'rough bugger', who commentator Don Mosey claimed would change the bowling on occasion with the words, 'Piss off down to long leg: I can do better myself.'

'He was often a very aggressive captain,' continued Cameron, 'focused and forceful. He could be a little impatient, especially with other off-spinners. He was the best there was under certain conditions, a bit like John Bracewell if it was turning, though he wasn't quite suited to flighting it. In my years he knew when to bowl.'

In 1991, John Reid and Clive Lloyd led a coaching seminar in South Africa. They emerged with a 20-point plan of what a captain should be.

1. Must have the trust, respect and confidence of his players.
2. Must be a leader.
3. Must know his players.
4. Must have discipline on and off the field.
5. Must know the laws of the game.
6. Must know the strengths and weaknesses of the opposition.
7. Must sort out field placings beforehand.
8. Must be able to motivate team-mates.
9. Must anticipate what will happen during the game and be aware of the game situation.
10. Must communicate with the bowlers all the time.
11. Must lead by example.
12. Must be a strong character.
13. Must be able to read wickets.
14. Must take a leadership role in training.
15. Must be calm in tight situations.
16. Must have a good relationship with the manager/coach.
17. Must always know how much time (or overs) is left in the match.
18. Must sometimes be firm and take the initiative, even when making decisions against the views of the team.
19. Must not be afraid to try different tactics in order to get a wicket.
20. Must play fair and not let the team get involved in intimidation.

These 20 commandments tell a lot about Reid's attitude towards his responsibilities and his reluctance to delegate, as well as what his strengths and preoccupations were as a captain and are as a referee.

In the end, Reid wrote in 1966, 'I had devoted my time and energy to cricket almost from the day I left school, and in recent years such application had been increasingly difficult.' Tony MacGibbon, New Zealand's leading bowler for much of Reid's reign, said, 'I remember that Lord Cobham told John Reid, if he wasn't enjoying his cricket as captain he should get out of it.' By 1965 it was time for Reid to move on.

He later became a selector (1975–78), when Howarth and Wright made their debuts. He had been a selector from 1958 to 1965 but, curiously, the captaincy was left in disarray in the first series without him against England in 1965/66. Reid's preferred choice, Barry Sinclair, took over from Murray Chapple, who was injured after captaining the first test. Reid expected him to 'take over from me and go on longer than he did'. But by 1967/68 Graham Dowling, Reid's 1965 deputy, was available to begin his tenure.

Reid opened a squash club in Wellington, then emigrated to South Africa where he worked for Toyota and coached Northern Transvaal (1983–89), Transvaal (1990) as well as South Africa (1985–86), seemingly oblivious to apartheid. He returned to New Zealand in 1992, and in 1993 became a high-profile ICC referee. Chuckers were anathema to Reid, who spoke his mind when refereeing, criticising the action of Pakistani Shoaib Akhtar when it was not his place to do so, according to a fellow referee. Reid also managed the New Zealand Under-19s on tours in 1994 and 1996.

On his role as a referee he commented, with typical Kiwi understatement, 'I'd played a bit of cricket and I think I can read a game even as a referee.'

Reid now lives in Taupo with his wife Norli. He has three children, one of whom, Richard, represented New Zealand as an international cricketer.

Reid has commented that he will probably be remembered as 'an all-rounder, a cricket captain who knew what he was about and a tough old bastard'. He went on to elaborate, 'I was tough for a start and got the team firmly behind me. It took five years, until 1961, for things to be ideal.'

However, as Reid himself wrote, 'a captain can't do it alone'.

9. MURRAY CHAPPLE 25 February 1966 – 1 March 1966

A vice-captain par excellence

With the retirement of 37-year-old John Reid and 41-year-old Bert Sutcliffe on their return home after the disappointing 1965 tour to Pakistan and England, New Zealand was short of experienced players. Graham Dowling, then aged 28, and John Sparling, 27, were being groomed for the captaincy, but they were currently unavailable. As a consequence the selection panel of Ken Deas, Jack Kerr, Walter Hadlee and Murray Chapple made the surprise choice of Chapple himself as captain.

The first test match of the post-Reid era brought in Grahame Bilby for the unavailable Graham Dowling, and the only player with a test century behind him was Sinclair. Even the positive pen of Dick Brittenden could find little to be optimistic about in 'the lack of quality' and 'very thin' batting of the chosen team.

Chapple had begun his career with Canterbury in 1949/50, and was now 35. His one match in charge was to be his final test (of 14) after making his test debut in South Africa as Bert Sutcliffe's opening partner back in 1952/53. He actually went on to represent New Zealand once more in 1972, when he was team manager, a role that was well suited to the 'essentially practical cricketer' that Chapple was, according to Brittenden. He continued as a selector from 1965/66 until 1969/70, after which he served as deputy chairman of the New Zealand Cricket Council. Chapple managed tours to the West Indies and to India and Pakistan in 1976, and was to manage New Zealand's tour of England and then become chairman of the Cricket Council when he died suddenly in 1985.

In Christchurch club cricket, Chapple played 95 senior matches for Lancaster Park. He was lauded by Brittenden, who wrote in the club's centenary history, 'His ability to size up a player or a situation has been widely recognised throughout New Zealand; there are few shrewder judges of the game anywhere.' As a captain, Brittenden reckoned Chapple 'did not have

the bold, brassy approach of Ian Cromb and Ray Dowker to his captaincy duties, but he achieved excellent results and, like the others, had a very good record for Canterbury'.

The strong on-side right-handed batsman, and left-arm bowler, came to prominence in 1952/53 aged 22, when he hit a career-best 165, as well as 88 in the second innings, for Canterbury against South Africa. Selectors Jack Kerr, Bert Sutcliffe, Ken Uttley and captain Merv Wallace picked him to play South Africa the following week. Opening, he scored 22 and seven in the drawn game, but won selection for the 1953/54 tour of South Africa under Geoff Rabone.

Batting at three, he made one and one, then 8 and 22 as an opener, before a test best 76 in the third test, held at Cape Town. Scores of 4, 42, 8 and 18 completed the run, and Chapple played tests only occasionally thereafter. He played (scoring three and one) in New Zealand's first test win, and it was a surprise when he was chosen to tour South Africa again in 1961/62.

Captain John Reid was keen on 'retaining experience', and Chapple's ability to 'anticipate many of the pitfalls and unusual conditions we would strike' was a factor in his selection.

'Murray Chapple was magnificent as vice-captain. As a highly successful captain of Canterbury he knew the ropes and did the job of vice-captain as I have never seen it done before. He took over practice so that I was free to look to my own form and to keep a more careful eye on the other team members.' On the tour where Reid believed he reached maturity as a test captain, Chapple was instrumental in taking the weight off Reid's shoulders off the field. And, with 69 and 33 in the third test, his first for nearly six years, he played a key role on the field in New Zealand's second test win.

'There was a feeling at one stage that Murray and I were at loggerheads,' Reid said later. 'It was not true. He was a good competitor and as captain of Canterbury we had battles on the field, but not off it.' In South Africa in 1953/54 the two men were in opposite camps, but they were both more mature tourists eight years later.

Before the 1961/62 tour Reid asked the selectors to pick Chapple. 'I needed a vice-captain who was not necessarily going to play in tests, and Murray was the best one available.' The 31-year-old was now more thickset than in his youth, an avuncular figure with Brylcreemed hair and an easy smile.

The selectors suggested Reid telephone Chapple, although the meeting had already run on to 11 p.m. 'He got out of bed and came down and we told him what we wanted. He did a hell of a good job and scored some good runs. He looked after all sorts of things, such as practices and looking after players, as the captain has a hell of a lot of other things to do, with the press and everything else,' said Reid.

The Springboks featured large in Chapple's international career, with matches against South Africa on the tours of 1952/53 and 1961/62, as well as at home in 1952/53 and 1963/64, making up 11 of Chapple's 14 test outings. However, it was against England that he played his single game as captain.

Chapple first led Canterbury in 1957/58, and in 1961's *New Zealand Cricketers* Dick Brittenden wrote, 'Chapple has shown the same flair for leadership with his club team Lancaster Park, as he has with Canterbury. Chapple seldom makes a thoughtless move, or a bad one. Nothing is done merely by instinct. He is almost certainly the best tactical captain in New Zealand at present.'

Captaincy was probably Chapple's major strength as a cricketer. 'No-one understood the game, or his fellow players, better,' wrote Joseph Romanos in *A Century of Great New Zealand Cricketers*.

In all, Chapple played in four different decades, with a highlight being his leading of Canterbury to Plunket Shield success in 1959/60. Of the 21 games he led between 1957/58 and 1960/61, the team won seven, lost eight and drew six. He played for Central Districts from 1950/51 to 1951/52 and then between 1962/63 and 1965/66. His last game was to be for an injury-struck New Zealand, who he managed on a tour to the West Indies in 1972, although the match with the Windward Islands was rained off.

In Chapple's sole test in command, MCC captain M.J.K. Smith won the toss and elected to bat. From 47/4 in 85 minutes on a soft wicket, the tourists recovered to make 342. Bevan Congdon's maiden test century (104 with seven fours in 320 minutes) helped New Zealand to a five-run lead, only the fifth in tests between the two countries. On the final day, Smith's declaration set Chapple's men 196 to win in 140 minutes. Chapple, at number seven, fell caught behind for a duck, and his team 'was soon undermined' (*Men in White*) after making no attempt at the target. They hung on for a draw at 48/8, thanks to Victor Pollard's six not out in 93 minutes. Chapple pulled a leg muscle and was replaced by Sinclair for the next test. He retired that season.

In addition to his numerous cricketing roles Chapple was a schoolteacher, and at the time of his death he was the district senior inspector of primary schools in Hamilton. He left his wife, Frances, and three children, Susan, Murray and Mark.

10. BARRY SINCLAIR 4 March 1966 – 20 February 1968

A fairly pragmatic approach to things

In the vacuum that followed John Reid's retirement as New Zealand captain, Barry Sinclair emerged to become New Zealand's third captain in as many matches. Characteristically, his first act — when thrown into the job he did 'out of a sense of obligation' — was to raise his game and top score for his team with 72 runs in the drawn test against England at Dunedin in March 1966.

Sinclair grew up with New Zealand cricket's peerless historian Don Neely. From boyhood days practising on the roadside with apple boxes as wickets, the pair went on to Rongotai College and Wellington club cricket at Kilbirnie together. 'Neely was always captain then,' recalled Sinclair. 'Subconsciously I learnt from him as a captain. He was always more innovative than I was — always trying to do unusual things. That was not part of my nature. You learn just by being there. I also picked up a lot from John Reid, but without sitting down and talking about how to captain.'

In 1956 Sinclair toured Fiji with Kilbirnie under guest captain Walter Hadlee, who had been recruited by 1949 England tour manager and long-time Kilbirnie member Jack Phillipps. Sinclair had to return home with a poisoned mouth, the first of a series of unfortunate ailments during his career that included a bad squash injury that almost lost him an eye and prevented him playing in a World XI against England in 1967.

The diminutive Sinclair, New Zealand's shortest captain at five foot three inches (160 cm), provided a valuable bridge towards the successful era of Graham Dowling, who had deputised for Reid in England in 1965 but was unavailable for the return series because of work commitments. At 29 years of age, Sinclair was now in his seventh season of first-class cricket, but had captained his province only once. Similarly, Wellington had plucked him from second-grade cricket as a teenager, after just a single game for first-grade club Kilbirnie (now known as Easts). 'Imagine how hard that was,' Sinclair said later.

New Zealand captain Barry Sinclair puffs out his chest in serious mood, April 1967.
Christchurch Star

'I had no ambitions to be captain. I was just concentrating on playing as well as I could. I put a huge amount of time into developing my own game, because I wasn't a natural player.

'In 1965 John Reid had retired. He was 39 and had given it away and there wasn't anyone particularly obvious to be captain. I wasn't thinking to be captain, I was just thinking how many runs I could make to stay in the team.

'The most experienced player you had was made captain. New Zealand cricket always chose a batsman. Harry Cave was the exception, and he did a pretty useful job, but we were struggling for someone at that stage.'

There were some unusual circumstances surrounding Sinclair's elevation. In 1965/66 Wellington beat Auckland and won the Plunket Shield. On the train back to Wellington, chairman of selectors Walter Hadlee approached Sinclair. 'We've got a captaincy problem, and we're thinking of you mid-term,' he told a surprised Sinclair.

Hadlee continued, 'We'll make you vice-captain against England and let you captain the President's XI against the MCC at Wellington.'

'In those days you didn't debate — you tended to say to yourself, "Whatever",' Sinclair later said. 'It [the captaincy] was something I hadn't studied intensely, like Neely studied it.

'When the test side was announced they made Murray Chapple captain. He was at the end of his career and probably shouldn't have been in the side, but we went to Christchurch and saved the game. In those days New Zealand had taken a fair hammering from England in 1958 and 62/63 and 65 and they were a pretty strong side, so to come out with draws was seen as not doing too badly.

'At Dunedin there was rain. I came off the field from practice at 10.35 to go to the dressing room for a cup of tea. Murray Chapple was going out to toss — it was the usual story — when someone came to me, I can't remember if it was Dr John Heslop, a board member from Dunedin, or Martin Horton, who I think was our manager. I was putting my bat down and getting a cup of tea. They said, "Murray Chapple's not playing and you're captain." I said, "Okay," and just grabbed a blazer, because I knew you had to do that. It was twenty to eleven, and M.J.K. Smith, who I knew because I'd been at Warwickshire in 1960, went out to the middle with me. He said, "Got a coin?" The umpires had one, I think, so we tossed. That was my introduction to captaining New Zealand. There were no preliminaries, no support. In those days no one talked to you, you just talked to your players.'

Sinclair won the toss, batted and struggled to 33 out of a meagre 192 all out. On a 'capricious wicket' the home side were put back in on the final afternoon after England declared at 254/8. Only 36 minutes remained with the score 112/9, 50 runs ahead, but Eric Petrie and Tom Puna followed Sinclair's attacking 39 to hold on for a draw.

In Auckland, 'for three and three-quarter days' Sinclair was 'in the headlines every day, for the right reasons'. He made 114 in 229 minutes with 11 fours, in what he described as 'only my second test and I had been captain of New Zealand only a week'.

His third test century included his thousandth test run, in his nineteenth match. Only Sutcliffe (13 matches) and Reid (21) had achieved this before. 'It was my best in terms of a fluent innings. It wasn't always like that,' recalled the nuggety right-hander.

Dick Brittenden regards his best as his 138 against South Africa in 1963/64. 'Sinclair distinguished himself with other test centuries, but his battle at Eden Park must rank as one of the epics of New Zealand cricket.'

'Peter Pollock hit me down the left side a lot of times. He'd hit me and then I'd hook him for four. It was a fair battering,' Sinclair later recalled.

Back at Auckland in 1967 a first innings lead of 74, after Sinclair threw England captain Colin Cowdrey out from cover ('I knocked the sticks over') for 59, was followed by collapse as New Zealand made 129 in 103.3 overs. Ever fast on his feet, Sinclair specialised in the cover position. He also used his agility effectively, particularly against the short ball, in his stroke play.

'England went very defensive. Higgs and Jones had a long on and long off and it was a real struggle,' commented Sinclair.

After requiring 204 in 272 minutes England was 84/3, now needing 120 in as many minutes. Even the normally circumspect Arthur Carman called the finish 'disappointing'. As Sinclair said himself, 'I decided to make it harder for them by using my pace attack rather than winkle them out by spin.' Although criticised by the *New Zealand Herald* 'for want of imagination', Sinclair's long-serving predecessor (Reid) and his successor (Dowling) also had an aversion to using spin.

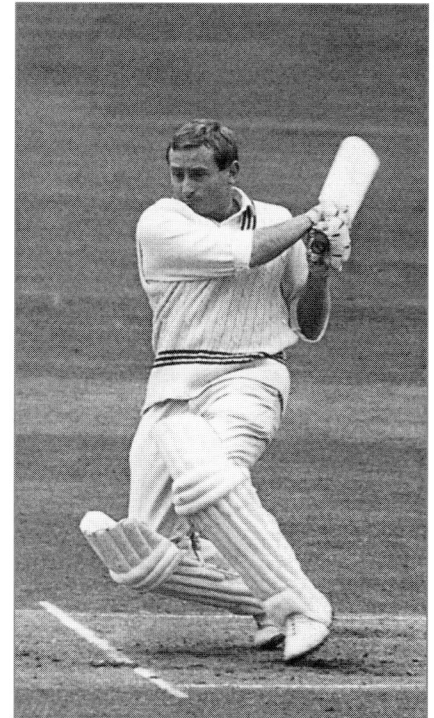

On the first match of the England tour in 1965, Barry Sinclair hits out of Jim Laker's bowling as New Zealand play London New Zealand at the Oval. It was Laker's first match at the Oval since leaving Surrey in 1959.
Christchurch Star

Barry Sinclair, the New Zealand captain, cuts the ball through the slips for an Invitation team chosen by Canterbury and New Zealand selector Mac Anderson in an early season warm-up, October 1967.
Christchurch Star

Sinclair: 'I took some flak, but I also gave a bit back. Some of the things the critics said had some validity. But we had sat down — Motz, Taylor, Pollard, Congdon and me — and decided we didn't have a great spin attack. If England can't make 204 in 280 minutes we're not going to give them the game, we said. It may seem ultra-defensive now, but in 1966 it didn't seem all that bad a thing. That's how it was.

'We didn't have much faith in the spinners. Vic Pollard just threw the ball into the wicket and Tom Puna was a pretty ordinary off spinner. We didn't have an attack capable of bowling England out. We just made it hard for them.

'I may have called the shots differently at Eden Park if I had had more experience as skipper. There were some mitigating circumstances. There was no advice given by anybody. We sat down and worked it out for ourselves. In hindsight, if we'd tried to bowl them out and lost, what would it have mattered? But no one liked losing in those days. Maybe if we'd had Alabaster or someone. Take it whatever way you like.' Revealingly, the dapper and overtly competitive Sinclair said later, 'I'm too proud to say that I probably didn't do it right.'

Unfortunately, this game became the defining one of Sinclair's tenure as test captain. To go on the defensive when a win was possible was no longer acceptable to many observers. These included the chairman and secretary of the Australian Cricket Board, who had been brought over at the New Zealand Cricket Council's expense in order to establish a closer playing relationship after 20 years without a trans-Tasman test.

Sinclair retained the captaincy for the ground-breaking return series against Australia at home at the start of 1967 and away at the end of the year. Although there were no tests, New Zealand's performances were a revelation, particularly at Pukekura Park in New Plymouth, where spinners Pollard and Bryan Yuile took 18 wickets between them and brought about a win by 159 runs.

'The team was probably the best I have played with,' Sinclair commented. 'For most of my ten years in big cricket myself and others have been overshadowed by Bert Sutcliffe and John Reid, but in this side we had 11 players all equal. If we didn't do it right in Auckland we certainly did it right at New Plymouth.'

The return series was scheduled for November. 'This was obviously too early in the season as we'd had no cricket,' Sinclair recalled. 'I put a lot of pressure on as we needed some practice, and a game against Canterbury at the beginning of November was arranged. I was pretty rusty and finally got John Guy to set up a weekend in Gisborne, where there is a drier climate. New Zealand Cricket finally agreed, but said, "You're captain — you want it, you organise it!" Martin Horton and I did it all and New Zealand Cricket paid.

'In those days you didn't have anyone to do anything else. The captain ran the practices and if there were any problems, the captain dealt with it. Everyone had problems at various stages on the Australia tour. There was no one to delegate to. The management got you from A to B. It's all different now.'

Where did it hit you? Sinclair rues a missed hook off Mufasirul in the first innings of the third test against Pakistan at Lancaster Park, 1965. He retired hurt, but recovered to make 46, and was there at the close to see New Zealand to a draw.
Christchurch Star

A new era had begun, but it was almost the end for Sinclair. The 1967/68 tour by India began at Dunedin with a defeat by five wickets for New Zealand, with Sinclair scoring nought and eight. An attack of boils put the diminutive right-hander out of the second test, against India at Christchurch. Dowling took over and scored 239, a New Zealand test record and the highest score by a test captain (the previous record was Reid's 142 against South Africa in an innings defeat in 1961/62). New Zealand beat India for the first time, and recorded their fourth test win — the first for six years, since beating South Africa on 4 January 1962.

'The Board asked me if I was happy to play on under Graham Dowling. I didn't push returning to be captain and neither did they, and I was quite happy to play under him.

Barry Sinclair pushes
forward, November 1967.
Christchurch Star

I didn't know how long I'd carry on. I had two kids and couldn't get time off work. I'd worked for Goodyear from 1962, but in 1969 they had a change to new American management, and they weren't interested in cricket so I couldn't go to England in 1969. There was no financial reward to keep playing and suddenly the huge desire that I'd had ran out. I was pretty driven right through my career.'

A royalty cheque for £32 from Gray-Nicholls bats was 'pretty good'. 'We got £7.50 a day in England in 1965. You didn't make any money. It was an amateur game basically.'

Scores of 20 and 12 in the fourth and final test against India (lost by 272 runs) signalled the end to Sinclair's test career, and a brief return against Australia in 1969/70 under Bevan Congdon's captaincy showed the 34-year-old 'the competitive edge was slipping away. I realised I wasn't enjoying the game any more.'

Sinclair retired from first-class cricket at the end of the 1970/71 season, having made more appearances for Wellington than any other player. 'I wouldn't say I'm over it yet,' Sinclair said on leaving cricket, adding, 'I just didn't want to spend another Christmas playing Central Districts in Wanganui.'

Sinclair continued to play President's grade cricket until he was 57, and has always coached — at Takapuna Grammar, King's prep school in Auckland and at the North Shore club in Devonport, where he now lives. He and his wife Helen have two sons, Mark and Jeremy, and in his mid-sixties he still managed an export company selling mainly meat and butter to Pacific islands and Papua New Guinea.

Commenting on the players he coaches, Sinclair says, 'They all want to bring the bat from third slip. They can't understand when they get caught at second. It's getting harder,' he groans.

One of his protégés is Richard Jones, who has blossomed after a move from Auckland to Wellington, arranged by Sinclair. 'We set targets and talk about what he is in Wellington for — to score runs. I have a fairly pragmatic approach to these things.' It's a worthy summation of one of New Zealand's cricketing heroes.

11. GRAHAM DOWLING

22 February 1968 –
14 March 1972

He was the mildest-mannered man / That ever scuttled ship or cut a throat

Graham Dowling has bridged generations in New Zealand cricket and even in his sixties still had an influence in the game as an international referee. He looks back fondly to his debut for Canterbury in the amateur days of 1958, but forward to the 'development of New Zealand cricket'.

Dowling's record on the pitch is a fine one. On his debut as test captain, playing against India at Christchurch in 1968, the right-handed opener set a new New Zealand test best of 239. In 1967/68 he scored a New Zealand domestic season record 968 runs. He was captain of New Zealand in 19 of his 39 tests. The team won four tests and an away series for the first time, against Pakistan in 1969. The wins included New Zealand's first at Christchurch and Wellington, as well as their first against India and Pakistan.

While Dowling paved the way for the national side's success in later years, the magnitude of his team's performances cannot be easily forgotten. A studious, methodical and accomplished opener, in the mould of fellow Christchurch accountant Walter Hadlee, the black-haired, jut-jawed Dowling became as thoughtful a test captain as Hadlee had been 20 years before.

But there were downs as well as ups during his career. He was not as successful as he would have liked in tours to England in 1965 and 1969, either as a player or as a captain. While leading the team in 1969, and chasing a rare New Zealand victory, Dowling experienced the dreadful frustration of a downpour when India were 76-7 and on the edge of defeat. Trousers rolled up, he tried to mop up the water, but the match was abandoned despite his efforts.

In Australia in 1970, while deputising for wicket-keeper Ken Wadsworth, Dowling broke a finger so badly it had to be amputated. Yet he fought back to captain the side again, until a career-ending back injury forced him home during the 1972 tour to the West Indies.

His role as a cricket administrator began in 1974. He became secretary of the Cricket Council's Board of Control in 1981, and was executive director from 1984 until 1995. Dowling also managed the Mark Burgess-led team that reached the semi-finals of the 1979 World Cup. He has also had a successful career as a chartered accountant, and was a partner in KPMG Peat Marwick from 1962 to 1981. He and his wife Leila have three children, and he is currently Bursar at College House in Christchurch.

New Zealand appears to be in a stable period following a radical change in governance in New Zealand cricket when Christopher Doig ascended to Dowling's chief executive role, a change in personnel that also marked a change in the character of the post. Mark Greatbatch has described Dowling as 'a sincere man who liked to be distant from his players'. Portraying Dowling as an 'us and them' type, Greatbatch believed he 'moved out at an appropriate time' as the 'transformation of this role to what it has become today was rapid'.

In his autobiography *Someone Had to Do It*, Don Cameron wrote: 'One of Dowling's great assets was that, as a former international captain, he was automatically a member of the influential class at the meetings of the International Cricket Conference, and his stature as a former test player opened many doors that were shut to many non-playing administrators. Another was Dowling's in-built affection for the game.'

Dowling regards Walter Hadlee, who led the first national sides he watched, as one of the greatest of New Zealand's cricket captains, and says Hadlee shaped his approach in years to come.

'He was hugely analytical. Immediately postwar the game was different, but he was a very shrewd, calculating captain, who handled his resources extremely well and pretty successfully. Although they didn't win any test matches in his time they didn't have too many opportunities either. He might have played about eleven test matches and there he is, the grand old man of New Zealand cricket.'

Graham Dowling, one of the Christchurch cricketing accountants, along with Walter Hadlee and Jack Kerr, who led New Zealand to more test victories in four years than in their previous 47.
Christchurch Star

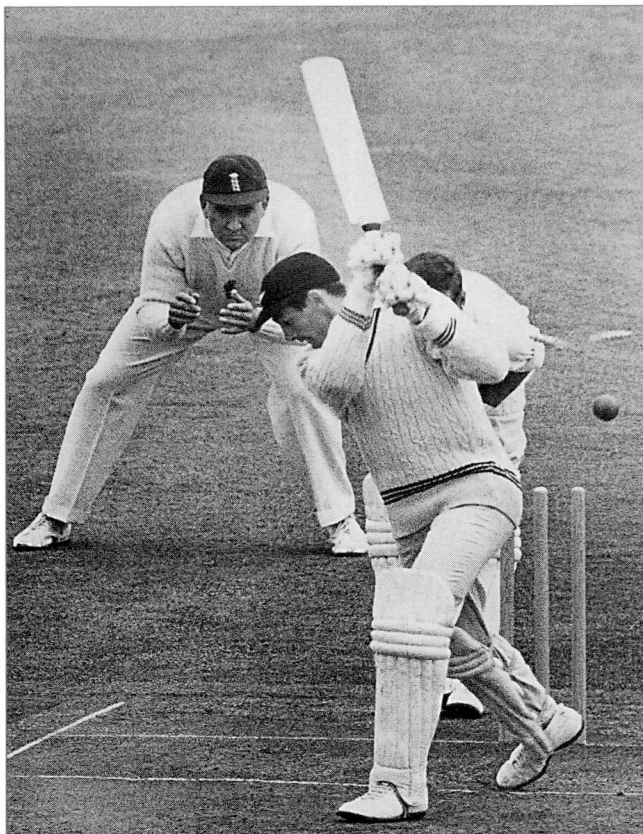

Dowling out! Fred Titmus bowls Graham Dowling for 32 in the first test at Edgbaston, May 1965. Colin Cowdrey is at slip and Jim Parks is the wicket-keeper.
Christchurch Star

Another who commands his respect is John Reid, who was captain when Dowling first played for New Zealand.

'I've played a lot of my cricket with John Reid senior. He'd lead from the front, would have been a wonderful one-day cricketer, in the current scenario. He could do it all. He would have been right up there with the best all-rounders in world cricket without a doubt. He did things by example; you wanted to get rid of someone and off a short run he'd be bowling bouncers with the keeper standing up to him or smash the hell out of the opposing bowler as he did in 61/2 in South Africa. Fielded magnificently as well, everything. Maybe not quite as shrewd and calculating in terms of the way he changed his fields and set his bowlers and that sort of thing, but did wonders for New Zealand cricket. He led at the time when we managed to get our first and a couple of other test wins that I was involved in and always had the greatest of respect for his team-mates. We were all pretty well making up the numbers who occasionally contributed and he was the world star.'

Dowling takes great pride in spanning the generations in his many cricket roles. The fond memories he has of a cricket career that stretched from the naive amateurism of the fifties to the opportunistic commercialism of the nineties are rare rewards for a lifetime's involvement in the game. When he says he has no regrets, one senses Dowling really means it.

Graham Dowling followed a similar path to men such as Tom Lowry and Walter Hadlee — first a batsman, then a leader, and finally an administrator and manager. Like Lowry and Hadlee, 'Dowls' was at his best as a skipper, and it was as a captain that his slender figure and defined features first became well known. He first toured internationally as vice-captain of New Zealand Colts back in 1955/56, and 12 years later he would become captain of the national team.

Although Dowling was vice-captain to John Reid on the 1965 tour to India,

Graham Dowling

Pakistan and England, he was rarely consulted by his captain. Reid preferred the counsel of Frank Cameron, who later selected national teams with Reid in the seventies. As his successor, Reid recommended Barry Sinclair, although Murray Chapple was the surprise choice as captain for the first test after Reid's retirement, against England at Lancaster Park.

Chapple had captained Canterbury from 1957/58 to 1960/61 and Central Districts thereafter. He was 34, lacking fitness and out of form. A pulled leg muscle gave Sinclair, an inexperienced skipper even at club level, the national job for the next two years. In the mid-sixties Dowling was establishing his career in accountancy, and he did not play in the 1965/66 series against England because of work commitments.

In the meantime he did lead Canterbury, as he had done since 1962/63, when he took over from Tony MacGibbon who had captained the province for a year after Chapple moved to Central Districts. Dowling's 43 matches as Canterbury captain produced 16 wins, equal to Dan Reese, who had led New Zealand from 1907 to 1914.

When Sinclair's indisposition finally gave Dowling the chance to captain New Zealand, he had already led Canterbury in 28 first-class games and played in 20 tests. Despite scoring two test centuries, including a 143 that included two sixes and 16 fours on the first day of the first test just a week before his momentous 239 at Lancaster Park, Dowling, now almost 29, had

Dowling turns the ball to leg during his 239 against India at Lancaster Park, February 1968. He was soon to reach the first double century scored by a New Zealand captain, in his first test in charge.
Christchurch Star

failed to reach his potential. He was often unavailable because of his accountancy career, which he took at least as seriously as his cricket, or because of troublesome finger injuries.

Two of his best test innings were a five-hour 78, which helped set South Africa 313 to win in the fourth innings of the fifth test at Port Elizabeth in February 1962, and 129 at Bombay in 1965. New Zealand won the Port Elizabeth match by 40 runs, giving them their third test win. The next was not until Dowling's belated promotion to the captaincy six years later. In Bombay Dowling's century helped New Zealand to 297. Bruce Taylor, in his second test, took 5/26 giving his side a first innings lead of 209. Following on India declared at 463/5 and reduced New Zealand to 80/8 in the two-and-a-half hours before the end of the match.

A gently spoken, considerate and polite man, in some ways Dowling's inner fire was hidden under a surface of mildness, similar to Mark Burgess, who batted at number five in the first test team Dowling led. Later known as an administrator who liked to play safe — or in the opinion of more harsh critics, to sit on the fence — Dowling's passion overflowed just once on the playing field.

'We'd been done in the first test match in Bombay on an ill-prepared pitch because there'd been riots in the venue further up north so we had to stay in Bombay. The ball turned square, absolutely square and we got cleaned out. We went up to Nagpur and won the test match there, and then went on to Hyderabad. It was a sunny afternoon, then all of a sudden a cloud comes over. Suddenly the grounds flooded. We had a whole lot of people trying to mop it up when the showers disappeared, but then gradually they diminished and I got a bit bolshie. I'd actually lost my cool a few times and I started trying to get rid of the water with stumps digging into the ground and that sort of thing. But their efforts were just ridiculous; no one really tried that hard. There were twenty-five or thirty thousand people watching, because they loved cricket. They were booing the Indians and wanted to see the finish of the match but we couldn't get play in the finish and it was probably a hopeless case but I vented my spirits, because we were right on the verge of a series win, which we deserved, the boys deserved. We got the victory two tests later, when we got a test then held on. So that was a great thrill, great team work in that side and I was honoured to walk out first.'

This was just before Dowling's team won the first overseas series for New Zealand in Pakistan in 1969. He believes, 'We should have won the one before that, in India, too when the rain robbed us. It was sort of a nightmare when I think back on it.'

Wins were few and far between in those days. In 40 years New Zealand had won just six test matches before they beat Pakistan by five wickets at Lahore in 1969/70. It took almost another 30 years for a repetition, during the 1996/97 tour by Lee Germon's team, which also won in Lahore.

Dowling reaches 200 during his 239 against India, Lancaster Park 1968.

There are some similarities between Germon and Dowling. Both have strong associations with St Andrew's College in Christchurch (Dowling as an old boy and former member of the Board of Governors, Germon as director of development) and both were indirect victims of the new regime of Christopher Doig, New Zealand Cricket's revolutionary chief executive from 1995. Doig took over when Dowling chose to resign after the 1994/95 South Africa tour, while Germon was sacked by the selectors and Steve Rixon, Doig's appointee as coach, early in 1997.

However, in Dowling's time far fewer test matches were played than now. There were no major tours between 1961/62 and 1964/65, when New Zealand toured India, Pakistan, Great Britain, Holland, Bermuda and the US, making it virtually a world trip. They were away for nearly six months. In 1969 they undertook a similar tour.

On Dowling's first tour, to South Africa and Australia in 1961/62 under John Reid, things were very different for a New Zealand captain. 'There was nowhere near the media focus at all. I mean you went overseas and in the early sixties there were no New Zealand journalists on tour. Even Dick Brittenden wasn't on that one. The other tours in 1965 and, as captain in 1969 and 1971/72 to the West Indies, just one journalist travelled with you.

'You had to make the odd speech, but media pressure was just minute

The New Zealand team in England, 1969. Left to right, back: B.D. Milburn, B.F. Hastings, K.J. Wadsworth, H.J. Howarth, B.A.G. Murray, M.G. Burgess, D.R. Hadlee, R.S. Cunis, G.M. Turner. Front: B.R. Taylor, R.C. Motz, V. Pollard (vice-captain), G.C. Burgess (manager), G.T. Dowling (captain), B.E. Congdon, B.W. Yuile, R.O. Collinge.

compared to what it is these days. I feel sorry for Stephen Fleming because every day you've got to stand in front of the media.'

Dowling's major tours as captain were to England in 1969, followed by India and Pakistan in 1969/70, and the West Indies in 1971/72. Around these tours were Dowling-led home series against India in 1967/68, the West Indies in 1968/69 and England in 1970/71. Dowling had already met all these teams, as well as South Africa, and it was this international experience — along with that of players such as Glenn Turner, Bevan Congdon, Vic Pollard and Bruce Taylor — that helped New Zealand come of age at around this time. Although Dowling never played a test match against the Aussies — 'They wouldn't have us on until 1973/74' — one of the satisfying things about his cricket career was that the New Zealand team started winning the state one-day knockout competition in Australia.

After a back injury sent him home from the West Indies and brought about his retirement as a player, Dowling had the chance to observe his successors' approach to captaining the national team.

'I always thought that Geoff Howarth was a very good captain. He had a manner about him, an authoritative manner, he looked the part, he was the first to really get involved in the one-day circus in Australia, and you could see on TV he did run the ship extremely well. He nurtured his resources and manipulated them as you had to do. I mean it's a real game of chess, this one-day thing, and it was only just beginning.

'Howarth was highly respected and successful, a very astute captain I thought, and Crowe as well, slightly differently. He was a very deep and sound thinker on the game and successfully led the country. It was a tragedy that injury curtailed things for Martin, when he had a lot more left in him I think.'

Dowling does not agree that the same could be said about him, although he was still a fine batsman and leader when he was forced to retire.

'I was probably about 35 and it was time to develop a career and whatever else was in front of me. I'd been there. I'd sort of hung on. I'd broken my finger, proved to myself that I could play with only nine and a half fingers, and went on to captain the side to the West Indies, the first New Zealand side that went there. I didn't last that tour, but it was great being involved in it.'

Dowling has no inclination to record his experiences in the game in book form, as many of his successors have done.

'Unless you come up with something no one's ever heard of or get stuck into your team-mates, or come up with something about no balling or chucking, or some behind-the-scenes stuff that should never be made public then, you know, you're not going to sell it are you?

'It's not me. I was totally happy with my lot. I was so fortunate to have my luck and all the things that came from getting the odd extra chance as a first-class cricketer then at test cricket. There were times when as a first-class cricketer I thought my stay here would be over shortly, then I was given another chance — you get 100 and away you go again, so I've been very lucky, and I'm happy with that.' Before his retirement as a test referee in 2001 he said: 'I've got no more ambitions. I will be totally happy if I don't referee another test or one-dayer. It won't worry me at all, because I've done a series, I've been to three countries in that capacity, and done a couple of test matches at Lord's, which is the ultimate. The most recent one was the hundredth ever at Lord's, so if it all comes to an end tomorrow it won't be the end of the world for me.'

Tragically for Dowling, the centenary of New Zealand cricket clashed with

The end result is the same, the sideburns longer, in December 1971. But injuries were catching up with Dowling, and he would not last the forthcoming West Indies tour, returning after the second test when his back gave way. Congdon took over, and Dowling retired after 19 tests in charge, the most successful New Zealand skipper yet.
Christchurch Star

Net practice for the New Zealand touring team. Padless captain Graham Dowling at Eastbourne.
Christchurch Star

the shambles of the infamous 1994/95 South Africa tour. But Dowling has moved on since those days.

'I've kept my distance and avoided sticking my nose in. I think things have turned round without a doubt. From a playing point of view we're always going to have problems. It's the same for the All Blacks. It annoys me, so much of the sports-loving public has such short memories and they are so quick to be critical; most of it is out of ignorance. They're getting a heap of wonderful sport thrust at them and the moment someone fails it's "Cut his head off", "Sack the coach", and I think that's just pathetic. In my humble opinion it's very sad to hear.

'New Zealand cricket has probably got its administration formula pretty right and got some good people in their key positions. I'm sure of that and it's looking good, they're doing wonderful things for cricket. It's great that that's happening and I can be proud as a Kiwi going overseas in the knowledge that New Zealand cricket is doing pretty well. It's had its ups and downs, that's the story of professional sport, it will have its disasters, but they've done pretty well, in recent times.'

Perhaps Dowling's greatest legacy as a captain was pinpointed by Dick Shortt, a test umpire from 1959 to 1973.

'I think one turning point for New Zealand cricket occurred in the [1968] Indian test at Lancaster Park,' Shortt revealed in a 1977 interview with Don Neely. 'Graham Dowling was appointed to captain the game and, in my experience, he was the first New Zealand captain prepared to isolate the umpire from his New Zealand context, into another point of the game, and to use him in every way permissible under the law, to achieve the end of winning the game.

'He came to the dressing room on the last day, so meticulous was he in his intent of victory, with a look of thunder on his face, saying I must insist on the Indians using a new ball in case they wanted an old one. Since Dowling a new attitude towards test cricket became apparent in New Zealand sides.'

So, the first captain who really believed New Zealand could win? Or who knew he had the team under him who could win, at least. Certainly Dowling's later reputation for conservatism, even for sitting on the fence, as an administrator, and the charmingly mild manner he displays now, belie his Walter Hadlee-like planning and attention to detail, his beady eye on the professional development of the game and his generous rapport with his players.

12. BEVAN CONGDON 23 March 1972 – 5 March 1975

A fatalistic view

From mutiny to majesty, Bevan Congdon's graph as New Zealand captain would be one of continual improvement. With his unrelenting desire to avoid defeat and toughen up New Zealand cricket, Congdon won few friends when he succeeded Graham Dowling in 1972, but the professionalism he showed in an amateur era was a sign of changes to come. The punctilious, precise Congdon gave his team a jolt that led it to acquire the attitude necessary for a modern era of constant training, one-day internationals, contracts and competitiveness.

'If the team loses, the captain is at fault because he did not use his bowlers, batsmen, fielding positions, toss, rain and the elements etc., etc. If the team wins the players rightly receive praise, but so often the captain's contribution is overlooked,' Congdon has said.

'I guess I have a very fatalistic view of captaincy.'

Always tough, often terse, Congdon believes the roles of captain, coach and players should be analysed 'to place responsibility and accountability' where it properly lies.

'Too often now the team's support structure seems to absolve the players from actually performing.' Hard-hitting words from the granite-jawed hero of New Zealand cricket.

Yet another player to play his best cricket when appointed to the captaincy, 34-year-old Congdon was unpopular when he first led the team. However, he evolved into a cricketer of world stature and took his team to their best performances yet against their oldest enemies, England and Australia. Dick Brittenden wrote in 1970 that 'Congdon should make a good captain — because he is essentially a practical cricketer'.

Precise, immaculately turned out, unforgiving of those who did not try as hard as he undoubtedly did, Congdon was the hard man of New Zealand cricket. An amateur with a professional attitude, indulging in no fripperies,

A stony-faced Congdon at New Zealand House in London on 17 April 1973, looking forward to a marvellous tour.
Christchurch Star

no concessions to the fashions of the 1970s, he was a leader with an almost military bearing.

After Graham Dowling was forced out with a back injury, Congdon was the obvious choice to take over as captain for the third test against the West Indies at Barbados in 1971/72. Congdon scored 126, emulating Dowling's century on his debut as test captain. He had also scored 166 not out and 82 in the previous match, and averaged 88.50 in the tests, as well as taking 13 wickets with his medium pace bowling.

Ever the pragmatist, Congdon said he was not surprised to be given the job, simply because 'I was appointed vice-captain for the tour'. He went on to elaborate: 'To a large number of those appointed captain, their selection is "by default" — being the most appropriate person at the time, when for whatever reason a new captain is required.'

Straddling the era between John Reid and John Wright, Congdon was already in his mid-thirties when he became captain. He was New Zealand's second oldest new skipper, behind Merv Wallace who was 36 when he had his two tests in charge. When Congdon, aged almost 37, passed the captaincy on to Glenn Turner, he was 46 days younger than Reid was when he retired almost ten years earlier. Congdon was a new test player then, having already waited since 1960/61, when he made his Central Districts debut, for international recognition. He had also played successfully for Nelson since 1959 as the minor association resisted a record 28 challenges for the Hawke Cup. Congdon averaged 54.34 in this competition, and learnt from fine players such as Ian Leggat, who had toured South Africa with New Zealand in 1953/54. Perhaps more importantly, former Derbyshire and England player Les Townsend had settled in the area and was able to pass correct coaching techniques and a professional outlook onto the young Congdon.

In his book *Caribbean Crusade*, Don Cameron later wrote: 'When Congo [Congdon] retires from cricket, said one of his players, he certainly won't get

The New Zealand team to tour the UK, 1973. Left to right, back: J.M. Parker, D.R. Hadlee, R.W. Anderson, H.J. Howarth, R.J. Hadlee, R.E. Redmond, E.K. Gillott, K.J. Wadsworth, V. Pollard. Front: R.O. Collinge, B.F. Hastings, G.M. Turner (vice-captain), J.C. Saunders (manager), B.E. Congdon (captain), M.G. Burgess, B.R. Taylor.
Surrey Cricket Club

a job in the diplomatic service. Congo had evidently just given the players a blunt message or two before they went to field against West Indies.' He continued by commenting that some of the players 'had less than total admiration for Congdon's methods and manner' against the 1969/70 Australians, after Congdon replaced the injured Dowling.

Congdon said at the time, 'I think I have steadied my play a lot. The whole basis of my attitude at present is to make the bowler work.'

Despite the fluency of Brian Hastings and Mark Burgess, and the orthodoxy and watchfulness of Graham Dowling and Glenn Turner, Congdon was reckoned to be New Zealand's most dangerous player. A report in *New Zealand Cricketer* of April 1972, written just before Congdon's accession to the captaincy, asked with uncanny foresight, 'Who knows how far he will get in the Caribbean?'

'In the majority of instances a new appointee is untried and therefore there is an element of risk,' said Congdon. In his case the gamble paid off, for as a player whose success came as a result of application and dedication rather than natural ability, in the words of Don Cameron, his 'achievements established him as a great man and almost as a great cricketer'.

It was Congdon's record as a captain that took him to this new level. Congdon himself has made the comments, 'My batting and bowling, and

The century at Trent Bridge that began Congdon's phenomenal series was full of defiant shots. But even a career-best 176 could not prevent a 38-run defeat when New Zealand were chasing 479 to win.
Christchurch Star

fielding and appreciation of the other members of the team's performance improved; my most successful performances were while I was captain.'

The figures bear this out. In his 17 tests as leader Congdon made 1067 runs at 41.03 and took 33 wickets. Before assuming the role he had played 31 tests, scoring 1569 runs at 26.59 and taking 12 wickets.

'It's attitude that becomes very much more significant,' Congdon said of his approach to test cricket. 'It's what you are trying to achieve and how you play the game, knowing your own physical and mental capabilities. It's a major, major step that takes you up the ladder into international cricket, an ingrained factor of whether the person has real goals.'

He listed those goals as:

- Getting selected.
- Learning and competing well enough to justify and hold one's place in the team.
- Playing so well as to become an important member of the team.
- To perform so well as to compare one's performance with one's team-mates.
- Having achieved this level of performance there are a number of players who respond to captaincy as a further motivation to their own game. Equally, there are similarly qualified players who are so focused on their own game that they do not respond well to captaincy.

Vic Pollard, who played against the 1969/70 Australians in New Zealand, later smilingly spoke of the 'near mutiny' on the West Indies tour, although those who were there, such as experienced batsman Brian Hastings, were more circumspect.

Hastings commented that Congdon 'kept to himself more than Dowling and wasn't quite as close to the team. Captaincy seemed to get the best out of Bev — he made even more runs. He was a very underrated cricketer. It wasn't easy for him. Bev in those days wasn't the most popular person. He wasn't as outgoing as a lot of the other members of the side. It wasn't an easy situation for him but Bev was tough — he was a real fighter. A lot of the guys thought he was a wee bit aloof and didn't have a great sense of humour, but for all that he served New Zealand terrifically. He led the side pretty well really.'

With time Congdon undoubtedly won the respect of his teammates, for as Don Cameron wrote, '— it was a hard time for Congdon in his first full test captaincy.... if New Zealand had not had the luck to win the third test they certainly were not going to lose the fourth and fifth.'

In his autobiography *Someone Had to Do It*, Don Cameron noted, 'Bevan Congdon was a curious man. He was born with some cricketing talent and worked so hard on his game that he became a genuine test all-rounder, and a rattling good gully catcher. Perhaps because he had to work so hard, Congdon had little patience with some other players who did not make the same effort, but perhaps were lucky enough to have more natural ability.'

Bevan Congdon on tour in England, 1973.
Christchurch Star

The veteran journalist continued, 'Whatever the reason, most of the players respected Congdon's ability, but not many would regard him as a warm or close friend. For the possible edification of New Zealand readers I put together a piece saying that while Congdon had the talent to hold his place as captain, he faced the bigger problem of attracting all the players so they would play together under his leadership.'

Congdon commented in his forthright way, 'I actually believe that players can perform better and learn better if they accept responsibility for themselves.'

Cameron's story appeared unexpectedly quickly, on the following morning, in a Barbados paper that found its way to Congdon's breakfast table. 'Congdon gave me an angular look as he left the dining room,' Cameron recalled. 'Then he proceeded to make a liar out of me.'

Indeed, at the end of the third test, after a New Zealand record first innings lead of 289, Sobers (142) and Davis (183) were dropped by Jarvis and Turner respectively and went on to reach centuries to rescue the West Indies. 'Congdon sat in his playing gear staring into space while most of the others had changed and were pursuing the handiest beer,' Cameron wrote, as the new captain failed to emulate Graham Dowling with a victory in his first test in charge. 'We played well enough to win,' recalled Congdon of the devastating near-miss.

Congdon hits his England counterpart Ray Illingworth over the top as Alan Knott looks on during the New Zealand captain's 175 against England in the epic Trent Bridge defeat in 1973. *Christchurch Star*

The next two tests were also high-scoring draws, highlighted by Turner's 259 New Zealand record at Georgetown, and Bruce Taylor's eight wickets in the match at Port of Spain. Left to score 401 in 605 minutes to win the rubber in Gary Sobers' record thirty-ninth successive test captaining the West Indies, Congdon (58), Taylor (42 not out) and Ross Morgan (40 not out) batted the game out.

'In the West Indies I batted for a long time with Glenn Turner. I'm sure my game benefited. It was in approach as much as anything,' revealed Congdon. New Zealand's cricketing maturity was taking place, 'brought about by a lot more exposure to overseas cricket and overseas conditions'.

Two draws book-ended an innings and 166-run defeat at Carisbrook against Pakistan. Mushtaq Mohammed (201), Asif Iqbal (175) and Intikhab Alam (11/130) starred in Pakistan's first test win in New Zealand.

While there was just a single win in Congdon's 17 consecutive tests in charge, New Zealand almost achieved a long-awaited breakthrough on the 1973 tour of England.

'Congdon's gallant band', as Dick Brittenden described the tour party, scored a record 440 in the fourth innings at Nottingham, in pursuit of 478 to win. Congdon's 176 was the epitome of a captain's innings, as he added 177 for the fourth wicket with Pollard who made 116.

'Though the belief among English critics,' noted the magazine *New Zealand Cricketer*, was that 'New Zealand has its best ever chance of taking a test from England'. Would there be another so good?

The second test almost provided another opportunity, following the 38-run loss in the first. Congdon's 175, along with another century from Pollard and 105 by Mark Burgess, helped New Zealand to 551/9 declared, their highest total until 1985/86. More importantly, it gave a first innings lead of 298. However, England responded with 463/9 to save the match. In hindsight, Congdon could have attackingly declared at 492/6 at the end of day three to give more time to bowl out England on a perfect Lord's pitch.

But New Zealand's chance was gone, and the Leeds test was lost by an innings and one run, with Congdon's run ending with nought and two, both caught Alan Knott, bowled Geoff Arnold.

Alan Richards, the NZBC radio commentator, said, 'One advantage enjoyed by England was Illingworth's superiority to Congdon as a tactician — splendid individual cricketer that he is, and likeable personality that he possesses, Congdon lacks the flair for adventure or attack which New Zealand seems to need in order to emerge completely from the slight inferiority complex which has plagued our test team for so long.'

On the 1973 tour Congdon was described as 'a thoughtful captain, who has tried to give everyone a chance to run into form'. This didn't include young slow-left-armer Eric Gillott, who bowled just 136.5 overs on the tour.

Congdon later commented, 'The 1973 team that went to England was, with minor exceptions, one of the strongest batting sides we'd seen for a long time. But it's appropriate to note that in that area, although we didn't lose many tests, we didn't win that many either.'

He believed the missing element was a match-winning bowler, citing England's Geoff Arnold, whose swing and seam took 16 wickets in the series, and the inimitable Richard Hadlee as the men who would have finished the job for New Zealand.

The next mission for the New Zealanders was their first ever test series in Australia, which came about in 1973/74. The matches at Melbourne and Adelaide resulted in innings defeats, but at the SCG Australia were 425 behind with eight second innings wickets left when rain washed out the final day. Again Congdon had waited until the game was safe before declaring late on day four, after the third day was also washed out. The match was Jeremy Coney's test debut.

The pressures of the media, as New Zealand captain Bevan Congdon prepares to drive during net practice at Lord's, April 1973.
Christchurch Star

A seventh test century in the making for Congdon, now playing as a senior professional under Glenn Turner. His 107 not out saved New Zealand in the first test against Australia in 1976/77.
Christchurch Star

'We were in an extremely strong position but for virtually two days of rain stoppages,' Congdon said later. Always balanced, he continued, 'One cannot place too much emphasis on such occurrences without in fairness remembering those games where we benefited from rain disruptions.'

But revenge came just three months later when Australia played their first tests in New Zealand since 1945/46. The Basin saw 1455 runs scored for 24 wickets, with Congdon making 132.

New Zealand won the next match at Lancaster Park, their eighth win in 113 matches. Turner became the first to score a hundred in each innings of a test for New Zealand. He wrote, 'Congo would be the toughest guy I've come across. Dour and uncompromising.' Congdon scored just eight and two, but took 3/33, including Greg Chappell's wicket in the first innings (Chappell had scored a record 380 runs in the first test). Congdon: 'It was a really good contest, a lot closer than it actually looked.' New Zealand won by five wickets. The third test, held at Eden Park, was lost by 297 runs.

Eleven months later England stopped off in New Zealand, having been thrashed 4-1 by Australia and their speed demons Lillee and Thomson. They preferred the New Zealand attack and the Kiwi pitches, winning at Eden Park by an innings and 83 runs, in the match where Ewen Chatfield almost died when Peter Lever hit him on the head with a bouncer. At the time he and debutant Geoff Howarth were 44 runs into a last-wicket partnership, trying to make England bat again. The other test at Christchurch was drawn. England lost just eight wickets in the two tests.

Congdon had always been a slow-burner. He made his first first-class century in 1964/65 and played against Pakistan in a test in the same season, adding 109 in 97 minutes with John Reid in his first innings. He second top scored to Geoff Howarth — 'the only other batsman to make a real fight of it', according to *Men in White*. His last match for New Zealand was in 1978, at the age of 40. On the 1978 tour to England he averaged an impressive 34.75 with the bat and 27.08 with the ball.

The way Congdon used his experience helped a generation of New Zealand cricketers, as he alone bridged the gap between Reid and Sutcliffe and those of the future generation such as John Wright. 'Not many have had Congdon's confidence in his own ability. He does not talk a lot. But he thinks. He learns. It all seems to be paying off at present,' wrote the author of a 1972 piece in *New Zealand Cricketer*.

Bevan Congdon

Another editorial in the same magazine, before Pakistan's 1972/73 visit, wondered if Glenn Turner 'should assume a role for which he has clearly been cast'. While Congdon is described as 'the sort of cricketer who has it in him to respond to a challenge: and captaincy in the West Indies test series was certainly that — it would seem to be a cruel and unjust rebuff to a fine cricketer to relieve him of the captaincy now that it seems to be his by right of succession'. However, 'taking all things into account, Turner would appear the better choice. He is going to lead New Zealand very soon; and there seems no reason for delaying the appointment any longer.'

An OBE and a rare smile from Bevan Congdon, pictured with his wife Shirley at Government House in November 1975. *Christchurch Star*

But the appointment of 25-year-old Turner, who would have been an 'extremely popular choice as captain among New Zealand players', was withheld until Congdon made himself unavailable for the 1975 World Cup.

'I actually did not see sport as a career and had contracted myself to a company [Wills Tobacco] on the basis that if sport interfered with my work commitments then work came first. I had reached a level of senior management which required me to commit to work from 1975,' Congdon wrote.

Congdon became one of just seven players to represent four provinces or more (John Guy played for five) when he made his Canterbury debut in 1974/75. He was fourth on the New Zealand list of run scorers when he retired in 1978, as well as having taken 204 wickets and 201 catches. He had also averaged 54.71 in his 12 one-day internationals.

In club cricket Congdon showed his impressive stamina when, aged 41, he bowled 47 overs in a day for Lancaster Park in the championship final of 1979/80.

In *A Century of Great New Zealand Cricketers* Joseph Romanos wrote, 'Never particularly outgoing, Congdon was not well-suited to captaincy — team-mates said they found it hard to get close to him and he was too defensively minded.' Radio commentator Alan Richards agreed, saying, 'Younger players had difficulties in getting close to him. He was intolerant of mediocrity.' John Wright was, as ever, candid on the subject: 'I'd always admired his attitude — in England in 1978 I roomed with him once and he drew a line down the middle of the room — he was rather more meticulous than me. The cultural divide between Congo and 18-year-old Brendon Bracewell was even more yawning and it couldn't be said they established a rapport.'

New Zealand Test Cricket Captains

Frank Cameron, who was a member of the selection panel that chose Congdon as captain, has said, 'Congo was a bit more pragmatic and more obviously aggressive than Dowling. Dowling wouldn't show impatience. Congo liked things to happen, a bit like John Reid. If bowlers weren't bowling well he'd think, "I'll bowl and get these fellas out." He was very intense, very hard, very shrewd.'

Described by Brittenden as 'a cricketer's cricketer', Congdon was business-like in all aspects of the game. The captaincy brought out the best in his play, and that was enough to sustain New Zealand during his tenure.

One of the finest all-round cricketers produced by New Zealand, Bevan Congdon was a player of immense character and a fine ambassador for his country. He now lives in Auckland with his wife Shirley, and has two daughters.

Congdon was a New Zealand selector in 1993. 'I would be less than honest if I said this was an enjoyable task,' he said. 'Everyone, repeat everyone, believes they have the answers and the facts or situations are unimportant, especially if one doesn't have the accountability for making decisions.'

13. GLENN TURNER
24 January 1976 – 1 March 1977

My way

One of the dominant figures of recent New Zealand cricket history, Glenn Turner is New Zealand's greatest first-class run scorer, and is regarded by many as the best cricketing tactician the country has produced. Yet he captained only ten tests, and played just 41 in his career, missing six years as a test player between March 1977 and a two-test swansong against Sri Lanka in March 1983.

That Turner should abandon New Zealand cricket while captain made his decision to quit and concentrate on his benefit year with Worcesterhire even harder to understand. A sort of across-Tasman Kerry Packer figure, Turner professionalised the game in New Zealand, after making his first-class debut aged 16 back in 1964, when there were no full-time pros in the country.

Turner's early days were spent in Dunedin, where Frank Cameron, later one of the selectors who appointed him New Zealand captain, was his coach at Otago Boys' High School. 'He was an outstanding schoolboy captain and later I played for Otago with him. I followed his career very, very closely. In the early days of one-day games we were a little behind. Turner had the experience,' Cameron commented wryly. 'I remember flying from Dunedin and back with him [for the Eden Park eight-wicket test defeat against India in January 1976] and getting off to look at the Lancaster Park wicket, because you were never too sure what you were going to get there.'

This incident is typical of Turner's conscientiousness. He liked to cover all angles, and prided himself on his research and planning before games.

Turner began his test career with a duck against the West Indies in the 1968/69 series, but in the second test hit 74 to help New Zealand to victory, their fifth in tests and second under Graham Dowling. Another 50, in a 'vital stand of 65' with Vic Pollard, helped the team to a first test win in India in 1969/70. Turner's battling skills were emphasised by his first test century (110) later in the tour against Pakistan, which took more than seven hours. His

Glenn Turner, pictured in 1975.
Christchurch Star

seven-boundary 'Herculean effort' helped bring about a first series victory overseas, after he had been dropped for the first two tests.

Turner's progress, shaped by Otago coach Billy Ibadulla and by playing for Worcestershire from 1967, was such that by the end of the 1971/72 tour of the West Indies he was New Zealand's top batsman. Ten first-class centuries in the 1970 season, then two test double centuries against the West Indies, followed by a thousand runs by the end of May on the 1973 tour of England confirmed Turner as a world class player.

Bevan Congdon's unavailability for the 1975 World Cup brought Turner the captaincy. New Zealand reached the semi-finals, with Turner making a record 171 not out against East Africa, as well as 114 not out against India. His early lack of strokes had long since gone, with the demands of the English one-day competitions ensuring freer scoring.

The home series against India in 1975/76 was drawn 1-1, Richard Hadlee's record figures of 7/23 in an innings and 11/58 in the match providing Turner's sole win as captain. By 1977 Turner's career as a test captain was over, at the age of 29.

'New Zealand's most disastrous tour' was how radio's Alan Richards described the 1976/77 India and Pakistan tour. Turner had given 'serious thought' to withdrawing due to worries about the itinerary and his payments. He said he only went in the end because his wife's parents, who lived in Bombay, expected him to.

Turner scored 60 runs in four innings as New Zealand was outplayed in the first two tests against Pakistan. In the second Turner lost the toss, 'and we lost heart', wrote Lance Cairns. After being struck on the arm in the first innings at Hyderabad Turner withdrew from the third test ('I wasn't going to be able to hit "pussy",' Turner wrote in his autobiography *Opening Up*) giving John Parker his sole test as New Zealand skipper. The game, held at Karachi, was drawn.

However, another pair of losses followed against India, with Turner criticised for putting the Indians in, to make 399, in the first test at Bombay. A home series of two tests against Australia marked 'a new era in New Zealand test cricket', as the Kiwis began to compete with their neighbours.

But Turner's 1978 benefit season with Worcestershire created a rift between him and the New Zealand authorities, particularly Walter Hadlee. In 1977 Hadlee, who was then chairman of the Board of Control, was quoted in the *Listener* as saying, 'I would expect our chaps to go out there and die. After all, they are playing for their country.' Hadlee categorically denies ever having said this, but the article had already run when he received proofs and requested it be withdrawn.

Turner responded, 'The people who say we must go out there and die usually say it from the safety of their XJ6s en route to their $70,000 houses. That honour and glory stuff doesn't pay the bills and it's bloody hard work.'

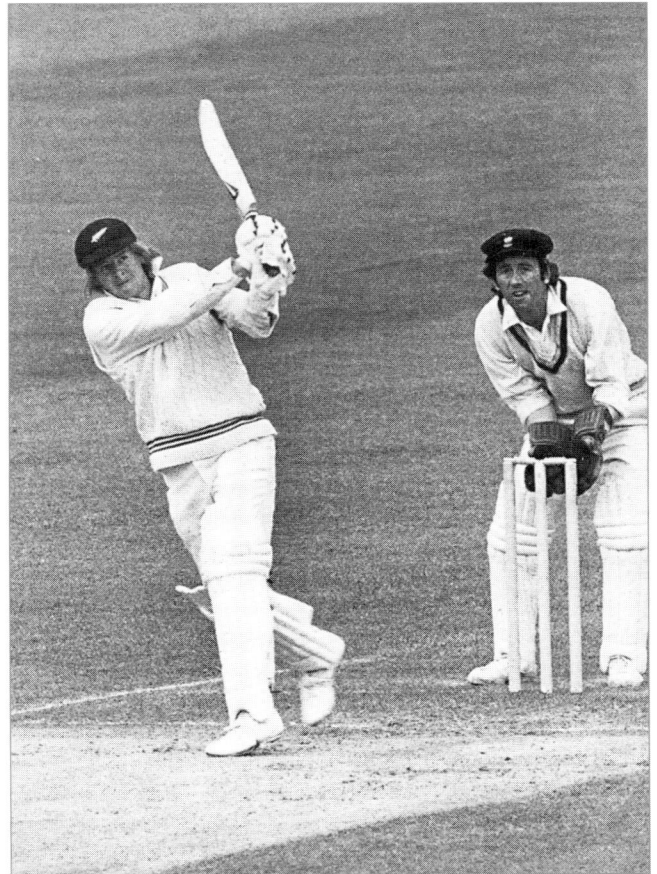

Glenn Turner drives Jack Birkenshaw for six while playing for New Zealand against the MCC at Lord's, April 1973. Turner went on to become the first New Zealander to score a thousand runs before the end of May. The wicket-keeper is Bob Taylor.
Christchurch Star

Turner was to miss the next 21 tests as his feud with the board intensified. A close parallel could be drawn with Geoffrey Boycott, with whom Turner had been compared as an accumulator, tactician and diligent practiser. Boycott's single-minded dogmatism kept him out of the England team from 1974 to 1977.

Mark Burgess took over as captain for England's 1977/78 visit. John Wright made his debut in the first test, Hadlee took ten wickets and New Zealand beat England for the first time.

Turner said later, 'In some ways I wish — with the programme that New Zealand's got now, I wouldn't have needed to play as much county cricket. You couldn't make a living out of playing cricket for New Zealand, which you can now. And therefore the amount of first-class cricket that I did play, and I played a lot, particularly as New Zealanders go, and because of the lesser international programme, I only ended up playing 41 tests and 41 ODIs. I would

Batting with a broken finger, a courageous Glenn Turner turns a ball to leg off Derek Underwood during the first day's play in the third test against England at the Oval, 21 August 1969. Watching are slip Phil Sharpe and wicket-keeper Alan Knott. Later Sharpe caught Turner off Underwood for 53. New Zealand lost by eight wickets.
Christchurch Star

have liked to have played a lot more than that. If that had been the case then from a captaincy point of view there would have been a lot more than ten.'

Turner did not have a successful time as captain, although the team did win against India at Wellington in Turner's third test as skipper. In an amazing game Turner's 64, along with Mark Burgess' 85, gave New Zealand a first innings lead of 114 runs. In India's second innings, without Sunil Gavaskar, who was in hospital after having been hit on the right cheekbone trying to field a shot from Lance Cairns, Richard Hadlee took 7/23, a New Zealand test best, to dismiss India for a record low of 81. This levelled the series, but eight months later New Zealand lost four out of six tests on the subcontinent. The drawn games came in the third test against Pakistan at Karachi (from which Turner had withdrawn, having an injured arm) and a month later, in November 1976, when Turner made 113 and Warren Lees and David O'Sullivan survived for almost two hours to earn a draw at Kanpur against India.

Turner's reputation suffered against Australia in the two-test home series in February 1977, as he made 78 runs in four innings.

Glenn Turner

England captain and fast bowler Bob Willis wrote that Turner was 'not the bravest of batsmen' — which seems an inapt description for a batsman who was dismissed twice by leg spinner Kerry O'Keeffe after seeing off the extreme pace of Dennis Lillee and the new ball in the first test at Lancaster Park. Bevan Congdon's five-hour 107 not out ensured a draw for Turner's side. The second test, in Auckland, was lost by ten wickets, as Lillee took 11/123 in the match. In contrast, Hadlee's 2/158 showed he was not yet the brilliantly consistent bowler he was later to become.

After this series the slight right-hander disappeared to England to play county cricket. Following a dispute over airfares he was banned for a time from playing tests. 'I was New Zealand's first professional captain,' Turner protested. It has been said that he was also the most professional cricketer produced by New Zealand.

Turner, erudite and never lost for an answer, said this of his time in Britain: 'I found that playing the game day in and day out, if you were observant and taking an interest and there are only so many players that do that, then you got to know angles, you got to know different options and tactics that were open to you. Therefore there's no doubt the education one received playing the county circuit was invaluable. When I look back on it, I found that when I was involved in coaching in the mid-eighties, when we played Australia, most New Zealanders seemed a little overawed by the Australians. I felt that from the knowledge point of view one had a much better grasp and advantage having played so much cricket in England, and I saw the Australians as part-timers who I thought made pretty fundamental mistakes and didn't play the odds very well. I certainly didn't suffer from an inferiority complex; if anything I had to pull myself back from feeling a bit arrogant about it all.'

This perceived arrogance often polarised public support for Turner as he progressed from the 16-year-old who refused to pack the Otago team kit bag in 1964 to his difficulties as captain more than a decade later. While his vast knowledge and prodigious run scoring have commanded admiration, a fastidious, near-obsessional and occasionally immodest manner have at times made even some of his most devoted admirers waver.

Turner names no local men as influences on his captaincy, but he has said, 'I thought Ray Illingworth — he was always known as a moaning grumbling bugger, but he did try and play cricket, and he set decent declarations — I thought he had a very good grasp of tactics and I had a regard for him in particular.

Future New Zealand captains and Worcestershire team-mates Glenn Turner and John Parker practise at Lord's, April 1973.
Christchurch Star

'The disadvantage New Zealand's captains had comes into the same category as the Australians of the time, and that is I don't think they were playing enough to get the odds working for you. There are so many different ways to achieve something, that what you've got to work out is to get the odds to work in your favour. To me that too comes with a lot of experience, playing and playing and playing day in and day out, and our captains didn't have that advantage. The more you know about the game, the more you realise there is to know, and that's why it does come down to trying to get the odds to work for you in the decisions that you make, and that's the best you can do.'

In answer to a question about selection, Turner was blunt. 'I don't know how selectors went about choosing captains. I suspect it wasn't particularly sophisticated.

'I know that the support around sides now is much greater than it used to be, but the assumption is that those support people are dominating, but they shouldn't be.

'They are just to me a reference point for a captain. If you've got a new captain or a young captain, then in particular the coach will play a more significant role. But if the coach is successful then he does himself largely out of a job fairly quickly. You've still got to give lots of responsibilities to the captain. You can't captain the team from the sideline.

'I had a particularly good relationship with Jeremy Coney in the mid-eighties, where we talked at the end of every session. We talked through what had gone wrong, planning the next session, going over the different possibilities.

'Jerry saw it as useful to have someone off the field who was detached from the heat of the battle and can have a different perspective. He was probing enough in his own mind to want those other opinions, but at the end of the day, whether or not that is then applied by the captain is very much his decision. To have that reference point is very useful. The problem we have is getting people who have enough knowledge to be able to assist the captain.'

Talking about himself, Turner said, 'I don't have what they call normal reactions. I would like to think I could put cricket in perspective to life. I just gave it my best shot at the time, whether it be a test match or a World Cup; every match, I tried very hard, even in county cricket. Every game was important, but in the overall perspective of things not that vital.'

Regarding his other career as a coach, Turner said, 'I would like to think that when I was coach of the 1995 World Cup team we tried to educate our players instead of looking at this place [India] as a problem. If you can get yourself interested in their culture than you'll be happier. India's a place where you can go downhill very quickly if you don't have a smile on your face. I've been back there 25 times and I'm comfortable in the place and I try to get that across.'

In Turner's opinion very few New Zealand captains stand out. For him experience is the key, but only for certain types of players. 'Geoff Howarth had the training of playing a lot for Surrey and had the experience, but in every team you're lucky if you get more than one or two [of those players]. He hasn't got the experience unless he's been thinking like a captain.'

In 2001/02 Turner became coach of Otago, succeeding Denis Aberhart who had been promoted to the national job that Turner held for two stints. He lives in Dunedin with his wife Sukhinder. They have two children.

14. JOHN PARKER   30 October 1976 – 4 November 1976

It was all I had waited for

John Parker, the fourteenth man to be appointed captain in 46 years, was leader for a single test. At the time he was New Zealand's youngest captain, at 25 years 252 days. Parker was only ever a fill-in, stepping in to captain the third test on the 1976/77 tour of Pakistan and India after Glenn Turner was hit on the elbow during the ten-wicket second test defeat.

In *Men in White* it is said that 'Mushtaq's decision to bat virtually decided the side would not lose the test'. Majid Khan became the first non-Australian to score a first-day pre-lunch test century, and Pakistan made their highest total against New Zealand of 565/9 declared (Javed Miandad 206) which meant the tourists needed a big score even to secure a draw. John Parker's older brother Murray opened to become the first (but not the last) player to be skippered by his brother in a test. At 10/2, John Parker and Andy Roberts 'overcame the immediate crisis', according to *Men in White*, to reach 67 by stumps. Warren Lees (152) and Richard Hadlee (86) set a New Zealand record of 186 for the seventh wicket, ensuring Parker's team could hang on for a draw on the final day.

The match had its controversial moments, with Sadiq walking after being given not out when caught by Burgess at slip off Hadlee, and Mushtaq being given not out by the notorious Shakoor Rana after apparently being caught by Parker at first slip in the same over. Mushtaq went on to 107, and added 252 for the fourth wicket in 295 minutes with Miandad.

Parker's career had followed Turner's in other respects. The pair both played for Worcestershire and for Northern Districts, they opened together, and now Parker had replaced Turner as New Zealand captain. Parker was the youngest of three brothers who played first-class cricket, while Turner was brother to hockey international Brian and top golfer Greg. Parker's county career was over by 1975, and it had begun before he played for Northern Districts, where an MCC coaching certificate won him a job with the association. He had his Turner-like battles with sports administrators as the first professional New Zealand representative cricketers began to establish themselves, later claiming that Turner 'was an example of that. They made sure his career was finished before they listened to him.'

Speaking of his promising Worcestershire debut of 91 against the 1971 Indian tourists, Parker said, 'It was everything I had waited for and dreamed of when I was young.' He was fortunate, he said, that his 'trial by fire' took place, as he was the second to last overseas cricketer to get into county cricket, paying his way to England before the law was changed so that existing players had to have played ten years rather than just five to come off the list of cricketers classified as overseas players in England.

He scored 869 runs at 39.80 in 1972, and in New Zealand his form was also good, with 503 runs at 41.91 in his first season at Northern Districts, including a career-best 195 against Canterbury. But Parker scored just 23 at 4.60 in the test series in England the following year, despite having made his first century for New Zealand, 106 against Somerset, prior to the tests.

The trappings of success. John Parker celebrates a ton along with half the crowd at the Sydney Cricket Ground, playing for New Zealand against New South Wales in December 1973.
Christchurch Star

A pioneer of the reverse sweep, Parker scored three test centuries in 36 tests, and was never dropped from the test team between 1973 and 1981. He was also known as a good player of spin.

Parker's wry sense of humour developed during his five years on the county cricket circuit. Worcestershire's secretary, Yorkshireman Joe Lister, who was renowned as a powerful tyrant of the old school, once asked Parker to bowl to him in the nets. 'His first-class victims could be counted on the fingers of one hand of an incompetent sawmiller,' wrote Dick Brittenden of Parker's bowling successes. But, in Parker's words, '— as a pro my leg spinners, googlies and top spinners were slightly more consistent than they became later in my amateur days. Turner and D'Oliveira decided I should try and bowl

Jeremy Coney and John Parker celebrate a wicket against the West Indies in 1980.
Christchurch Star

him a googly. As cricket followers should be aware, Yorkshiremen are notorious for their inability to pick googlies.'

Amid great hilarity, Parker twisted Lister up 'like a pretzel' time and time again. Back in the dressing room, after a moment's silence, Lister boomed at Parker, 'Shit is hard to play.' Then he turned away to have a shower.

After the unsuccessful 1973 tour to England, Parker said in reference to the forthcoming tour to Australia, 'I knew I had to do it on this trip.' Parker did do it, with 108 in the Sydney test, and was the team's heaviest run-scorer with 627 runs on the tour.

He and Turner also made half-century opening stands in each innings in the first win against Australia, in 1973/74 at Christchurch.

In 1974 he was part of Worcestershire's championship-winning side, and in 1974/75 he scored mainly behind the wicket to make 121 against England in an innings loss. Parker then had his best year for Worcestershire, with 1061 runs at 34.22, including three centuries, one of which was hit up before lunch against Nottinghamshire. After 1975 he dropped down the order after having problems with the new ball on or around the off stump.

In the words of Trevor Bailey, 'Parker is a good honest workman steadily making himself a more reliable player by correcting earlier errors. He is the type of batsman who, because of his temperament and application, will score more runs than many with greater talent.' Parker became a professional coach at Northen Districts during the seventies, a role New Zealand captains Geoff Howarth, John Wright and Glenn Turner, as well as 1955/56 West Indies vice-captain Bruce Pairaudeau, took at various times.

In 1975/76 Parker became captain of Northern Districts after finishing with Worcestershire, but he made just 229 runs at 17.61 for his province. Then came his appointment as vice-captain on the 1976/77 tour to India and Pakistan.

Prior to the trip Parker took what was then the unusual step of training for games. 'Before then cricket training consisted of things like stretching down to strap on your boots or lifting a heavy bat once or twice,' he joked. Parker happened upon a bodybuilder at the YMCA gym in Hamilton where he was working out. 'I hate cricket,' said the weightlifter, 'but I saw a game once.' Eventually the muscleman divulged that he might have been in England in 1973, and he was probably at Lord's for the test match. Parker sensed what was coming in the characteristic tale told against himself. The forgetful bodybuilder finally recalled, 'All I do remember was that Turner didn't make many and Parker got his usual duck!'

Parker took part in New Zealand's first test win over England, at the Basin Reserve, in 1977/78. He was also one of the selectors for the tour to England in 1978. He agreed that his back would affect his fielding in the first test, and scored just 55 runs in the other two tests.

'Motivation to play for New Zealand isn't always there,' Parker said in 1979, and he played just six more tests, three against the West Indies and a final trio on the 1980/81 tour to Australia. His 182 runs in 11 innings were unimpressive and, now aged 29, he declared himself unavailable for India's visit in 1980/81. He proudly said, after non-selection for the 1979 World Cup, 'I have never been dropped from the test side.'

He played in 75 first-class games for Northern Districts, scoring 4611 runs at 38.42. This was the second highest number at the time, behind Andy Roberts, who retired at the same time as Parker in 1983/84, seven years after being led by Parker in his only test as captain. He also captained Northern Districts in the 1976/77 and 1977/78 seasons.

'When the Roberts and the Dunnings and the Gibsons and the Mountains were playing for Northern Districts they were only too pleased to talk and share their experiences and knowledge,' he lamented at the end of his career. 'I don't think it's the same now.'

Parker went on to become a popular radio commentator, working for Radio New Zealand for over a decade. It was a role in which his characteristic honesty was appreciated by most listeners, his fellow commentator Bryan Waddle describing him as 'forthright', and offering 'comments at times which don't meet with universal approval'.

15. MARK BURGESS

10 February 1978 –
14 December 1980

First to beat England

The last amateur New Zealand test captain, Mark Burgess was an experienced test player when he was matched against Geoff Boycott's English tourists in 1977/78. Burgess had replaced Glenn Turner, who had controversially decided to stay in England to organise his benefit year. Boycott was a replacement too, for Mike Brearley, who had his arm broken by a delivery from Sikander Bakht of Pakistan in January 1978.

Brearley is acknowledged by many as the greatest test captain in history, and in his book *The Art of Captaincy* he details his ideas, which stem from his training as a psychoanalyst, otherwise known as a 'degree in people'. However, instead of facing perhaps the best captain in world cricket, Burgess had to contend with one of the least successful man-managers in test history.

Burgess was 33 when he became the fifteenth test leader, with ten years and 38 tests behind him. Boycott, 37, had led England just once, in his seventieth test, which was the last of the series held the previous month in Pakistan.

'It sort of happened because I just happened to be the last man standing at that time,' Burgess said modestly. 'Glenn Turner had disappeared and Bevan Congdon had done the job and didn't look like he was going to play that much longer.'

Burgess lost the toss at windy Wellington and the New Zealanders were sent in to bat. John Wright, making his test debut, scored 55, while Burgess took nearly an hour to score nine, but 153/3 at stumps was a fair score. New Zealand had past, present or future captains batting between opener and number six in Wright, Howarth, Burgess, Congdon and Parker. Only Wright's fellow opener Robert 'Jumbo' Anderson split the run. A New Zealand first innings lead of 13 eventuated, with Boycott grinding out 77, bringing up 50 in 277 minutes. The deteriorating pitch accounted for New Zealand, who made just 123 in the second innings, with Burgess caught Boycott bowled Botham for six.

Set 137 for victory Boycott, with a shot that was strangely out of character, played across the line to Collinge's fourth ball and was bowled. Hadlee took

6/26 and, for the first time, New Zealand beat England. Burgess bowled Richard Hadlee and Richard Collinge straight through, apart from one over from Dayle Hadlee. Collinge again removed the top order, and Hadlee the rest.

Giving credit for the historic win, Don Cameron looked back to Walter Hadlee, 'who has worked harder than anyone in the cause of New Zealand cricket'.

Hadlee commented, 'New Zealand cricket has looked forward to this moment for so long' — 48 years and 48 matches to be precise. But it was Burgess who had led the team, beginning his reign with a win as Dowling had done ten years earlier. Reid, Turner and Wright also had early wins (all in their third match in charge), and later Howarth's first test as captain ended in a one-wicket win.

Despite this success Burgess felt, 'If I'd been better prepared and if I'd had more time I think I'd have done a better job. I can't give the reasons, but I just have this feeling I was not doing the best job I could have done.'

Mark Burgess during the New Zealand tour to England in 1973.
Christchurch Star

In the second test at Christchurch Botham became the second England player to make a century and take five wickets in the same game. After England decided to make a declaration without informing their hesitant skipper, Boycott, Burgess' side was left needing 280 to win. The New Zealand captain later confirmed that Botham deliberately ran out Boycott as England neared the time to declare. Burgess retired hurt after being struck on the left elbow while offering no stroke at a delivery from Bob Willis with the score at 18/2 in the second innings, but bravely returned to the crease at 95/9. Botham soon dismissed last man Ewen Chatfield, who had earlier, while bowling, run out Derek Randall who was backing up.

Burgess scored a 50 in the final match of the series, which was held at Eden Park. This game was notable for Geoff Howarth's emergence as a player of top quality — Burgess' successor made 122 and 102 in the drawn game.

NEW ZEALAND TEST CRICKET CAPTAINS

Mark Burgess poses, bags packed, at the beginning of his biggest tour, as captain to England in 1978.
Christchurch Star

Basin Reserve saw Burgess' only victory as test captain, although he had nine more games as leader. He kept the captaincy for the tour to England, his third, in 1978, Turner's benefit year. The test series ended as a 3-0 loss. Burgess commented, 'We had good positions and lost them. We didn't bat well enough.' Only Howarth prospered, with 94 in the first test and 123 in the third. Burgess and Congdon (who retired at the end of the tour) were past their best and Wright and Edgar were yet to reach theirs. 'A horror story,' recalled Burgess. 'It wasn't the most fun time. I looked forward to the tour because we'd played very well against Boycott's side, then we got over there. I don't know what made us as bad as we were, but we were very ordinary. I've got to accept responsibility as a captain for the poor performance of the players. We were never completely dysfunctional, but never really got to play at a good enough quality in the tests.'

Burgess was captain at the time of Kerry Packer's World Series cricket, which affected other test countries adversely, but in New Zealand only flirted with Richard Hadlee.

The visit of Pakistan in 1978/79 was controversial, with both Burgess and Mushtaq objecting to some of the umpiring of Fred Goodall. Burgess was criticised for not going through the proper channels by the New Zealand Cricket Umpires Association. Don Cameron wrote that, 'The NZCUA is being rather severe on the New Zealand captain', as 'the tiresome tactics' of the Pakistanis might have been legitimised by the time spent going through the proper channels.

The emergence of Edgar and Wright, along with the return of Jeremy Coney and the excellent play of the professionals Howarth and Hadlee, failed to stop Pakistan winning the series 1-0, with Javed Miandad (81 and 160 not out at Christchurch) a match-winner once more. The Pakistanis were missing four players to Packer, but could still field Imran Khan, Zaheer Abbas, Mushtaq Mohammed, Majid Khan and Asif Iqbal — all past, present or future test captains.

A nine-run semi-final defeat to the hosts England in the 1979 World Cup ended a good run, with Burgess commenting that 'it was disappointing to get so close and not to make it'. Graham Dowling, by now a selector, said, 'Looking back, Burgess' performance had a lot to do with the success of the side. One-day captaincy is possibly more demanding than leading a team in a five-day test. It is a ball-by-ball change of situation, which is depending on so many factors. I don't doubt that Geoff Howarth and Glenn Turner contributed to the decision making; there were some earnest conferences in the field. But the pattern that emerged reflected considerable credit on Mark's captaincy, which had been subject to criticism at times.'

Burgess was injured before the 1979/80 visit of the West Indies, and the Howarth era began.

Dick Brittenden, in an article calling Burgess 'to arms' after a period where a lack of enthusiasm meant he was effectively replaced by Howarth for the 1974/75 tour by the MCC, described Burgess as having 'more natural gifts than any of his contemporaries, perhaps even Glenn Turner'.

Burgess' career as a captain began early when in 1955, as an 11-year-old, he captained the Auckland schoolboys' team. The team was coached by Don Cleverley, and contained future internationals Graham Vivian, Rodney Redmond, Terry Jarvis and John McIntyre, as well as future national selector Ross Dykes. From Auckland Grammar School, Burgess followed his father Gordon, an Auckland opener and New Zealand manager on the 1969 tour that his son went on, into big cricket. Through his father Burgess was given coaching by Merv Wallace, 'technically the best batsman New Zealand had produced other than Bert Sutcliffe'. Sutcliffe's parents lived not far from Burgess' grandfather in Torbay on Auckland's North Shore, and these family connections, as well as an admiration for the 'almost godlike' John Reid, fuelled Burgess' desire to play cricket at a high level.

A first-class debut for the New Zealand Under-23s in 1964 preceded a three-year gap that included his National Service, before he was selected for Auckland. He scored, wrote Cameron, 'a rather modest' 270 runs at 33 in 1966/67, but won selection for the trip to Australia the next summer. Burgess made 98 not out on his New Zealand debut, against Victoria, and made his test debut against India in their first test in New Zealand in February 1968, scoring 50 and 39 in the lost game at Carisbrook. In the next game, Dowling's first as captain, New Zealand won, for just the fourth time in tests. The third test was lost by eight wickets, but Burgess confirmed his promise with his team's top scores of 66 and 60. This was probably where he won the tag of a 'cavalier', which stuck throughout his career. 'With a couple of years' more experience I would have gone on,' he said. 'In my mind I was not a cavalier and played with a very high degree of responsibility compared to what the team's needs were and I feel I've always been pretty honest with myself.'

Burgess went on to lead Auckland, sharing the job with Vivian and Hedley Howarth. 'I suppose in my early days I thought one day it might be great to captain the national side,' said Burgess. But when it came, '— captaincy wasn't something that at that stage in my career particularly suited me. I don't know if that was because I was unable to do the job well, but it inhibited me tremendously as a player. I cut at least two major scoring shots, [including] square cuts outside the off stump, because if I nicked one it would be seen as irresponsible as a captain.'

The other was the hook shot that Burgess eschewed after becoming skipper. 'If it was short I'd drop my hands and let the ball go. We were not shotless, but almost so. To restrict myself in a personal sense certainly didn't suit my own play.'

Burgess represented New Zealand at soccer once in 1967, as had New Zealand cricket team-mates Vic Pollard and Grahame Bilby. (Ces Dacre — soccer 1922–24, cricket 1921–27 — was an earlier double international in the two sporting spheres.) In Christchurch, New Zealand's soccer team, featuring Burgess, lost 11-0 to a Manchester United team that included George Best, Bobby Charlton and Denis Law. 'My real passion was always football,' Burgess said. He regretted having to turn down an invitation to play for Essex in England for the sole reason that 'they were a really good bunch of lads — mostly West Ham supporters like I have always been'. Despite the temptation, 'the incentive money-wise simply wasn't there. I would have been getting less than half what I made working back here,' Burgess revealed, 'as well as giving away career opportunities.'

Burgess silenced his critics before being out lbw to Mohinder Armanath in the third test against India in February 1976. He made 95, after a recall had given him scores of 31, 6 and 31 in the first two tests.
Christchurch Star

In common with many New Zealand players of his generation, Burgess stresses, 'We need to remember we weren't playing full-time. In 1969 we toured for over six months and became a very good unit on the way home. In the last test, at Dacca, I scored a century. I missed the next test in 1970/71 against England at Christchurch, but as there was Sunday play in the Auckland game Vic Pollard didn't play. I played and scored a hundred. It was 1972 in the West Indies when I next played a test.

Burgess hit in the chest by a bouncer from Willis on the 1978 England tour. He was certainly not the cavalier he is often portrayed as being.
Christchurch Star

'Things were fairly intermittent. To expect us to produce a lot of consistency was asking more than we were capable of producing.'

Three successive test centuries against Pakistan (1969), England (1970/71) and the West Indies (1972) marked the peak of his form. Dacca in 1969 was the 'finest moment of his career', in the words of Joseph Romanos, as Burgess came in at 25/4 with New Zealand just seven runs on in the second innings, later slipping to 101/8. His maiden test century of 119 not out, and nearly two hours of dogged resistance from Bob Cunis, secured an honourable draw in the last test Pakistan played in Dacca, as in 1971 it became the capital of the new nation of Bangladesh.

Burgess was not always a solid starter, but once going he was a cultured stroke player, driving and cutting with skill. He retired briefly in 1973, and was intermittently available thereafter.

Romanos considered Burgess 'a surprisingly defensive captain considering his attacking tendencies as a batsman', while Lance Cairns wrote, 'He was a stroke player, and to my mind that is not the proper sort of background for a captain.' Perhaps it was the softly spoken Burgess' fair hair and good looks, and his stroke play, that gave the impression that he was a cricketing cavalier.

Frank Cameron portrayed a more robust cricketing personality. 'He was very intense, but a very likeable fellow. He was very, very determined as a captain. He was intelligent, not a cavalier, a stylish stroke maker, classy and lovely to watch. We had a few who could grind it out in those days — he didn't grind it out. He was an outstanding sportsman — he could play anything. But he took his cricket very seriously. He and Ken Wadsworth were two of our better-known bat-throwers. He used to express his disappointment.'

Burgess ended his career in 1980/81 after a final tour of Australia, 13 years after his first, in which he stepped in to captain the second test after Geoff

Howarth injured his hand. He had finished with Auckland the season before and said, 'If you only had to cope with the success side of the game it wouldn't seem right. The best thing to know is that you've given it your best shot.'

No one can say he didn't do that. Except Burgess himself, that is.

'I sold myself a bit short I think,' he said in his refreshingly frank and reflective manner.

Burgess has four children, two from his second marriage to Susan, and has been a director of Brittain and Wynyard, sports goods dealers, since 1973.

16. GEOFF HOWARTH
8 February 1980 – 8 May 1985

Before the gods that made the gods had seen their sunrise pass

Geoff Howarth was the most successful New Zealand captain in history until Stephen Fleming eclipsed his 11 wins and 30 tests in charge over 15 years later.

Following the career path of Glenn Turner, Howarth first played for Surrey in 1971, at the age of 20, and for Auckland in 1972/73. A move to Northern Districts in 1974/75 brought 498 runs in ten innings and a test place.

He made his test debut against England on their 1974/75 tour to New Zealand, although his 51 not out in the second innings failed to stave off an innings defeat. The England win was completed when Ewen Chatfield nearly died after being hit by a Peter Lever bouncer. Howarth was at the other end. His brother Hedley, seven years older, had first played tests in 1969 and was in the team with Geoff.

Howarth's parents had emigrated from Britain, and after he had made his first-class debut at 18 in the 1968/69 season for the New Zealand Under-23s his cricketing ambition led him back to the UK and a long apprenticeship with Surrey. The slim, handsome, fair-haired Howarth made his first county team debut in 1971, when he was 20. Bigger contributions, with delightful off-side strokes typical of his stylish batting, earned him a county cap in 1974, and brought 1554 runs at 37.90 in the hot summer of 1976. That cap was to lead to the inevitable benefit after ten years' service. This tax-free reward has been the pension fund for generations of county cricketers, but it has meant that players hang on until they are past their best in order to gain the prize. In the case of Howarth, and Glenn Turner before him, it stood in the way of New Zealand captaincy. It also brought into focus the new professionalism of these men, which contrasted with the loyal unpaid administration of the New Zealand game.

After the experience of the 1975 World Cup, Mark Burgess was preferred to Howarth as a batsman for India's 1975/76 visit. But Howarth was picked to join the 1976/77 tour to Pakistan and India direct from Surrey at the end of the English season. He failed to score a half century in five tests under Turner, but kept his place, this time as an opener for Australia's 1976/77 tour. In four innings, 131 runs represented a better return, although many thought his omission from the team was imminent. Then, in the month of his 27th birthday, March 1978, he made an outstanding breakthrough with a pair of centuries, 122 and 102, his first test hundreds, in the third test of the home series against England. Only the second New Zealander to achieve this double, after Turner, Howarth's feat was another highlight of a series that included the maiden test win over England.

By then Burgess had replaced Turner as captain, and Howarth was a regular in the test team. The dual centuries against England, which saved the match on a worsening Eden Park pitch to draw the series 1-1, boosted Howarth's confidence, which was often curiously fragile considering his outward air of assurance. On the 1978 tour of England, scores of 94, 0, 31 not out, 34, 123 and 14 not out equalled 296 runs at an average of 74 in the tests, and made up part of his 816 at 45.33 on tour.

A fourth century in six matches (114 in the inaugural test at Napier) was not enough to stop Pakistan winning the 1978/79 series, which was to be Burgess' last as a test captain. Eventually Howarth, now almost 29, was chosen as skipper by the selection panel of Frank Cameron, Graham Dowling, Burgess and Don Neely after Burgess declared himself unavailable for further captaincy roles after the semi-final run in the 1979 World Cup, when Howarth was New Zealand's vice-captain.

'The appointment of Howarth as a captain was simple,' revealed Neely, a national selector from 1979 to 1993. The meticulous Neely then gave an insight into New Zealand Cricket's version of the white smoke that ritualistically emerges from the Vatican when a new pope is elected. Neely detailed

What with John Walker's tresses, Bob Moodie's kaftan and now Geoff Howarth sporting an ill-judged perm — can the New Zealand sporting psyche take the strain? Howarth had previously claimed he was a stickler for neatness as a captain. *Christchurch Star*

The World Cup semi-final at the Oval in June 1975. Howarth pulls a ball from Bernard Julien to the rope. *Christchurch Star*

Howarth's 736 runs, scored at an average of 49.06, scored in the last three series, adding, 'Howarth had established himself as the country's finest batsman.

'We [the selectors] met at Wellington on January 18th 1980. We stopped at the Basin Reserve and looked at the reconstruction that was converting an oversized rectangle into a circular oval. We sat in the sun in front of the old grandstand and Frank said, "We need a new captain." It was unanimously decided in less than five minutes that Howarth was the one. From memory, there were no other contenders.'

During the 1979/80 tour by the West Indies, New Zealand followed a one-day win with the famous one-wicket victory at Dunedin in Howarth's first test in charge. Howarth wrote, 'I remember standing in the sawdust at Carisbrook watching those final overs. The whole country stopped to watch the live television drama that was acted out in front of them. The road that runs above Carisbrook was packed with people — such was the interest in the outcome. Boock and Troup gamely pushed and prodded three runs before the winning run came with a leg bye — in hindsight it was the start of seven or eight years of glory for the new regime and for New Zealand cricket.'

A test best of 147 followed in the second test draw, and the controversial series was won after the third test draw — New Zealand's first home series win after 50 years of trying.

'The saga of a man stepping out of nowhere to perform and orchestrate heroics is in the realm of legend, but it actually happened to Geoff Howarth,' wrote Don Neely in the *DB Cricket Annual* of 1980. That season Northern Districts won a clean sweep, but it was for New Zealand that Howarth's 'something special' emerged. Neely summed up: 'Howarth is a proud man with a sense about his special ability and by sheer strength of his personality he transformed a questionable New Zealand side into something of a family and proved to be the power behind their glory.'

New Zealand lost the first test of their 1980/81 tour to Australia by ten wickets, and then Howarth hurt his hand in a bush match in Wagga Wagga and Burgess replaced him for a last test in charge. The series was lost 1-0, but New Zealand reached the finals of a three-team one-day competition, losing 3-1 to Australia, who infamously had Trevor Chappell bowl underarm to ensure Brian McKechnie could not hit a last-ball six to tie the third final. Howarth diplomatically welcomed Australian captain Greg Chappell, who had ordered the 'Aussie bowl', to the wicket in the next game. Sir Donald Bradman described Howarth's captaincy as 'able and inspiring' and his sportsmanship as 'quite outstanding, especially in a moment of extreme provocation, a blot on the spirit of the game which no apology from an Australian captain could ever erase'.

A first series win against India followed in 1980/81, New Zealand's second successive series win at home. Howarth's 137 not out in the first test, at the Basin Reserve, was the only score over 50 that New Zealand managed in the match. The fourth test victory against India came within four days, as India failed by 62 runs to reach the 253 required to win. Better still was to come, with Hadlee, Wright, Cairns, Edgar, Chatfield, Coney and Howarth forming an outstanding team for the eighties.

They drew 1-1 against Australia in 1981/82, scoring a second win against the local rivals, with Howarth in quite commanding form. Australian wicket-keeper Rod Marsh described a trip to New Zealand as being 'as attractive to us as a trip to Ethiopia', summarising generations of trans-Tasman rivalry in one sentence.

The series began with a rain-affected draw at the Basin Reserve on Martin Crowe's debut, followed by New Zealand's thirteenth victory in their 147th test. The match at Eden Park was characterised by Bruce Edgar's 418-ball 161, which built a 177 first innings lead. Howarth made 56, adding 154 with Edgar for the fourth wicket. Hadlee finished off a promising Australian total with four wickets for five runs, as the last six wickets fell for 39 in 80 minutes. Edgar made another 29, Howarth 19 and Cairns 34 off 32 balls to see the Kiwis home to their 109 target with five wickets to spare.

Another tri-nation one-day competition, in which New Zealand made a disappointing 2-0 loss in the best of three finals, preceded a 2-0 thrashing of test newcomers Sri Lanka, which included New Zealand's first test innings win. Another World Cup semi-final appearance ended in a narrow 11-run loss to Pakistan, but in the following test series against England an historic five-wicket win at Headingley marked New Zealand's first win in England.

'It says here Howarth got a hundred the other day —.' The New Zealand captain's demeanour on the field was influenced by countless days with Surrey, enjoying the bonhomie of the English county game.
Christchurch Star

Although the series was lost 3-1, the first loss since Australia two and a half years earlier, revenge was immediate with a 1-0 series win, New Zealand's first against England in 21 attempts, in the return rubber.

'What little success we had achieved had created an astonishing upsurge of public interest in the game all around New Zealand,' Howarth wrote in the foreword to Bob Willis' account of the 1983/84 tour, *A Captain's Diary*. 'It might have added extra strain to my job, through the unusual pressure of being expected to produce the goods by an ever-expecting public, but I could easily put up with that for the pleasure of being followed by huge crowds.'

Willis' team, which he believed was just as good as New Zealand, lost the second test, held at Lancaster Park, by an innings and 132 runs. It was New Zealand's seventeenth test win, and the third against England, who failed to reach 100 in either innings. Ironically, the last time this had happened in a test was between the same teams, when New Zealand were crushed by the spin of Tony Lock and Jim Laker, scoring just 47 and 74 at Lord's back in 1958.

Geoff Howarth

Among Howarth's strengths were his instinctive bowling changes, 'hard to understand but very often successful', as Don Neely put the Lowry-like intuition.

'In the early days of ODIs he was probably the best captain in the world,' Neely asserted. 'He made sure that the team got through its early overs quickly so that when the pressure came on in the last 30 minutes he had time on his side to make careful field placements. His opponents were often panicking to get through their overs in the allotted time. Because he understood time so well he appeared ice-calm in the midst of the tempest that surrounded his opponents and the large crowds.'

New Zealand's next tour was to Sri Lanka, their first, where Howarth again led his team to a 2-0 win. Another tour to the subcontinent followed, which Howarth decided to avoid due to 'fear of health problems there'. He had found the 1976/77 tour 'exceptionally trying', according to captain Glenn Turner, being concerned with his health. 'I didn't enjoy the sights, the smells, or the food — the lifestyle on the subcontinent was so foreign to me that I never felt able to relax and concentrate on my job as a professional cricketer. As my career progressed I would learn to put up with such external pressures. It would become a case of put up and get on with the job.' This lesson was one that Howarth would later preach as a captain and coach.

It was the beginning of the end. Howarth would lead New Zealand's best-ever test team in just one more winning series. Fittingly, they won 2-0 against Pakistan in the return series, but Howarth could only make the team as an opener, such was its strength. Hadlee passed 250 wickets in the clinching win at Carisbrook, which was won by Coney's 111 not out in the face of Wasim Akram, playing in his second test.

Coney had led New Zealand to a 2-0 defeat in the previous rubber in Pakistan, another fraught trip. Now he avenged himself and the New Zealand team by scoring the winning runs. It was his second test century, and was another heroic innings after his 174 not out against England a year earlier. Coney added 50 off 132 balls for the ninth wicket with Ewen Chatfield to reach the target of 278 after Lance Cairns had been hit on the head and was unable to bat on. Coney's form was one of the factors that led to Howarth being ousted after a tough swansong in the West Indies.

'Towards the end of his time he was perhaps a little demanding of the younger players. He found it easier to be negative than positive with his comments to them,' noted Don Neely.

NEW ZEALAND TEST CRICKET CAPTAINS

The World Championship one-day series in Australia was not a success, and things did not augur well for the forthcoming tour of the West Indies. The home side was still bitter about the poor umpiring back in 1980 and New Zealand also lacked key batsmen Bruce Edgar and John Reid. Howarth was having problems making the Surrey team, and on the tour scored 74 runs in six innings before a last knock of 84 failed to stop a ten-wicket loss to make the series 2-0. But a final five-hour 84, opening against Marshall, Garner, Davis and Walsh, reminded everyone of his class when New Zealand followed on at Sabina Park 225 behind. Howarth and Jeff Crowe, who succeeded Coney, took the visitors to within two runs of the West Indies' 363 first innings total.

Howarth and Coney, who had his left forearm fractured by Garner in the first innings, were critical of the number of bouncers bowled, but this was simply the shape of things to come. Ken Rutherford had a miserable tour, scoring just 12 runs in four tests.

Frank Cameron, who was assistant coach and selector on the tour, became Howarth's confidant. 'I explained some of the pressures that I had been under as captain and that I couldn't keep doing all the jobs and bat at the top of the order,' Howarth wrote in his 1998 autobiography *Stirred but Not Shaken*.

The title of the book 'does him a disservice', in the view of Walter Hadlee, who suggested Howarth 'had been badly advised' to make this reference to his drinking. Howarth wrote, 'I could not continue to be responsible for the coaching, the captaincy, the public relations thing, the net practice and bat in the top three. It was asking too much. The pressure had taken its toll.'

The underarm incident against Australia, Martin Snedden's disallowed catch off Greg Chappell (both in one-day games), even the first test win at Carisbrook in 1980 were all stressful situations that were coolly handled by Howarth. But now the end was near.

Eyesight worries and a poor benefit year with Surrey were factors that made it a sad end to a great career. The culmination was when Graham Dowling, then secretary for New Zealand Cricket, phoned Howarth in the UK shortly after Surrey failed to renew his contract after 16 seasons of service.

'Geoff, it's my job to tell you that you won't be captain of the team for Australia,' Dowling said. 'In fact, you are not even required as a player.'

Howarth was in the classic situation of a sportsman 'lost in the wilderness'.

'It was like my life had ended,' he wrote, in an eerie echo of many stories from David Frith's studies of the disproportionate number of suicides by cricketers.

Geoff Howarth

It went thataway. In 1978 Howarth came of age as a New Zealand batsman, with 296 test runs at 74, and 816 at 45 on tour. He had made the breakthrough at Auckland earlier that year with centuries in each innings against England, to propel himself into the ranks of the world's best batsmen.
Christchurch Star

It didn't get much better than this. Howarth is swamped by the crowd after reaching his hundred at Lancaster Park in February 1980. Against Roberts, Holding, Garner and Croft he made a career-best 147. On 68 Howarth had survived a confident appeal for a catch behind the wicket. After tea, with Howarth on 99, the tourists did not emerge due to their anger with the umpires. Walter Hadlee reminded the West Indies of their contracts, and threatened to report them to the ICC. The ice-cool Howarth brought up his century off the next ball.
Christchurch Star

'Though he appeared totally in control and at ease he invariably started the day in a despondent mood. I don't think sleep came easily to him,' observed Neely. The 'huge void in my life' was filled only when Howarth was rescued by being given more opportunities at the top of New Zealand cricket.

He had more than doubled New Zealand's test win record, and had become the first captain to win more than he lost. Six series wins, with just two losses, two draws, and 1491 runs as captain meant Howarth left New Zealand cricket in a more prosperous and respected position than it had ever previously known.

Later, in 1993, he became New Zealand's first full-time coach, after successfully guiding the 1989 youth team. He coached the 1988 Young New Zealand team, using the phrase, 'If you're good enough you don't need your hand held', which perhaps said a lot about his style as a leader. Danny Morrison, Chris Cairns, Adam Parore and Chris Harris all emerged from these teams.

During the 1993 tour to Sri Lanka several players, as well as coach Warren ('Wally') Lees, had returned home early following an incident in which a bomb exploded outside the team's hotel. Lees was subsequently replaced by Howarth as coach of the national team, much to captain Martin Crowe's chagrin, and the acrimony between the pair remained throughout Howarth's time as coach.

As a schoolteacher Lees had spent six months on a part-time cricket contract that was worth $10,000 a month. Howarth's was a full-time appointment.

Commenting on his role as coach, Howarth said, 'I've been going at it since 1987 and now I've got it I don't intend to lose it easily.' In fact he had coached since 1974, when he moved to Gisborne, scored almost 500 runs for Northern Districts and won selection for a Gillette limited overs contest in Australia.

But after 22 months as New Zealand coach he was replaced by Glenn Turner, whose career he had followed so closely 20 years before.

Ken Rutherford had replaced the injured Crowe, but when Howarth went Rutherford went too, replaced by Lee Germon.

While Martin Crowe 'never really developed a warm regard' for Howarth, he did learn from his quick-thinking style. Ken Rutherford wrote, in reference to the contradictions in Howarth's nature, 'Geoff was one of those good old Kiwi blokes who played their cricket hard on the field and enjoyed themselves off it. It was a case of getting out, competing and then having a few beers afterwards. Fitness, other than match fitness, didn't mean much. Yet as a player he was a hard-nosed professional and his achievements back that up.'

The Otago batsman continued, 'Getting out and doing it for the side, your team-mates or the country seemed to be the gist of his planning and that came through in his team-talks. In one breath he would be exhorting the team to go down together and in the next espousing the easy-going English county cricket philosophy of enjoying the game.'

The effect of the county scene was again shown to be double-edged, just as it had been with Turner, as Howarth was caught between eras of old and new professionalism.

A 'disaster' of a benefit season with Surrey in 1983 landed Howarth just £27,000, and he described 1984, when he led the county, as 'a big learning curve, but an enjoyable experience' — a somewhat odd description coming from an experienced test captain. Little did he know it, but Howarth was also in his only season as Surrey's playing captain. He was deemed dispensable under English overseas player rules, when a new fast bowler, Tony Gray, was signed to replace Sylvester Clarke. Howarth played for the seconds in 1985 and the 35-year-old veteran of 16 years of top cricket was not re-signed for the 1986 season. Worse was to come.

The process of sacking a New Zealand captain was later unveiled, again by Neely. This procedure has become increasingly frequent in recent years. The first test captain to be dropped was Harry Cave in 1956. Others who were pushed before they jumped, in the style of English soccer managers, were Jeff Crowe, Ken Rutherford and Lee Germon in the eighties and nineties. New Zealand was becoming increasingly competitive, and demands for success from viewers and sponsors meant that winning equals money, and losing means clearing the tables and starting again.

'The dropping of Howarth was badly handled,' Neely disclosed. 'Bob Vance [New Zealand Chairman] and Graham Dowling [Executive Director] were in England at an ICC meeting. Selectors Cameron, [Neely] and John Guy were meeting in the Russley Hotel in Christchurch in July or August 1985, several months after the NZ tour of the West Indies, where FJC [Frank Cameron] had been assistant manager. We were preparing for a tour of Australia with three tests before Christmas with a team build-up beginning in Auckland in October 1985.

'During our meeting at the Russley it was decided that GPH [Howarth] had lost his batting edge — in spite of the fact he had scored 84 in his last test innings in the West Indies. FJC rang from the Russley Hotel and told RAV [Vance] and GTD [Dowling] that Jeremy Coney would be captaining the team in Australia. They were asked to tell GPH [Howarth] the next night when they were due to have a meal with him. Unfortunately, neither told GPH and apparently throughout the meal he discussed ways in which the Australians' weaknesses, as he perceived them, could be exploited.

'There was much sympathy for GPH when the team was announced because he was dropped without prior warning.'

A codicil from Neely appends the tale. 'A fortnight later I was in London on business and rang GPH from the Charing Cross Hotel. The phone exploded with his pent-up frustration (justifiably) and he came around for a meal. He was terribly upset. We talked for some hours in the company of my wife, Paddianne. The next day [29 August] I joined him at the Oval to watch the first day of the sixth test between England and Australia and watched Gooch (179) and Gower (157 not out) end the day at 376/3. He was charming and most hospitable.'

Frank Cameron, a selector from 1968 to 1986, had a huge role in the selection of Congdon, Turner, Burgess, Howarth and Coney as test captains. He wrote, 'Cricket historians in the future will no doubt give high marks to Geoff Howarth. But does the captain make the team, or the team make the captain? A strong team may carry along a rather limited captain, while the skipper of a weak side does not make the headlines. Yet in my time we were fortunate to have men of the calibre of Graham Dowling, Bevan Congdon, Glenn Turner and Mark Burgess to lead our teams.

'The title of a publication based on this era, *The Howarth Years*, may well sum up the feelings of followers of the game — some would change the title from *The Howarth Years* to *The Hadlee Years*.

'It was probably the toughest decision I've ever had to make,' said Cameron. 'I was always for the status quo, but the other two selectors were adamant his time was up. People used to say Howarth must be sleeping with bloody Cameron, but he'd reached the end of the road. Geoff was a very emotional sort of person, who often performed best when he was on top of the world. In county cricket he was struggling and he'd lost confidence. It was about the right time to finish.'

John Morrison has spoken of 'the dangerous side of cricket'. Ian Smith said, 'Howarth liked the social side of the game. I think that was a legacy of county cricket. I don't think anyone doubted his ability to captain a cricket side. I felt Geoff Howarth predominantly got it right. I don't know any cricketer who did not like to celebrate success. He was enjoying cricketing life at the end just as at the start.'

17. JEREMY CONEY

16 November 1984 –
15 March 1987

A single arrow is easily broken but not eleven in a bundle

The gangly, affable Jeremy Coney has been one of the characters of New Zealand cricket ever since his emergence with Wellington in the early seventies. His playing career spanned the halcyon days of New Zealand's greatest cricketing period during the eighties.

Even today, Coney is an instantly recognisable figure on Sky TV's cricket coverage. His series of documentaries, *The Mantis and the Cricket*, filmed in 2001, are of immense value to the history of New Zealand cricket. The moustached, lanky (1.92 m) all-rounder has thus brought up a quarter of a century of service to the game in which he looked like becoming an also-ran in the mid-seventies.

Communication has always been his forte perhaps because, like current test captain Stephen Fleming, he is a trained teacher. Perhaps significantly, Coney's subjects were English and drama. Unlike Fleming, the long-limbed and loquacious Coney developed slowly, making his New Zealand debut at 21 (as Fleming did) but not becoming a regular until 1979 when New Zealand, under the captaincy of Mark Burgess, hosted Pakistan. Up to this time Coney had played just four test matches in five years. This was after an outstanding Rothmans Under-23 tournament in Auckland back in 1969 when, aged 16, he followed his older brother Chris into representative cricket. He made his first-class debut in 1971 and first played for New Zealand two years later.

'Mantis', as he became known on account of his lanky body and long limbs, replaced the injured Turner on the tour of Australia in 1973/74. After helping New Zealand to their first test victory over Australia (under Congdon in 1974), he was dropped for the next match (being replaced by Burgess, who came out of a short-lived retirement).

A lack of decisive scoring kept him out of the team, but scores of 6, 36, 69, 82 and 49, as well as taking three wickets with his medium pace, finally cemented the 26-year-old Coney a test run, despite the 1-0 loss in the

Australian series. He effectively replaced Congdon as the batting all-rounder in the team.

New Zealand played no more tests for almost a year, one of the last such lengthy gaps in their playing calendar.

A couple more good scores (80 and 49 not out in drawn tests) by the man Don Cameron described as 'that astonishing fighter' helped New Zealand win their first series against the West Indies. Coney's reach and height helped him get behind the ball and score through the cut and hook. This was New Zealand's first golden era as a test-playing nation, and Coney was now an essential part of the side. He was missed when out injured for the first test of the tour of Australia in 1980/81, and scored 50s in each of the next two tests, as well as taking 3/28 in the last.

After the 1-0 series home win against India in the 1980/81 season, Coney was at the wicket for New Zealand's second test win against Australia, achieved at Eden Park in 1981/82.

After playing in the two wins against Sri Lanka in 1982/83, which gave Howarth a record number of victories as captain, in 1983 Coney was again at the crease during a Kiwi triumph, hitting the winning run when the New Zealanders beat England away for the first time. It was their first overseas win since Dowling's team beat Pakistan at Lahore in 1969/70. Even better was to follow in 1983/84 when New Zealand won their first series against England after 54 years of trying.

New Zealand have just gained their first victory in Australia, November 1985. At the Gabba Coney's New Zealanders won in style, with Hadlee taking 9/52 and 6/71, and Martin Crowe making 188.
Christchurch Star

Another 2-0 win against the Sri Lankans, this time away, preceded Coney's test captaincy debut at the age of 32, when Howarth opted out of the 1984/85 tour of Pakistan. It was to be a nightmare beginning to his career as captain.

The team lost 2-0, with the umpiring gaining more headlines than the cricket. Pakistan won the first test, held on a grassless pitch at Lahore, by six wickets. Coney's experiment in swapping Jeff Crowe for Wright as opener was a one-off failure — they made one run between them and quickly reverted to their old positions.

Spin again dominated the following week in Hyderabad, with Pakistan triumphing by seven wickets. Coney and manager Ian Taylor prepared a statement about the standard of umpiring after John Wright, Ian Smith (when the square leg umpire overruled the umpire at the bowler's end), Evan Gray, Wright again, and Jeff Crowe all suffered dubious decisions from Khizer Hayat and Mian Mohammad Aslam. A committee, formed under Pakistan great Hanif Mohammed, found that four decisions against the New Zealanders were 'confusing'. The results were released after the Kiwis had gone home. Taylor commented, 'To those who have been watching the game closely it was quite apparent the decisions in the match went against us — the whole team is disappointed.'

In the last test notorious umpire Shakoor Rana, later to be half of an infamous on-field argument with England captain Mike Gatting, refused to give Pakistan's best batsman Javed Miandad out caught behind off Bracewell.

'I swear to God I am not a cheat,' he told Coney, who was eventually persuaded to stay on the field by the other umpire, Javed Akhatar.

Many years later Pakistani journalists joked that Coney was the man 'who called us a cheat'. Again, cultural differences were at the heart of the dissatisfaction.

In his droll, inside-looking-out book *The Playing Mantis*, Coney described the nation thus: 'Pakistan is the Bible. Travelling through its cities brings back memories of Sunday-morning request sessions with stories like "The Small One Going to the Tanners". Pakistan is dust. It is everywhere. It enters every conceivable part of the body, more particularly the nose, hair and eyes. Pakistan is a vast drab colour. It's waking up at 4am to wailing prayers. Pakistan is waving to friendly, interested people. Pakistan is bright imitation-chrome buses with broken axles.

'Pakistan,' he said, 'is not an easy place to tour anyway, but the fact that we were without Richard Hadlee, who was our main wicket-taker, and Geoff Howarth, has been bypassed.'

He continued, 'It was somewhat of a surprise when I was initially selected as captain, both I think from the expectations of others and also from myself, having only captained Wellington for two seasons some years before.'

Coney had led his province in 1976/77 and 1977/78, and later was captained by John Morrison in domestic competition. During his debut season of 1971/72, Coney had been part of a Wellington team led by Bevan Congdon. The serious, taciturn Congdon's style contrasted markedly with Coney's emphasis on

Jeremy Coney

Coney (80) survives the wrath of the West Indians, who refused to take the field at one point during the game at Lancaster Park in February 1980.
Christchurch Star

Jeremy Coney was an expert in public relations. Here the former teacher could be forgiven for thinking he is back in the classroom marking books. The scene was Lancaster Park, during the rain-affected draw against India in March 1981.
Christchurch Star

discussion within the team and fun off the pitch. When he was captain of Wellington both Coney's batting and the team's performances were often inconsistent. A patient innings of 63 not out against Auckland in 1972/73 was heralded as Coney's coming of age, but harmony in his play was a long time in arriving. First he had to establish himself in the test team, which took him until 1980, after he went through a Stephen Fleming-like mid-career century drought. It was his lanky idiosyncrasies, such as jumping in the air to play pace bowling, and his deceptive saunter when coming in to bowl, that won crowds over. Coney's series of match-winning performances was to make him an even bigger favourite with the public in the eighties as New Zealand, for the first time, became a team of consistent winners. However, there were those, such as rival for the job John Wright, who did not always see Coney as a likely candidate for the captaincy.

'I had always been one of the generals if you like in the team hierarchy,' Coney explained. 'And while I'd been consulted at times when Geoff Howarth was captain, it was very different when you're suddenly thrust into the position of taking your team and I was certainly nervous about that.

'It was in the days when there wasn't a coach as such and to be fair we struggled a bit on the tour although, in the first innings in most of the games, we did pretty well. We fought back quite hard. We were beaten in the record books 2-0, but at the same time we saw some good things happen.'

'I have never been with a tighter-knit group or happier players,' star batsman John Reid wrote. The Aucklander continued, 'We were prepared at times to do anything for each other.' This ethos was down to Coney, who wrote to all the tourists before the tour began. 'Because I'm not Geoff, things will inevitably change,' he stated. He also stated his belief that every member 'has the right to enjoy touring as much as possible'. Slow-left-armer and renowned wit Stephen Boock replied, 'I received my training programme this week and I am impressed with the accuracy of spelling.' With characters such as Boock in the team, Coney's wish for an enjoyable tour was to come true at least in some respects.

Coney revealed, 'I enjoyed the experience to a point. I did feel that all of us had worked very hard because we knew that before we set off it was not going to be an easy assignment. In some of the games things went against us a bit; in the end I started to take it a bit personally, that every decision was going to be against us. And that's a mistake that I made and as I look back now I wish I could have another go at some things. I'd change a lot of things if I had the chance now. I had very little captaining experience and I think also following Geoff Howarth wasn't that easy. He had such a lot and we'd done reasonably well under him. I think there were expectations from the players and there were obviously going to be two different styles from two different characters.'

The appointment of a familiar figure was the key event that was to make Coney a successful and fondly remembered test captain. The man to make the difference, Coney said, was 'Glenn Turner when he came along after the tour of Pakistan. I didn't have a good tour with the bat and Glenn helped me work on aspects in my technique.

'By 1985 I was able to start an alliance with Glenn Turner and I used him a lot. Every session we'd sit down and plan the play.'

Lee Germon was to receive similar guidance from Turner as a test captain ten years later.

Selectors Don Neely, Frank Cameron and John Guy requested that Turner was included as cricket manager in the touring group to help Coney with the captaincy. Neely concurred that, 'The tour of Pakistan was enjoyed by all the players. JVC [Coney] was credited for generating a team spirit within the group that had been absent.'

Having led New Zealand through the frustrating tour of Pakistan, Coney, at 32, resumed his position in New Zealand's middle order in the ground-breaking 1980s test team of Geoff Howarth. However, Howarth's days were numbered, and after the 2-0 loss to Pakistan in the return series in New Zealand, Coney was in pole position to take over. Another 2-0 loss in the next series, against the West Indies, in 1984/85 resulted in the end of Howarth's unprecedentedly successful reign.

Despite sustaining a broken arm, caused by a delivery from Joel Garner in the fourth test, Coney became permanent leader for the tour of Australia in 1985/86. New Zealand's remarkable run of success was to resume after the disappointments of Pakistan and the West Indies. The team won the first and third tests then in the return series Coney's team won again, and then again, for the first time, in England in 1986.

New Zealand's first test win in Australia came with their seventh attempt. The stunning victory was achieved through Hadlee's 9/52 and 6/71, which the imperious all-rounder described as, 'A great moment for us all, especially for Martin Crowe, who made 188, while I took 15/123. That was the perfect test.'

'Imagine England beating the All Blacks by 40 points,' suggested Don Cameron, comparing this unlikely event to New Zealand's 'clear-cut and classical' victory by an innings and 41 runs. 'Here was a New Zealand team moving on with such polish, such poise, such dominating skill that by halfway — [only] one team could win the test.'

Initially considered no-hopers by the Australians, Coney was truculent when asked if he thought his team were underdogs. 'No, do you?' he replied.

Wicket-keeper Ian Smith summed up the team's attitude. 'There's a genuine will in this side to improve and fight for our positions,' although 'much more work has been spent on our catching and throwing practice.'

This discipline was down to new coach Glenn Turner. Turner also used his English county contacts, one of whom (as a player revealed when Turner was uncharacteristically tight-lipped) was England manager and former Worcestershire team-mate Norman Gifford, to assess the Australians' strengths and weaknesses.

'The test had unfolded very much as New Zealand had planned, step after progressive step,' wrote Don Cameron.

Reid scored 108 and Martin Crowe 188, at the time his test best. Coney made a useful 22. It was the greatest victory in New Zealand's 56-year test history.

'Going into the 1985/86 campaign against Australia, New Zealand had proved itself an effective force at home without managing quality success — no insult to Sri Lanka intended — abroad. That is why that wonderful five-day experience at the Gabba meant so much,' wrote Coney.

After the game Coney commented, 'I am delighted with the team performance and I must stress it was a team performance. There was a certain amount of humility about the victory but there is pleasure too. It was planned, worked out and it was earned.'

New Zealand became the first holder of the Trans-Tasman Trophy on 4 December 1985, when Hadlee's 11/155 forced a six-wicket win at the WACA. Coney was out just before seeing his team home yet again. He had now participated in 13 New Zealand victories out of the 23 tests the nation won.

Don Cameron described the New Zealand captain in his post-tour wrap as 'that rare sporting person — the thorough professional with the enthusiasm and patriotism of an amateur'.

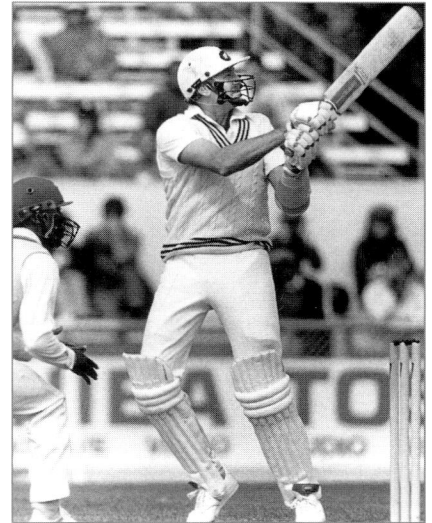
Captain Jeremy Coney hooks during New Zealand's five-wicket win against the West Indies at Lancaster Park in March 1987. Gus Logie is the fielder.
Christchurch Star

'Coney handled the public-relations side of the tour with aplomb,' continued the impressed Cameron. 'He — rather baffled some interviewers by dropping in words like "dichotomy" and "equanimity", and to the curly questions had the knack of making long, rather involved answers that took the spite out of the question.'

Even better was to follow, when Coney's team retained the Trans-Tasman Trophy by winning at Auckland and drawing at Wellington and Christchurch in the New Year.

After a match-saving 174 not out at Wellington in 1983/84 and a match-winning 111 not out against Pakistan in 1984/85, Coney achieved his only test century as captain, 101 not out, in the drawn first test against Australia at the Basin Reserve.

But it was his first innings high of 93, which kept the Kiwis in the match, 66 behind Australia, that led to John Bracewell's match-winning 6/32, and an eight-wicket win.

Coney's batting style favoured back-foot play, according to Don Cameron. Coaching expert and writer Ray Hunt went into greater detail, analysing

Coney's height was always a useful weapon, never more so than against the West Indies fast bowlers in 1987.
Christchurch Star

Coney's 'pre-delivery back-foot movement back and across to somewhere about off-stump or middle and off, and he can play forward from this position, or play balls on the leg stump'.

Hunt continued, 'What he does do, and so few have been able to do since Bert Sutcliffe, is to move his back foot a second time to bring himself more in line with a ball further outside the off stump. To do this he either does not have all his weight on the back foot, or, he has the time to rock onto the front foot so as to lift and place the back foot a second time. He did it many times in his long Basin innings. [The 1983/84 174 not out — a first century in 127 innings and one of the great rearguard actions.]'

The next series was also successful, with the first win in a rubber away to England. At Trent Bridge Hadlee's customary ten wickets, plus a maiden test century from Bracewell, led to Coney again being at the wicket when Martin Crowe hit the winning runs.

Coney displayed his affability by allowing England a replacement wicket-keeper for the injured Bruce French in the first test.

In the second came the second victory in 33 attempts against England. It was New Zealand's first test win in England.

'New Zealand's test history isn't littered with test victories, so we are naturally delighted to have won here. It's particularly pleasing for Richard Hadlee, who I know wanted to win here, having made Nottingham his home away from home. But I think the point I take most pleasure from is that we achieved victory in just over four days after coming back from a rather shaky 144/5 in our first innings,' Coney said during an unusually modest performance at the post-match press conference.

In the third test Ian Botham returned from a drug suspension, and passed Dennis Lillee's record of test wickets. Hadlee was to equal Lillee's figure in New Zealand's next but one series, against Sri Lanka, under the captaincy of Jeff Crowe.

'Coney's men — a team which, he says so accurately, tries a little harder — won the series strictly on their merits,' wrote Cameron after Coney's side returned with 'some delight in the way they threw England cricket into disarray'. At that stage, the team had played nine tests in ten months, winning four, losing one and drawing four. For the first time they had won three test series in a row.

'This has been a golden period of New Zealand cricket — by a great New Zealand team,' saluted Cameron.

Don Neely agreed. 'Coney grew with the role and absorbed the advice of Glenn Turner on the role of captain. The thespian in Jeremy came to the fore the bigger the occasion. He was quite masterly in handling the after-match media sessions. Like Howarth he won more tests than he lost.'

Coney delayed an announced retirement to lead his country in a drawn home series with the West Indies, notable for a falling out with the team's match-winner, Richard Hadlee. 'The vicious contretemps', as Hadlee described it, did not stop Hadlee taking 6/50 and 3/101 in what was to be Coney's final test. The fall-out came when Hadlee criticised disciplinary standards in a column he wrote in the newspaper *Truth*. Coney and Turner were upset, with Coney accusing his match-winner of being 'disloyal to the team'. In the end John Wright passed on Coney's messages on the field, in one of the more bizarre moments in New Zealand cricket history. 'The captain has asked me to find out which end you wish to bowl at and what field you require?' asked Wright as the third test began. Looking back, the humour of the situation appealed to Coney, although the signs are there that he was ready to retire.

Coney signed off with a win, his fifth as skipper in 15 games, when he put the West Indies in on a slightly damp Lancaster Park pitch. Hadlee and Chatfield had them 67/6 at lunch, but on the third day Coney could not quite finish off what they started, being caught off Garner, shortly before Martin Crowe and John Bracewell joined to hit the runs needed for the five-wicket win. 'It's hard to bat with tears in your eyes,' Coney said after striding off to a standing ovation. His technique had failed him with New Zealand needing just 33 runs to win the test and square the series.

Today Coney is a lively and respected commentator for radio and television, and has also been compiling footage of New Zealand cricketers talking about the game for Sky Sports. He has two children, Sarah and Ben, from his first marriage, and is now married to former New Zealand netball captain Julie Coney (née Townsend).

18. JEFF CROWE 16 April 1987 – 29 February 1988

Choppa

The second man, after John Parker, to captain his brother in the New Zealand team, Jeff Crowe had a cricketing background that groomed him for the top. His father Dave was a Wellington and Canterbury representative, and Jeff became captain of the national schoolboys' team, leading them in Australia. The team's coach was the recently retired test player Vic Pollard, who guided the youngster from the sidelines. Soon after this Crowe moved to Adelaide. He had begun the road towards a possible Australian cap with the West Torrens club aged just 18. Crowe made his first-class debut for South Australia in 1977/78.

In 29 Sheffield Shield matches for South Australia Crowe scored 1701 runs at 34.02, with eight centuries and five 50s. The best of his five seasons for the Redbacks was 1981/82, when he made 704 runs at 50.28 in ten matches. The highlight of Crowe's three-century season was his 126, which helped South Australia to 423 against Victoria in the end-of-season Shield decider. Set 161 to win, Crowe was at the crease to see his adopted team home to the title.

Crowe has said, 'The experience in Oz was simply A1. You don't get to play with and against great Australian and international players all that often when learning your trade. The Aussies taught me to play it tough, always competitive and with a great respect of the game and its traditions. They made it clear that it was critical to work hard at your game as much as possible and to take any offerings and opportunities. I tried to emulate the South Australian captains that I played under like David Hookes, Ian Chappell and John Inverarity when I captained New Zealand, but didn't have the form as a batsman to be confident in my role. In watching them they all led by example and exuded a great deal of confidence in themselves and support for their players.'

Crowe decided to come back to New Zealand a year after his younger brother Martin made his test debut. On his return, during the 1982/83 season,

Jeff Crowe

Crowe first played for Auckland against Otago, then was picked for New Zealand, all within two weeks. After moderate success against Australia's one-day side, Crowe began his test career in a winning team against newcomers Sri Lanka in March 1983. The 1983 World Cup and tour of England followed, including the first test victory in England. Crowe scored 0 and 13. Both Jeff and Martin made ducks in the first innings of the first test, which New Zealand lost by 189 runs. The brothers were to go on to play together 34 times in tests, the most by New Zealanders.

Maturity as a test batsman came with 128 in the third test against England on their 1983/84 tour, which followed 47 in the historic innings win in the second test at Christchurch.

'Crowe has been regarded as a possible successor to Geoff Howarth as New Zealand's test captain,' Don Neely wrote in his report of the Young New Zealand tour to Zimbabwe in September/October 1984. 'On this tour he must have enhanced his prospects of promotion. He showed an excellent tactical sense and a cheerful but firm control of his team,' he

Jeff Crowe in 1991.
Christchurch Star

concluded. The Young New Zealand tour led straight into a tour of Pakistan, where Crowe enhanced his reputation further with scores of 0, 43, 39, 57 and 62 in the lost test series.

With the exception of when he was dropped for Ken Rutherford in Australia in late 1985, Crowe was now a regular in the New Zealand team. Although John Wright had been the favourite to succeed Jeremy Coney, he was unavailable when Coney retired before the tour of Sri Lanka in 1986/87, and Crowe was named captain. Crowe led the team to Sri Lanka, with his brother Martin as vice-captain, and retained the captaincy even when Wright became available again.

The Sri Lanka series was abandoned after the first test because of civil unrest, but in this match Crowe scored 120 not out. Taking 516 minutes, which included an hour without scoring, it was test history's third slowest century. It

Jeff Crowe blocks a ball from Joel Garner during his 156-run partnership with brother Martin at Lancaster Park, March 1987. It set up a New Zealand victory.
Christchurch Star

was Crowe's third and last test century, and was also the third century to be scored in a first test by a New Zealand captain, following the feats of Dowling and Congdon.

The 1987 World Cup in India and Pakistan was a disappointment after recent test wins against England and Australia, with Crowe's 88 against Zimbabwe the best score of the tournament.

Unfortunately for Crowe, his leadership coincided with a collapse in his own form. After failing to secure a likely win over Australia in the third test of 1987/88, he was dropped during the subsequent home series against England. He later commented, 'I never won a test but did come close to it in Melbourne in 87. Some would say we were robbed!'

A crucial lbw decision towards the end of the test was not given, and Australia's last pair of Craig McDermott and Mike Whitney survived the final 29 balls to secure the Trans-Tasman Trophy. Richard Hadlee equalled Ian Botham's test record of 373 wickets with match figures of 10/176, but Whitney miraculously played out his final over. Crowe scored 6 and 25, and, according to Neely, 'throughout the tour struggled to find form but remained a popular captain within the team'.

Under Crowe New Zealand lost the Trans-Tasman Trophy, which they had held since its inception in 1985/86. Wright took over for the third test in England, and although Crowe toured Australia and England under Wright in 1990, he played just one more test.

Don Neely justified the decision to drop Crowe by saying, 'JJC's [Crowe's] test average in six completed innings was 13.00. When England toured NZ in February–March 1988 John Wright and Trevor Franklin were just beginning a good opening partnership. JJC's scores of 28 and 0, 11 and 1 in the first two tests highlighted his loss of batting form and the selectors [Neely, Gren Alabaster and Bob Cunis] were given no other option but to appoint JGW [John Wright] as captain for the third test at the Basin Reserve.'

Crowe said later, 'If anything I needed to concentrate on my batting more in the initial time and less on the needs of the team I was captaining. Once you have your own game in order then you can be more proactive in terms of the team and the tactics. If I had batted better and captained New Zealand a bit more then the confidence to captain astutely and with skill could have come through. In captaining Auckland I started to get the feel of what it is like to be a captain with some control over the outcome of the game.

'Each captain is a different person and did their job in totally different ways. They all had different strengths and weaknesses. You need to ascertain your way and what are your strengths in leading. I lacked confidence to be in the test arena as a player and it was always difficult to be comfortable in the same arena as a captain also. I had a reasonable understanding of the way the game should be played, mostly influenced by the Australian style, and latterly gained some flair and innovation in tactics. One area I was poor in was in the motivational area and being able to stimulate the players with good emotion and passionate words. The highlight was the honour of being a New Zealand test captain, albeit for a very short time.'

Crowe says that the responsibility of being New Zealand captain affected his play 'greatly!' 'Apart from my first test as captain making 100, I struggled to show any form which makes it almost impossible to lead from the front!'

Geoff Howarth described Crowe as 'the complete opposite of his brother, Martin'. According to Howarth, Martin is 'a basically insecure character who needed propping up', while Jeff 'speaks his mind bluntly and you know where you stand with him'. However, he believes Crowe was 'thrust into the role of New Zealand captain before he had the chance to establish himself in the side', despite Crowe's 29 tests in four years up to his elevation. It was more likely the pressures of captaincy that affected his form, rather than a lack of experience.

Since retiring from cricket in 1992 Jeff Crowe has run a corporate golfing holiday company in Florida. When he was asked to replace John Graham as New Zealand manager in 1999, at the age of 41, he said, 'I guess I always thought I would get back into the game sometime when the time was right. The way things worked out, it's right now. I've had a good break from the game and I'm ready to return.'

He added that he believed his experience organising the golfing tours, where he regularly guided people around the world and dealt with travel companies, would stand him in good stead in his new position. Indeed, 'Choppa' has proved the ideal man for the role.

England bowled too short. Jeff Crowe at his best, hitting 47 against England during the best-ever victory at Lancaster Park, 1983/84, when the tourists failed to reach 100 in either innings.
Christchurch Star

19. JOHN WRIGHT 3 March 1988 – 10 July 1990

I was a last resort

John Wright was possibly the most popular of New Zealand's test captains. He followed the path of Lowry (also a Christ's College old boy), Turner and Howarth in gaining experience in English county cricket, which helped him to success as a test player.

Wright was 32 when he succeeded Jeff Crowe as leader after Crowe had become the first captain to be dropped during a home series.

'I wished I had been given a chance to do the job earlier. I was a last resort and only got a chance because Jeff Crowe's batting form deteriorated,' Wright later said ruefully.

After the 3-1 test series loss under Howarth on the tour of England in 1983, Wright said in an interview, 'I had my own ideas but had to keep them to myself and apply them to my own game.'

Howarth, who was three years older than Wright, had captained the Brabin Cup selection team in 1973. Selectors Bert Sutcliffe and Martin Horton had overlooked Wright, and later Jeremy Coney and Jeff Crowe were to captain New Zealand ahead of the more established Wright.

'It takes time and experience to learn the job and the best way of learning is doing it. For why I wasn't given a chance earlier you have to ask the selectors. I was never given any reasons. Maybe they thought it would affect my batting. It was nice to get a chance to prove it to myself and others,' Wright revealed in 2001.

According to selector Don Neely: 'After Coney's stint, John Wright would probably have been captain, but he was busy arranging his benefit with Derbyshire.'

Wright later wrote, 'You're told you've been awarded a benefit a year in advance but I discovered a bit later than normal because a certain Derbyshire official, who may have been slightly, totally or even absolutely [drunk] at the time, sent me a letter [saying] I'd been awarded a benefit in 1987 by seamail.

If I'd been given the nod early on I could have done some preparation during the 1986 season.'

As it was, the New Zealand captaincy was lost and won through the incompetence of a drunken Derby administrator, as Wright was already committed to getting back to England when New Zealand's tour of Sri Lanka was arranged at six weeks' notice in January 1987. Jeff Crowe led the team, scoring 120 not out in what turned out to be a single test.

Wright captained New Zealand for the first time in March 1988 at the Basin, 11 years after his test debut, which was on the same ground and against the same opposition. He was the only survivor from either team. England equalled their record for successive winless matches (13) in the rain-affected draw.

Leading New Zealand to India in November 1988, Wright top scored with 58 in the first test at Bangalore as New Zealand failed to reach anywhere near the 337 required to win. Earlier, Richard Hadlee had Arun Lal caught at slip by debutant Chris Kuggeleijn with the first ball of the third over of the match, to pass Ian Botham's record of 373 test wickets.

John Wright, a DB mugshot.
Christchurch Star

Wright achieved his first test win as captain in the next test, held at Bombay. Hadlee, with match figures of 10/88, forced victory by 136 runs. It was New Zealand's second win in 17 tests in India. Wright, playing in his sixtieth test, became New Zealand's highest test run scorer, passing Bevan Congdon's 3448 runs, which were scored in one test more than Wright had played. He later called the Bombay win the 'best highlight — a wonderful team effort and a wonderful game of cricket. It could have gone either way three or four times during the match.' He paid tribute to all his players, who each made a contribution to the win.

India won the final test by ten wickets, with Wright batting throughout New Zealand's second innings for 61 in 189 balls, ensuring India had to bat again despite the away team's lowest score in India (124).

John Wright leg glances in the match against Pakistan, January 1985. New Zealand won the three-match series 2-0, recording their first home wins against Pakistan. Howarth captained; Wright had to wait three years for his chance.
Christchurch Star

Pakistan toured New Zealand in the first few months of 1989, playing out two high-scoring draws.

To Wright, cricket with Derbyshire, where he played from 1977 to 1988, had become 'a grind' that he didn't miss at all. He enjoyed the India trip, describing it in November 1989 as 'a great experience'. As ever Wright was positive about the team and their play, despite criticism that the 'results weren't that great'. His sympathy for his team-mates' skills and their fatigue ('We were knackered at the end of last season') helped the New Zealand team 'maintain its positive nature, so we have an attractive season and the game comes out better at the end of it all'.

Comments such as these may sound glib from some, but from the amenable Wright they seemed genuine, such was his reputation for integrity in the game. He continued his reign with a tour to Australia later in 1989, during which Mark Greatbatch's 485-ball 146 not out saved the one-off test held at the WACA ground in Perth.

India provided Wright with a second test win as captain when they toured in 1989/90, in a game that will surely go down in cricket history as the zenith of his career. This was Wright's finest match as a cricketer, in which he hit a 443-ball, 553-minute test best of 185, which included 23 fours. New Zealand won by ten wickets at 1.15 p.m. on the fourth day, gaining a twenty-eighth test victory, and a sixth in Christchurch.

The next two tests were drawn, with Wright scoring 113 not out in Napier, his ninth test century. 'I should have possibly declared on the last day of the final test against India,' he said later. New Zealand batted on to 483/5, but drew the game, winning the series. Perhaps the hardness Wright had gained in professional English cricket prevented 'an exciting final day'. Don Neely concurred that Wright 'verged on the side of caution. He had the option of making India a declaration — as it was the third game in the series and New Zealand were leading one nil, he preferred to bat for most of the fifth day and win the series.'

Wright had to deal with some of the most hostile bowling allowed in tests, but this bouncer came from team-mate Richard Hadlee in a Canterbury–Northern Districts provincial match. *Christchurch Star*

As a left-handed opener, Wright said, 'Over the years I've worked it out. I know I've got to stick around before I can play some shots.' At this time Wright reverted to a more conventional stance than formerly, placing his bat on the ground rather than in the air, a technique he had adopted to combat a longstanding back problem. 'It was the first time in ages I'd felt natural,' he said, and the improvement in results in his mid-thirties was marked. While admired for his skill, Wright was not known for his grace as a batsman, the raised bat combining with a two-eyed stance and a functional style of shot selection.

What could possibly have been the strongest New Zealand team yet was missing the world-class Martin Crowe, the only man with more test hundreds than Wright, when the team met Australia at the Basin in March 1990. Wright hit a third ton in four matches to see his team home by nine wickets, after they had bowled Australia out for 110 and 269. It was their sixth win against the Australians in tests, and ended an Australian run of 14 games without defeat.

NEW ZEALAND TEST CRICKET CAPTAINS

John Wright is all grim determination as he pushes for a single during the first test against India at Lancaster Park on 2 February 1990. By the close he had 127 not out, and went on to his highest test score, a 443-ball 185. Hadlee took his 400th test wicket as New Zealand beat India by ten wickets, and New Zealand have perhaps never been a better unit since.
Christchurch Star

This was the greatest success of Wright's career. He later said, 'No one gave us a chance and we were without our best batsman. Beating Australia is always a highlight.'

Like Walter Hadlee, Wright set targets before the England tour of 1990. His aim was to 'put ourselves under pressure all the time instead of just drifting aimlessly and waiting for the tests'. Wright knew that from 'living cricket', the New Zealand team could gain a lot from an England tour.

However, the tour brought an end to Wright's success as a test captain, with a defeat by 114 runs at Edgbaston following two draws. Richard Hadlee retired after that match, with a record 431 test wickets and a knighthood that had been announced in the Queen's Birthday Honours List.

Wright later said, 'If you want regrets, putting England in to bat in the last test in England is one. It was Hadlee's last test and it had rained for about two days before the test. We started late after lunch and as it was Richard's last test he was keen to bowl, but it was a mistake. It cost us the series.'

Wright's career as a test captain was over; when he opted out of the Pakistan tour that followed the team's return from England Martin Crowe took over. But the Canterbury and Northern Districts veteran had an Indian summer as a batsman, hitting centuries against both Sri Lanka and England in home series, before being recalled from retirement as one of four replacements on the 1992/93 tour of Sri Lanka. The tour had come close to being abandoned following a suicide bomb attack outside the team's Colombo hotel, in which five people were killed, and five New Zealand players, as well as coach Wally Lees, had returned home. Wright became the first New Zealander to pass 5000 runs in tests in this series, before ending his career with a top score of 30, then a final 50 in the nine-wicket defeat at Colombo.

He later became a successful coach for Kent in the UK, where he had played for the seconds back in 1976. From there Wright went to India, where he achieved hero status. An initial one-year $500,000 contract was Wright's reward for beating Australians Geoff Marsh and Greg Chappell to the job, after he had lost out to David Trist for the New Zealand job and Zimbabwean Duncan Fletcher for the England role. He coached his new team to a series win against Australia, who had a record 16 successive test wins. 'They're not that bloody good,' Wright was heard to mutter. India's old fire re-emerged when, according to manager Chetan Chauhan, Wright 'delivered a pep talk of such quality that it turned the series on its head'.

Wright was certainly one to call his players 'to play for the flag', in the words of Ian Smith, his wicket-keeper. Stories from Derbyshire mention a fearsome temper, unexpected in the laidback Wright, but any outbursts were always quickly regretted.

Don Neely comments, 'John Wright was a great team man — always very friendly — and went out of his way to make newcomers feel welcome. He cared for every member of the side from the youngest to the oldest.'

If Wright had a weakness it was that he found it difficult to decide on a team. 'John always wanted plenty of cover,' says Neely. 'He would have preferred 15 at the ground. After he stood down I still consulted with him on the team make-up. The first occasion I did this he spat out the eleven as quickly as a computer. When I commented that it was a pleasure to have such a clear, concise comment, he answered by saying, "That's because I'm not captain." '

'Captaincy is a lonely job,' the self-effacing Wright wrote in his entertaining autobiography *Christmas in Rarotonga*. 'Especially when you're losing and more so when you're confronted with off-field troubles. Captaincy is also a personal job. You get all the accolades when you win but, just as if you're in charge of any type of organisation, losing can be a personal slight.

'I loved representing my country,' Wright concluded. 'It was always a great thrill walking out. It's what I played for.'

Regarding the captaincy, Wright summed up, 'I don't really know how it has affected my life. It was a great learning experience and a huge honour. I loved working with the boys; they were good people.'

20. MARTIN CROWE

10 October 1990 – 16 April 1993

Captaincy is the complete summary of the way the game should be played

Martin Crowe was already the finest batsman that New Zealand had produced when he was given the job of test captain in late 1990. But the captaincy proved to be a poisoned chalice. New Zealand's match-winner Sir Richard Hadlee had retired after the tour of England earlier in the year, and the team struggled to find success.

Crowe later summed up the impact of Hadlee's departure. 'Regrets? Not having Hadlee to chuck the ball to,' he said succinctly.

In 1981, aged 18, Crowe spent a summer on a scholarship with the Lord's groundstaff. In 1982 he played league cricket for Bradford, and the following year he toured England as a test player. In 1984 he moved into Ian Botham's Taunton house as Somerset's new overseas professional.

In New Zealand Crowe made his test debut during the 1981/82 series with Australia. In his own words, it was 'way too soon! — My confidence and belief in myself was gone,' he wrote after test scores of 9, 2, 0 and 9 showed him to be out of his depth.

He describes team-mate John Wright as 'great' in the situation. 'He would talk to you, advise you, tell you that you were a great player.' Captain Geoff Howarth 'was pretty tough on me', attempting to motivate Crowe by making comments such as, 'You're just a show pony, Crowie', which the 19-year-old hated.

Martin's brother Jeff, who had been playing for South Australia, decided to come home to attempt to play for New Zealand after watching the second test against Australia. He replaced Martin for New Zealand's next test series, with Martin twelfth man in Jeff's debut match, which was won by an innings. In 1983 both brothers toured England, achieving little in a series that was lost 3-1, although both played in the first New Zealand test win, which came in their twenty-ninth attempt in England. The tour also won Crowe his county contract, replacing Viv Richards, who was touring England with the West Indies.

Crowe broke through at test level during England's 1983/84 tour, scoring 100 (along with Coney's 174 not out) to help save the first test. A second win in six matches against England followed in the next test, the famous innings and 132-run victory at Lancaster Park.

On the late summer tour of Sri Lanka a broken thumb and salmonella poisoning immediately preceded his first county season and began a long string of health problems that were eventually to end Crowe's test captaincy, and ultimately his career. In the second test, handicapped by illness and injury, he scored 19 in 217 minutes off 157 balls, eight of the runs coming off the last three balls, to bat out one of the dullest days in tests. But the innings did show his growing mastery over the bat, as he developed the ability to attack or defend as required.

While flatmate Ian Botham won the headlines at Somerset, Crowe gained the experience that had helped Lowry, Turner, Parker, Howarth and Wright in their paths to the New Zealand test captaincy. Botham's booze-fired leadership was a good example of what not to do, but captain Peter Roebuck welcomed Crowe's input. In 1984 Crowe formed the Young Nags, a club for young county players to 'Strive for perfection to earn the cap'. Roebuck: 'It was quite amazing — Martin's effort to give a discipline and standard that wasn't happening because Somerset is such a haphazard club. It wouldn't occur to you that he was younger than some of the other Nags.'

Crowe played in the New Zealand series in Pakistan, led by Coney, that was lost 2-0, before Howarth's last hurrah, the 2-0 win in the return series.

The West Indies were to dominate Crowe's career in contrasting ways in 1985 and 1986. First they beat New Zealand 2-0, although Crowe passed 1000 runs in tests during his 188 at Georgetown. In 1986/87 Crowe's 83 and 9 not out at Lancaster Park helped level the three-match series against the West Indies in Jeremy Coney's last test as captain. In the calendar year of 1987 Crowe gained a reputation as one of the world's best batsmen, scoring more than 4000

Martin Crowe in November 1992.
Christchurch Star

Crowe hit in the face during his 137 against Australia at Lancaster Park in March 1986.
Christchurch Star

runs, including 17 centuries and 16 fifties in 60 innings for Central Districts, Somerset and New Zealand.

Crowe had already played 51 tests between 1981/82 and 1990, prior to his appointment as captain, which followed John Wright's announcement that he was unavailable for the 1990/91 tour to Pakistan. Ian Smith, the only other candidate, magnanimously put Crowe's name forward to the selectors. In truth, Crowe had been groomed for the role ever since he captained Auckland Primary Schools back in the early seventies.

'It was my dream from an early age to one day captain my country,' said Crowe, who had been mentored by his father Dave, a former Christ's College pupil, and Canterbury and Auckland player. Crowe's ideas on captaincy are made plain in his book *Martin Crowe's Winning Cricket*: 'Being a captain is the complete role of a cricketer for he has to want to learn all there is to know. In some ways captaincy is the complete summary of the way the game should be played.'

Crowe's career as test captain began badly when the *Dominion*'s Peter Bidwell quoted him as being critical of Pakistan's umpires, after which Crowe was increasingly suspicious of the press. New Zealand lost their first test under Crowe, played at Karachi in October 1990, by an innings and 43 runs. Crowe batted for 250 minutes and 143 balls during an unbeaten 68 not out in the second innings, but a seam attack of Danny Morrison, Chris Pringle, Willie Watson and Crowe himself had been unable to prevent Pakistan making 433 for six declared.

The next two matches followed the same pattern, with Shoaib Mohammed adding two more centuries to his first test 656-minute 203 not out. Crowe made 108 not out (306 balls, 552 minutes) in the second match at Lahore, again failing to save the match, against 'the highest quality of swing and seam bowling I ever faced' from Waqar Younis (10/106).

The third test was closer, when Pringle's 7/52 (achieved through scratching the ball with a bottle top) removed Pakistan for their lowest total against the Kiwis (102). Waqar took 12/130, pioneering the art of reverse swing at New Zealand's expense.

A drawn home series against Sri Lanka brought Crowe's greatest batting achievement, a New Zealand test record of 299 (523 balls, 610 minutes, 29 fours, 3 sixes). In later years his disappointment at being caught behind off

Arjuna Ranatunga overshadowed his achievement, illustrating for many Crowe's intense personality. 'It was like climbing Mt Everest and pulling a hamstring on the last stride,' Crowe commented drily.

In 1991/92 England won their first series in New Zealand since 1974/75, the first win by any team in New Zealand since Pakistan in 1978/79. The success of the Hadlee years was already just a memory for New Zealand cricket fans. Crowe's woes were epitomised by the first test against Graham Gooch's England team at Christchurch. Entering the final over an innings and four runs behind, Crowe 'gambled and failed' by trying to hit Phil Tufnell for four to save the game. Crowe choked and was caught by Derek Pringle at extra cover.

In a television programme *Crowe on Crowe*, when Jeff interviewed Martin, the latter criticised the selectors for their lack of faith in him, citing his lack of enjoyment of the role and his batting form. Graham Gooch later wrote, 'I saw John Wright having a meeting with their selectors and it didn't take a genius to work out what they were discussing.' In the end the selectors didn't ask Crowe to resign, but he fell out with convenor Don Neely anyway.

Martin Crowe in full cry, 1986.
Christchurch Star

In 1992 Crowe captained the 'Young Guns' to a semi-final slot in the World Cup, one of the few highlights of his career as captain. During the World Cup Crowe implemented his finest piece of leadership, with the support of coach Wally Lees.

Wally Lees was an important element in Crowe's captaincy, but after his early return from Sri Lanka his days as coach were numbered, and in April 1993 he was replaced by Howarth. Crowe was 'devastated'; he had, he said, 'established a bond of understanding and trust that couldn't be ignored'. He later described his biggest disappointment as captain as, 'Seeing Wally Lees sacked for no reason, the catalyst for New Zealand's worst period that followed.' He was also suspicious of Geoff Howarth, under whom he had debuted in 1981/82.

Ironically, a judge as good as John Wright believes Crowe and Howarth were very similar as captains. 'Both were tactically very good, but not strong on their consistency of communication. Wally Lees worked well with Martin and knew how to get the best out of him. With Geoff Howarth it was never going to work.'

Don Cameron wrote in his autobiography, 'Crowe had grown into the

Martin Crowe, with the weight of the second test visibly on his shoulders, keeps the ball down as he pushes into the gully against the eager West Indies pace attack at Eden Park, March 1987. The game was an historic victory, with Crowe's 83 and 9 not out seeing his side home to a five-wicket victory.
Christchurch Star

captaincy under the canny coaching of Warren Lees, more the down to earth Kiwi than Howarth. Crowe tended towards the intense mind games of cricket. He preferred the personal coaching style of Lees to the more detached methods of Howarth, but they shared the same affection for the game — they probably agreed to disagree.'

'The success of NZ in the World Cup in 1991/92 was totally down to [Crowe's] foresight and planning. Not only was he the best batsman, but he was by far the most innovative and challenging captain,' said selector Don Neely. Off spinner Dipak Patel opened the bowling, there were unexpected and thoughtful field placements and bowling changes, and the captain led the tournament's run scoring.

Crowe made 100 not out against cup-holders Australia in the first match and 91 in 83 balls in the semi-final with Pakistan. But a strained hamstring forced him to watch as, in the field, New Zealand threw away the advantage he had given them with his batting.

The World Cup was followed by series against Zimbabwe and Sri Lanka that brought the mercurial right-hander's first success as test captain. The 13-match drought ended when Crowe's 140 and 61 gave him the chance to declare, setting Zimbabwe 315 to win in 71 overs. Spinner Dipak Patel took 6/50 and New Zealand won by 177 runs. The match was future captain Dion Nash's test debut.

From Zimbabwe the team went on to Sri Lanka where, in the second test, Crowe hit 107 in just 121 balls, with four sixes and 10 fours, which failed to stop Sri Lanka winning by nine wickets. On 39 he stood his ground after umpire Ignatius Anandappa upheld silly point's appeal for a catch that had not carried. Thammahetti Samarsinghe at square leg asked his colleague to rescind his decision.

In *Martin Crowe's Winning Cricket* Crowe lists nine keys that are necessary for a captain to succeed: knowing the rules and traditions of the game; representing the team; being a sportsman; leading by example; getting the best from the players; discipline; practice and training; using instinct; and being decisive. These principles were the basis of the outstanding leadership Crowe demonstrated at the World Cup (where he followed his elder brother Jeff, who had led New Zealand in the World Cup in 1987).

Crowe later spoke of his route to captaincy. 'My influences were Ian and

There was no better batsman to watch than Martin Crowe. Here he hooks the West Indies attack to the boundary, during his game-high score of 83, Lancaster Park, March 1987.
Christchurch Star

Martin Crowe felled. A missed hook off Bruce Reid hit Crowe's jaw, but he came back to make a superb 137.
Christchurch Star

Greg Chappell and Jeff Crowe. The only captain I played under that I rated was Jeff Crowe.' He certainly did not rate his successor, Ken Rutherford, believing his close friend Mark Greatbatch should have been his replacement when he withdrew with an injured finger on the morning of the Hamilton test against Pakistan in early 1994.

After Rutherford held the reins against Pakistan, Crowe returned for the daunting task of a series against Australia. The first match at Christchurch was lost by an innings and 60 runs, and Crowe offered to resign, 'to put a bomb under the whole team'.

This idea of being accountable seemed to be Crowe's way of reinforcing his desire to be wanted. He hoped he could return after two tests with soon-to-retire John Wright in charge, with the team performing again, and perhaps the team realising what they had been missing. The suggestion backfired on Crowe when selector Don Neely, who wanted Crowe to carry on, told the press of the gesture.

Surprisingly, following a rain-affected draw at the Basin Reserve (where Crowe made 98 in the first innings), one of the greatest highlights of Crowe's captaincy took place.

Playing at Eden Park, Australia never recovered from being 48/6, as Morrison and Watson swung the ball, making Allan Border regret batting after winning the toss. Eventually, after 29 minutes of the fifth day, New Zealand reached 201/5 to beat Australia in a test for the first time for three years. It was John Wright's eighty-second and final test.

However, New Zealand's next test, against Australia in Perth in November 1993, marked the beginning of the end for Crowe. An honourable draw was achieved at considerable cost, as Crowe aggravated a knee injury and had to fly home for surgery. Rutherford again replaced Crowe, who was now 31. He had played his last test as captain.

But Crowe was also losing the plot, accusing journalists of making up stories to do with his sexuality and personal life. 'There are lies being written. There are a lot of innuendoes which affect me personally, my marriage, my family. I wonder if it's worth it,' he said.

The strain of being such a high-profile sportsman was telling after a decade as a star. Crowe was the most talked about cricketer in the country, his profile especially high during his captaincy. But as Lynn McConnell wrote, 'Instead of reflecting on deeds of greatness, fans have picked at the man, overlooking the sheer skill he possesses.'

When he recovered from cruciate ligament surgery, which kept him out of six of the seven tests in 1993/94, Crowe told selector Ross Dykes, 'I don't wish to be captain any more — I read aloud my statement and felt the biggest sense of relief I have ever experienced. I was no longer captain of New Zealand.'

'A captain, like a teacher, cannot exert influence beyond the limits of his own inhibitions,' wrote David Lemmon, and as Crowe retreated, others were left to take control.

Crowe did not play in the test against India at Hamilton in March 1994 where Stephen Fleming, who was to become New Zealand's most successful leader, made his test debut, scoring 92 in the second innings. But a 1-0 loss to England in the 1994 away series showed Crowe was still one of the world's best batsmen. During his 142 at Lord's — his sixteenth test hundred — he passed 5000 test runs.

Crowe later overtook Wright's test record of 5334 runs and scored a further test hundred, before persistent injury ended his career on the ill-fated 1994/95 tour of South Africa.

Selector Don Neely neatly summed up Crowe's contradictions when he commented, 'He immersed himself totally into every aspect of the game and spent as much time on other players' games as he did on his own.'

On the other hand, 'Perhaps his major weakness stemmed from his greatest asset. He was a perfectionist at the crease. He knew how every shot should be played and was mortified if he didn't put the ball exactly where he wanted it to go. Sometimes he found it difficult to realise that not all players in the team could do what he thought they could do. Unlike his predecessors he never had the use of R.J. Hadlee.'

These days Martin Crowe is a Sky TV cricket commentator, and pursues a range of business interests.

21. IAN SMITH 1 March 1991 – 5 March 1991

Just a drummer in the band

The first wicket-keeper to lead New Zealand, Ian Smith captained the team in just one match, standing in for Martin Crowe in the final game of the 1990/91 home series against Sri Lanka. He retired after the 1991/92 World Cup, after setting New Zealand wicket-keeping records for test, first-class and ODI dismissals.

Shortish, round-faced and friendly, Smith attended Rongotai College, Wellington, the same school as former New Zealand captain Barry Sinclair, as well as 1979/80–1992/93 national selector Don Neely.

He began his career in 1977/78 as a 20-year-old, for Central Districts. He later moved to Auckland, but was never a provincial captain.

A long spell challenging for the wicket-keeping role at Central Districts (with Jock Edwards) preceded a time vying for the New Zealand job with Warren Lees. But by the end of the eighties Smith was established enough to be selected as stand-in for knee injury victim Martin Crowe, to become New Zealand's twenty-first test captain. The drawn game extended New Zealand's unbeaten home record to 13 games, dating back to Christchurch in 1986/87 against the West Indies.

'I enjoyed doing it; I would have perhaps liked to have done a bit more had I had the opportunity earlier on,' said Smith. 'At the time I was more interested in my role in what the side was doing — the keeping aspect with a bit of batting. It was not something I ever contemplated, being a full-time captain of New Zealand. I'd have enjoyed it better if we had won. We didn't play all that well in that test. We had conditions in our favour but we blew it on the first day.

'It's a test of a man's concentration to be able to think for ten other people, as well as concentrating on the very demanding role of wicket-keeping. You can't really afford to have too many thoughts going through your mind when you're keeping. You've got to pretty well focus on the ball and what the batsman is doing. To have a lot of thoughts going through your mind then push them aside and go back to them is quite demanding I would say. I take my hat off to those few that have done it.'

Smith is candid in his assessments of the test captains with whom he has played. 'The most influential captain I played under was Geoff Howarth. My first captain, he captained me for about four years until his retirement. The early years of your test playing career are the most important, when you start to be moulded, I've always thought. He knew the game very well. Having been in county cricket he lived the game so he'd been in and out of most circumstances, and he appeared on the park a pretty relaxed sort of a bloke. He had a bit of a Midas touch. When he tried something, something might happen. He had complete faith in his players. He didn't appear to be down on anyone in a team situation and was pretty supportive.'

As for the others: 'Jeff Crowe had a very mild manner about him and was very easy to play under, Jeremy Coney was a little bit more quietly demanding. He knew what would work. John Wright I think captained from the heart; a let's-do-it-for-the-country sort of captain. Martin Crowe was perhaps a bit of that, but get the best out of yourself and do it for yourself as well.'

Speaking as a commentator, his current role, Smith says of the current New Zealand skipper, Stephen Fleming, '— his record says he's as good as most of them though at times he hasn't had the playing riches that some of these captains have — it hasn't been easy for him. He hasn't had a first choice front line bowler of the ones he'd prefer to have. Several of the others were slightly more proactive, slightly more confident to try things. He's more of a "sit back and wait captain" rather than a "I'm going to try this right now" captain. The best captains have tended to be the ones who have hunches that come off. You can theorise until the cows come home but the actual game is won and lost out there and he is solely in charge and he should be able to take the credit for

A hundred comes up for Ian Smith. The New Zealand wicket-keeper, who was captain for one test, caught West Indies captain Viv Richards in the first test at the Basin in February 1987 to become the first New Zealander to make 100 test dismissals.
Christchurch Star

Martin Crowe and Ian Smith share the souvenirs; New Zealand v England, Lancaster Park 1984. *Christchurch Star*

those actions and to answer for them. Over here we've tended to have a lot of talk and controversy about our coaches. Coaches have tended to dominate a lot, more than our captains do, but it very much should go back to being a captain's deal.'

The test Smith led was unremarkable. Sri Lanka batted into the second day before New Zealand bowled the test minnows out for 380. Twenty-year-old Chris Cairns took 4/136 off 32 overs. Graeme Labrooy enlivened the match with 50 in 13 scoring strokes, a test record. John Wright (84) and Mark Greatbatch (65) helped New Zealand to 317 all out by batting much of the way through day three, while Smith was bowled by Rumesh Ratnayake for three. Aravinda De Silva's 123 and Cairns' 5/75 were the highlights of Sri Lanka's second innings 319 all out, which set New Zealand 383 to win. Andrew Jones set a home series run-scoring record of 513 when scoring 73 in New Zealand's 261/5, which was enough to extend the Kiwis' unbeaten home record to 12 games.

Smith's peak as a player coincided with the high point of New Zealand cricket in the 'glorious eighties', when Howarth and Coney, and later John Wright, led New Zealand to 19 test wins. It began with the one-wicket defeat of the West Indies in February 1980, and continued up to the nine-wicket win against Australia at Wellington in March 1990.

Smith became a regular in the test team after playing in two of the tests on the 1983 England tour, including the win at Headingley, New Zealand's first-ever test victory in England. Smith took seven catches, five off Ewen Chatfield. He took part in a further 13 test victories, out of the 29 achieved in the first 60 years of New Zealand test play.

Now a successful commentator, Smith's own view of his career is perhaps summed up in the title of his autobiography, *Just a Drummer in the Band.*

22. KEN RUTHERFORD
**29 November 1993 –
22 March 1995**

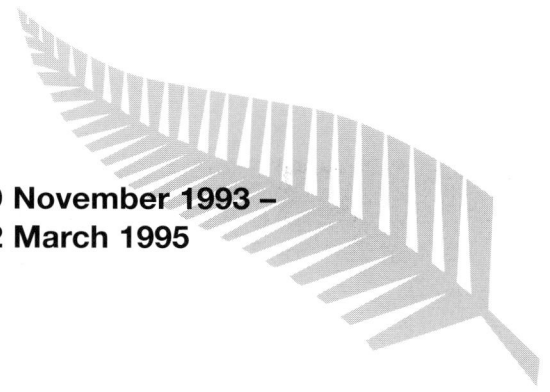

I wish I had the job again
knowing what I do now

For me the opportunity to captain New Zealand came as a complete surprise and something of a bonus,' Ken Rutherford wrote in his 1997 autobiography *A Hell of a Way to Make a Living*. Rutherford led his country for 18 of his 56 tests, but he was out of the job, and the team, by the time he was 30.

'You're it,' were the words coach Wally Lees used to announce New Zealand's twenty-second test captain. Rutherford's response gives considerable insight into how this felt. 'I was swamped with an overwhelming sense of self-doubt,' he wrote. 'What am I going to do? Who opens the bowling? Where does Andrew Jones field? Before I knew it I was out in the middle for the toss with Pakistan captain Javed Miandad.

'It was nothing I sought. There weren't too many players around to do the job after Martin Crowe's injury. I was in the right place at the right time,' Rutherford said later.

'I had a fair bit of international experience and felt confident on the field. Off the field in terms of the media especially and other obligations you have to learn as you go along. Off the field there are so many different things you are asked to contribute to, it's a case of having your own policy and sticking to it and learning as you go.'

In that first test against Pakistan in Hamilton, New Zealand was eventually set a modest 127 in two days, and 'a ferocious display of swing bowling destroyed us'. Rutherford's leadership was not generally successful in terms of wins, but two from 18 games is comparable to Crowe's two from 16 games and Germon's one from 12 games.

The post-Richard Hadlee era was a bleak one for New Zealand test cricket, which faced problems with injuries, suspensions, droppings and player unavailability, although after the glorious eighties the higher expectations of the public were partly to blame.

Ken Rutherford as captain in 1991.
Christchurch Star

Richard Hadlee wrote of Rutherford, '— from being one of the boys, he had to quickly elevate himself to meet the demands and the levels of responsibility and accountability that the position of captaincy requires'.

Rutherford had a difficult time as New Zealand captain, substituting for then succeeding Martin Crowe, before New Zealand's administration became fully modernised under chief executive Christopher Doig.

In his early career Rutherford was influenced by his elder brother Ian, an Otago stalwart, and Billy Ibadulla, the ex-Pakistan and Warwickshire player who moulded the young Glenn Turner as a batsman. Interestingly, Rutherford's early test career was during Turner's time as coach, but he later wrote, 'I was always the eleventh player picked in a Turner team.'

After becoming the 1984 Young Player to Lord's, Rutherford was selected for the 1984/85 tour to the West Indies as a 19-year-old. At the urinal at Auckland's Airport Travelodge he was curtly told by his new captain, Geoff Howarth, 'You've picked a hell of a job for the first one.' So it was, with the youngster scoring just 12 runs in seven innings as a test opener.

Billy Ibadulla was angry that his protégé was thrown to the lions, while in Rutherford's view convenor of selectors Frank Cameron was as much to blame as Howarth. He felt 'abused', while Cameron later admitted that he regretted picking Rutherford for his shattering career setback.

By 1992 Rutherford had scored 831 test runs at 18.46, disappointing even if you excuse the early West Indian failures. A perceived lack of maturity and discipline were seen as holding back the career of the enigmatic right-hander who, in 1986, had scored 317 in a day for New Zealand against Brian Close's XI at Scarborough. He was dropped from the pre-World Cup team, but won back his place for the last two tests in England prior to the big event.

The 1992 World Cup saw the turnaround as the 27-year-old Rutherford scored 212 runs at 42.40 with a series of responsible innings. He also scored heavily in Zimbabwe, where New Zealand achieved their first win of the post-Hadlee era, under captain Martin Crowe, then scored a second test century (105) in 54 test innings in Sri Lanka. His first (107*) was in the draw with England at the Basin Reserve in March 1988.

The early and mid-nineties were marked by a lack of playing strength and huge changes in the way the game was run, and notable for the contrasting styles of Lees and Turner, and captains Crowe, Rutherford and Germon. The role of the coach was also more significant than ever during this difficult and largely unsuccessful era for New Zealand cricket. While Crowe and Rutherford had little in common in terms of their personalities, they did share a distrust of Glenn Turner's methods, and a respect for Wally Lees' judgement. Rutherford felt Turner and Howarth lacked the interpersonal skills of Lees, a sentiment that went back to the beginning of his career. Jeremy Coney and Lee Germon, on the other hand, reacted well to Turner's coaching style.

It was Lees who had had the biggest influence on Rutherford as a youngster. They were in the same club side (Albion) in Dunedin and stayed close until Glenn Turner (who also played for Albion) took over as coach from Lees' successor Geoff Howarth after the 1994/95 tour of South Africa.

'[Lees'] contribution to the way I played was significant, probably more so at a younger age,' said Rutherford. 'In terms of captaincy, his attacking, positive approach influenced me. Wally ... would try everything [he] could to try and win a game, then probably think about drawing it ... most cricket supporters agree that's the way to captain sides. People don't want to watch a game of cricket that's going to be a draw.'

In Colombo 'that damn bomb' was an early distraction for Rutherford as he tried to rebuild his test career. The 1987 Sri Lanka tour had been abandoned after an explosion, and the 1992/93 tour looked to be going the same way. Rutherford was persuaded to stay in Sri Lanka by New Zealand Cricket chairman Peter McDermott, but there were repercussions for those who went home, including coach Wally Lees, who was soon replaced by Howarth. Others to leave included Mark Greatbatch, Willie Watson and Dipak Patel, who fell out with Rutherford over his change of heart. As a contracted player from April 1993 to 1995, Rutherford had won a concession from McDermott, which ensured his loyalty to the troubled tour.

In New Zealand's next test, the narrow loss to Pakistan a month later at Hamilton, Rutherford replaced the injured Crowe as test captain and completed his rehabilitation as an international cricketer.

NEW ZEALAND TEST CRICKET CAPTAINS

Ken Rutherford batting against Australia in a one-day game, March 1986.
Christchurch Star

Mark Greatbatch, who had lost out to Rutherford for the top job, made 133 in the first innings. New Zealand dismissed Pakistan for 174, their second lowest score in New Zealand, Danny Morrison taking five for 41, and the home team was left with a target of 127 to win.

From an overnight score of 39/3 New Zealand had been looking likely victors until Asif Mutjaba stuck a hand out at short leg and pulled in a superb reflex catch to dismiss Andrew Jones. Rutherford waited to number seven to bat, after using Danny Morrison and Adam Parore as nightwatchmen. Waqar Younis (5/22) had been in what was intended to be the last over of his spell when the wicket of Jones revived his spirits and he cut a swathe through the New Zealand middle-order, which when compounded with Wasim Akram's (5/45) control saw the home team all out for 93.

Recalling the 33-run victory Pakistani captain Javed Miandad said, 'We were losing the game, but we won the test.'

Of his tenure as captain Rutherford says, 'There weren't too many highlights,' echoing the honesty of his predecessor, Martin Crowe. The best moments were 'when we beat Pakistan in Christchurch and especially when we beat South Africa at the Wanderers. It was worth doing the job at those times.'

Recalling the game against Pakistan, Rutherford said, 'It was the end of the series and we had already lost 2-0. Maybe the Pakistanis weren't all out, but we'd played extremely well to get in that game. Bryan Young and Shane Thomson scored 100s and saw it through in good fashion.'

The 'Unlikely Victory' was how *Cricket News* magazine dubbed the win, especially coming after what were described as losses by 'embarrassing margins — the odds against a New Zealand victory were of gigantic proportions'.

In the match at Lancaster Park in February 1994 New Zealand were set an unlikely 324 to win after Morrison (4/66), Simon Doull (2/13) and Matthew Hart (3/47) bowled Pakistan out for 179.

Ken Rutherford

Recalling the historic win against South Africa, Rutherford comments, 'At the Wanderers the toss was important as the wicket became a mosaic with gaping holes all over it. In the fourth innings we would have struggled. As we tossed and decided we should bat on the wicket which was green the clouds opened and the sun came out.'

New Zealand made 411 and ended up with a first innings lead of 232. Hart (5/77) and Doull (4/33) bowled out the South Africans in the fourth innings for 289, giving New Zealand a first win in 33 years against South Africa.

Rutherford had little in common with Crowe, whom he described as 'the pin-up boy of New Zealand cricket'. Self-consciously unglamorous, Rutherford mocked Crowe's 'frequent' trips to the hairdressers, revelling in his own 'one-of-the-boys' persona and 'meagre assortment' of clothes in comparison with Crowe's Italian clothing labels. Rutherford also considered that Crowe had been the initiator in his 1991 dropping from the pre-World Cup squad.

'Throughout his tenure as captain I thought Crowe considered himself bigger than the job,' wrote Rutherford, who thought Crowe saw himself as 'Mr Cricket'. It was 'pie and pint versus champagne and caviar'. With reference to Crowe's concern that as a 'tall poppy' he received unfair criticism, Rutherford wrote, 'My career has been a battle, Crowe's a fairytale.'

After stepping up for the Pakistan test Rutherford's prospects as captain over the next two years were dependent on Crowe as he battled with injury at the end of his career. The entwining of their careers continued until the South Africa tour in 1994/95, when Rutherford blamed Crowe for 'the effect [the sour relationship with Howarth] had on the team'. 'When I took over the captaincy I felt the media corps breathed a sigh of relief,' he said. Even Crowe admitted that 'a big plus came from the media praise of Ken's captaincy in the field'.

When Crowe was injured again after the first match (of three) in the 1993/94 series in Australia Rutherford again took over. Australia won both matches by an innings, with Michael Slater, David Boon, Mark Waugh, Allan Border and Steve Waugh all making centuries. New Zealand's best individual score was an ultimately futile 86 by Rutherford in the innings at Brisbane.

Three months later New Zealand faced Pakistan at home, again without Crowe. Two more heavy defeats preceded the win at Christchurch when Young and Thomson guided New Zealand to 324/5 on the last day.

In March 1994 a one-off home test against India at Hamilton was notable for Stephen Fleming's impressive debut. Next came the 1994 tour of England, New Zealand's thirteenth.

Ken Rutherford lofts a hook shot as coach Geoff Howarth watches from behind during a New Zealand team practice at Lancaster Park in October 1993, prior to the disastrous tour of Australia. Rutherford's men lost two of the three tests by an innings and plenty, and had to say goodbye to Martin Crowe who aggravated a knee injury while saving the first test.
Christchurch Star

'Captaining the side to England in 1994 was especially poignant for me,' wrote Rutherford, conscious of his British roots (his parents emigrated to New Zealand from Scotland). Crowe decided to go as a player only, while Howarth was coach.

'I found the prospect of Crowe and Howarth meeting again unsettling,' Rutherford wrote after Howarth had unseated Lees. 'Crowe first came into the New Zealand side in the early 1980s under the captaincy of Howarth — he received little help or guidance, just as happened to me in the West Indies.'

The team that toured England was also notable for a number of newcomers. Rutherford's bowling attack was weak, consisting of rookie Heath Davis, the inexperienced Dion Nash, debutant Gavin Larsen and spinners Hart and Thomson. England won the first test at Nottingham by an innings and 90 runs. Former skipper Graham Gooch (210) and current captain Mike Atherton (101) added 263 for the second wicket on the second day.

However, Dion Nash (56 and 11/169 in the match) and Crowe (142) took New Zealand close to a pride-salvaging maiden win at Lord's, and another Crowe ton saved the third test at Old Trafford.

The England tour was followed by a tour to South Africa, where New Zealand won the first test by 137 runs as the home team collapsed at Johannesburg, losing eight wickets for 59 runs. However, New Zealand lost the next two tests — the first time since 1888 that a test team had lost a three-match series after being 1-0 up. There were rumours of a 'general lack of discipline and thereby an implied lack of leadership. Rubbish,' Rutherford wrote later. Lees and Hadlee also 'expressed to me concerns about Howarth's lack of ability to motivate and organise the players'.

Things came to a head at Paarl, where there was an incident that involved several players misbehaving at a social function. 'I thought I was coping with the job of captain quite well until the incident in Paarl,' Rutherford said later.

The management dealt with the incident on the tour, but Danny Morrison requested a meeting with New Zealand Cricket on his return, and stories of dope smoking and drinking came out. Rod Fulton, director of New Zealand Cricket, made a report. 'The Fulton Report was damning of myself and Geoff Howarth,' wrote Rutherford. The report noted: '[Rutherford's] personal example off the field needs improvement to encourage others to lift their standards — In respect of the team as a whole KR has some support. He wants to win and is one of the boys, but has failed to discipline his team or generate a cohesive unit.' Regarding discipline, the report regarded Rutherford's style as implying 'it's up to the individual'.

As a touring captain Rutherford faced difficult circumstances, both in South Africa and in England, and ultimately failed. New Zealand failed to win 17 consecutive series between 1990 and 1996/97, the era between Richard Hadlee's retirement and Stephen Fleming becoming captain. Rutherford was leader in 18 matches up to 1994/95, when Turner picked Lee Germon as the new leader, despite the fact that the Canterbury captain had never played a test. Germon had been appointed Canterbury captain by Fulton in 1990, noted Rutherford.

Perhaps the major innovation of Rutherford's tenure was his honesty with the media. 'I think the media appreciated that I was pretty up front,' he said. 'Maybe it was because they always got a story! If we played badly I said so and if we played well I'd expect them to reflect that.

'Looking back, I didn't really fulfil my potential at test level though I probably batted better as captain. In the last three or four years in South Africa I learnt things that would have made a big difference.'

The competitive and engaging Kiwi was adopted by Gauteng after burning his bridges in his native country, and was South African Cricketer of the Year in 2000. He wrote an outspoken autobiography, and after a stint coaching Ireland returned to New Zealand to work for the TAB in Wellington, thus involving himself professionally in his passion for horse racing.

'I'm actually quite enjoying being out of the game,' he says. 'It's good to sit back and reassess things and see what the future holds.'

Despite believing the provincial game 'doesn't mean that much any more', Rutherford doesn't rule out a return to coaching in New Zealand.

'Looking back, I'd have done things a lot differently,' he said in 2001. 'I learnt a lot about captaincy and learnt a lot through my experiences in the last four years. But I don't look back with regret — I wish I had the job again with what I know now.'

23. LEE GERMON 18 October 1995 – 10 February 1997

Left the room with silent dignity

Lee Germon achieved the distinction of being asked to captain his country having never played a test match. The Canterbury wicket-keeper was called up as Glenn Turner sought to bring a fresh approach to New Zealand cricket after the debacle of the South African tour in 1994/95. He captained New Zealand for 12 test matches, then was controversially sacked as yet another new broom, wielded by New Zealand Cricket chief executive officer Christopher Doig and coach Steve Rixon, swept through New Zealand cricket.

Doig's predecessor as chief executive of New Zealand cricket, Graham Dowling, describes Germon as someone who did a great job, observing that New Zealand cricket 'didn't have anyone as captain after that shambles when Rutherford was pushed out.

'Glenn Turner did a great job as well as a coach, pulling things back from where they were. And he obviously rated Lee as the one and only guy who had the ability to captain New Zealand, and turn things around on the field. Lee didn't deserve to be crucified in the finish with Glenn. The new broom came in after that and wanted further change and wasn't prepared to accept the Turner/Germon regime.

'Lee deserved to play for his country and did a fine job I thought, not a world beater as a player, but a gutsy cricketer, who went out and played extremely well. It was just a bit sad the way it all ended too quickly, but you're in the hands of selectors and that can happen in any sport.'

Germon retired from the game two years after losing the captaincy, aged just 29. He made a comeback captaining Otago in one-day games in 2000/01, and in all games in 2001/02.

When Germon made his test debut at Bangalore, he became the first player to captain New Zealand in his first test since Tom Lowry in 1929/30. Except for Ian Smith's appearance against Sri Lanka in 1991 as stand-in for the injured Martin Crowe, Germon was also the first wicket-keeper to captain the New Zealand team.

Lee Germon

While Germon, at 26, was the youngest player to captain New Zealand through a season, he actually had more experience as a cricket captain than almost all his predecessors. In 1986 he led the New Zealand Under-18s, in 1987 he captained Canterbury to national Under-18 tournament success under coach Bob Carter, and in 1988 he captained New Zealand Youth to the inaugural Youth World Cup in Australia. With him on that occasion were future stars Chris Cairns, Shane Thomson and Andrew Caddick. The *DB Annual* reported that Germon 'captained the side competently. His batting was effective against Australia where he scored 53 not out.' He had made his debut for Canterbury in November 1987, aged 19 years and 62 days, and was seemingly destined to take over from Ian Smith as national keeper.

Germon became captain of Canterbury in 1990/91, when he was 'probably too young', he says. 'It was a tough call actually, that I struggled with for two or three years, but one that I learnt a lot from.' The transition from the captaincy of loyal local rugby and cricket hero Rod Latham to

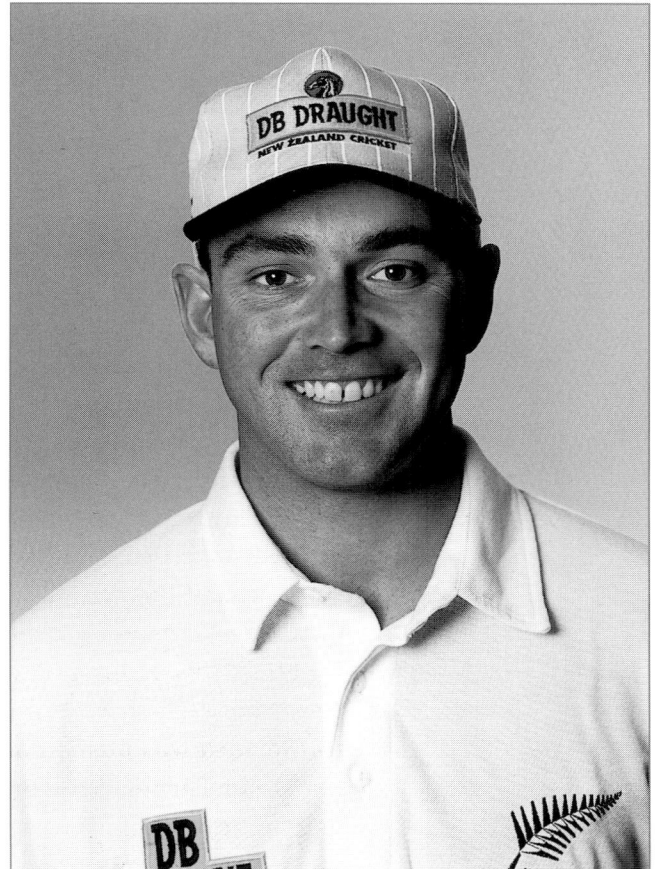

Lee Germon, captain of the New Zealand team, 1995. *Christchurch Star*

the confident upstart Germon was acrimonious. Germon's need to belong and to be respected were apparent, perhaps a reaction to his peripatetic upbringing as the son of an English immigrant in the New Zealand Air Force. Lee's father Ken Germon played cricket for Combined Services, and while he was based at RAF Woodbourne, near Blenheim, ten-year-old Lee was coached by Denis Aberhart, later his coach at Canterbury from 1992/93 to 1996/97.

Canterbury was a Shell Cup one-day winner in 1991/92, 92/93, 93/94, 95/96 and 96/97. Germon's leadership skills were therefore not in any doubt, as he successfully captained a team that had previously won the Shell Cup only once since its inception in 1980/81.

'Maybe initially we were a one-day team. We sought to resurrect Canterbury cricket through one-day cricket, so that's why we tended to excel at that in the formative stages of the team development; we saw it as a way of lifting ourselves. We were at the bottom, down in the doldrums so we took things a bit differently in one-day cricket, which not many teams have done, in terms of tactics and player personnel. And so we led the way in one-day cricket but then I think towards the end that we were just about unbeatable in both forms of the game with the players that we had. I'm trying to do the same with Otago now.'

The team also won the Shell (3/4-day) Trophy in 93/94, 96/97 and 97/98, again under Germon's leadership. However, it was to be a long wait for Germon to achieve his international goals, as first Adam Parore then Tony Blain kept him out of the national team.

In 1992, after Germon had been told by the selectors, then headed by Ross Dykes, that he was New Zealand's number two, Blain was called up ahead of him when Parore was hit on the head in the nets before the 1992/93 second test against Australia. Germon, who had begun working as a sponsorship manager at Canterbury TV, issued a media release criticising the selectors' poor communications. It was 1994 before Germon heard from them again, when he was picked as reserve wicket-keeper for the fateful tour of South Africa. In the fall-out from that tour he emerged as new coach Turner's choice as captain to follow Rutherford.

Turner appointed Germon as leader of the national side after considering his record and discussing his character, cricketing skills, leadership ability and knowledge with ex-captain Martin Crowe (now too injury-prone to be picked reliably as captain) and Denis Aberhart, the Canterbury and later national coach. It would be Aberhart who, with Turner as a selector, would resurrect Germon's career as a captain, this time of Otago, for the 2000/01 one-day season.

Germon's relationship with the team's coach has always been closer than that of other captains. Turner was accused of having Germon 'in his pocket', although this does not tally with Germon's character; Gavin Larsen commented that 'he was his own man' who 'didn't suffer fools gladly'. Turner himself used this same term, mentioning Germon's 'cutting tongue'. This suggests someone who knows his own mind, yet he was still perceived as having too close a partnership with Turner by several key players, which was subsequently to cost him and New Zealand dearly.

In response to Turner's observations, Germon says, 'I think that's probably a fair summation of me. He knows me pretty well. When I used to be in Otago on business with the bank, I used to make sure I popped in and saw him and had a chat and when he was up here we'd get him round home. I've got a huge respect for him so I really enjoy catching up with him.' In 2001/02 Germon became Otago's first-class captain, linking up again with Turner who had succeeded Aberhart as coach.

While Germon may be his own man, his relationship with Turner was crucial in his rise and fall as test captain. 'When we looked at choosing a captain, we wanted someone with a solid security of mind, someone with a strong temperament, not easily fazed; and also someone who was worth his place in the side,' Turner said in early 1996, midway through Germon's career as test captain. 'That was very clear in our minds, and when we chose Lee, it was a unanimous decision based on all those factors. In India, whereas he might have had concerns that the senior players would be a step ahead of him, it turned out he was a step ahead of them.'

The pair got on well, sharing a dry wit and a no-nonsense manner that alienated some players. To the accusation that Germon was 'Turner's puppet', Germon says, '— I think I was David Trist's puppet in my first few years captaining Canterbury.' Trist coached Canterbury from 1989 to 1993. However, the idea that Turner was in control remained. When Turner was appointed coach of New Zealand for a second time, replacing Geoff Howarth, he had demanded that he be convenor of selectors.

It was true that Germon seemed to have less autonomy than a New Zealand captain such as Graham Dowling, for instance. Germon explains, 'Often the captain was a coach as well, like Walter Hadlee; he took the coach's role and the captain's role. They played less cricket but they were away for longer. A lot of it comes down to the relationship you had with your coach.'

On taking up his new job Turner consulted a number of people, including Martin Crowe, Barry Milburn and Ian Smith. All said Lee Germon was the best gloveman in New Zealand at the time, and the incumbent, Adam Parore, played as a specialist batsman. Germon comments, 'I never really compared myself to others. I suppose I did when I was a bit younger, when Smithy was in the test team and Adam was there as well and I was sort of vying with Adam all the time. I'd sort of look and see how they did and when you played against them, I used to compare us, but towards the end I just concentrated on my own game. I think I kept reasonably consistently. When I first played for the Canterbury side I was quite inconsistent but then I managed to get some consistency of keeping and I suppose I was keeping pretty well at that stage.'

After being named captain Germon had some difficulties being accepted

NEW ZEALAND TEST CRICKET CAPTAINS

A confident and youthful Lee Germon, just turned 20, playing for Burnside West, appeals unsuccessfully for lbw against Ben Harris of St Albans, November 1988.
Christchurch Star

into the national side. As team-mate Gavin Larsen has said, 'The hardest task Germ had was gaining the respect of a number of players when he was given the skipper's job with basically no international experience behind him.'

Players such as Danny Morrison resented the fact that Germon had not yet served his time in the New Zealand team, having played no tests and having toured just once, on the 1994/95 trip to South Africa. Some resented the fact that Ken Rutherford had been summarily dumped as captain.

'I do expect etiquette on the field and discipline off it, and for people not to be big-headed, to treat other people with respect; I suppose this might be considered a rather old-fashioned virtue,' Germon says. 'We had South Africa hanging over us. There was some dirty laundry still floating around about who had done what and things that had been said, all this talk of Judas in the team and so on. I felt we needed to air it, so we had a gathering of all the guys who went to South Africa. Everyone spoke about how they felt and we cleared the air.'

Germon's keenness to present a clean image was understandable after the scandal of Paarl, but despite his competitiveness ('I'm not an angel on the field') he never succeeded in building the team culture that he thought 'critical'.

The team's overall record under Germon was unimpressive. He captained the 1995/96 teams to India and Pakistan (including the World Cup) and the 1996/97 team to Sharjah and Pakistan. He was also captain in the home series against Pakistan and West Indies. The team won the test against Pakistan at Lahore in 1996/97 by 44 runs, an impressive result, and drew the series 1-1. However, they had earlier lost to India and Pakistan (both 1-0) and failed to beat Zimbabwe in between, as well as losing to the West Indies, giving an overall record of one win and five losses in 12 tests as captain.

New Zealand lost their first test under Germon by eight wickets at Bangalore in October 1995. Germon top scored in both innings, with 48 and 41, but India won in three days. Rain ruined the second and third tests.

In the one-day internationals New Zealand went down 3-2 and competed well, scoring a record 348/8 at Nagpur.

In Germon's first home test as captain at his home ground Pakistan collapsed and New Zealand gained a first innings lead of 78. However, Pakistan recovered to set New Zealand 357 to win, too big a task against Mushtaq, who took 7/56. Germon was run out. The one-dayers were encouragingly shared 2-2 against the reigning World Cup holders.

In early 1996 Zimbabwe made their first tour of New Zealand. Rain affected

New Zealand team training — Lee Germon and Glenn Turner prepare for their first home test together, held at Lancaster Park in December 1995.
Christchurch Star

the result of the first test, but the weak Zimbabwe team also achieved a comfortable draw in the second. New Zealand won the one-dayers 2-1 and went to the World Cup with some hopes. Impressively beating England in their opening game, they lost to Pakistan with Germon batting too slowly at three. Making the quarter-finals, Germon almost made his name as New Zealand captain at Madras, as he and Chris Harris added 168 for the fourth wicket against Australia, until a Mark Waugh century put an end to their hopes of victory.

After the World Cup New Zealand made its third tour of the West Indies, losing the one-dayers 3-2 and the tests 1-0. However, they came back well in the latter part of the second test in Antigua and even had a chance of victory on the last day. The tour had its share of controversy when Chris Cairns, who had left the tour to seek treatment for a side strain, played for Nottinghamshire during the second test. Parore also left early, in what some described as a fit of pique.

Germon was averaging in the mid-twenties and keeping well, but all was not well with the team. Turner departed as coach, replaced by Steve Rixon, the former Australian wicket-keeper. Germon continued as captain, although the winning team in the first test of the Sharjah and Pakistan tour showed five changes from Turner's last test team. Nineties from Stephen Fleming and Chris Cairns in the second innings helped set Pakistan a fourth innings target of 276. Simon Doull and Dipak Patel bowled Pakistan out for 231, giving New Zealand its first test win since South Africa in December 1994. It was their first against Pakistan since Dowling's team won by five wickets at Lahore in 1969/70.

In the next match Germon made his highest test score of 55, but New Zealand lost by an innings and 13 runs. They lost the one-dayers against Pakistan 2-1.

As a batsman Germon loved to pepper the boundary square on the off side off the back foot, and his batting form as captain in India was ample proof of his ability to lead by example. At one-day international level, with the side in desperate need of a number three, Germon was occasionally pressed into service in this role.

But under Rixon, Germon's days as New Zealand captain were numbered. He was injured after another innings defeat, this time against England in the second test of their tour to New Zealand in February 1997. Stephen Fleming was appointed captain, at 23 the youngest appointee ever, and Parore returned as wicket-keeper. England won by four wickets.

Although he returned for the one-dayers, Germon was dropped for the next test against Sri Lanka in March 1997, which New Zealand won by an innings and 36 runs, with Fleming again appointed captain.

A Canterbury first-class record of 48 games as captain, with 19 wins and just seven defeats, is testament to Germon's success as a provincial skipper. After he replaced Rod Latham at the turn of the 1990s, Germon's men lost just one of their first 20 under his leadership.

Germon is still the Canterbury all-time leading wicket-keeper/batsman, scoring 2336 runs at 30.76, plus making 238 dismissals, in 76 first-class matches. He was probably still very close to his peak even when he left the game after the Shell Trophy final in March 1998, when he and Warren Wisneski added a New Zealand record 160 for the tenth wicket against Northern Districts at Rangiora. Germon made the final catch to give Canterbury an innings and 56-run victory.

'I think I'd probably kept better. I don't know. I think as you get older you become more attuned with your game and know what it takes and know how to prepare. And I think you'll find that with most players, their performance line increases until they get to a stage when they can't see quite as well or their wheelchair won't take them out as quick. Then they start going down, so I certainly think I got out when I was performing okay.'

Turner's influence on Germon, not only in his becoming captain of New Zealand but as a player, was fundamental to his development. He was undoubtedly a superb technical cricket coach. As Germon says, '— the coaching of Glenn Turner really helped me a lot with my batting and enabled me to work out the percentages of playing the spinners, what shots to use. Being a keeper helps in that you can read them a bit easier than other batters. I think it was a case of coaching.'

Germon and Turner both demanded high standards of appearance and behaviour from players. On the 1995/96 tour to India, for instance, there were extra fitness sessions as punishment for breaking team rules. Asked if he would approach things differently now, Germon says, 'Because guys had been on the turps the night before we decided that we would do an extra fitness session. It was a group decision, but I think I would do it differently now in the sense that we would all do it as a team rather than singling out those who had been out drinking. You still need to behave in a proper way when you're representing your country.' The strategy was reminiscent of Geoff Rabone's 6 a.m. session in South Africa in 1953/54, and was probably about as popular.

The Germon who captained Otago in the 2000/01 season was different to the Germon who captained New Zealand.

'I'm a lot more relaxed. The New Zealand team was in a similar position when we hadn't tasted a lot of success. And how do you go about instilling expectations of success in a side? So I was to take my learning from that and transport it into the Otago side, so it is similar in some ways.'

Germon believes the role of a test captain is changing. 'Now you've got coaches with every team and you never used to. Now I think a captain has got a large support crew around him. Whether it be a coach or a technical adviser like Gilbert Enoka who is with the New Zealand team. A manager who also has cricket skills. I think in some ways the captain doesn't need to play such a major role in the team, perhaps, and can fully concentrate on the park stuff. He's got someone who he can bounce ideas off all the time with as coach. I think it's a lot better now than perhaps it was, but having said that maybe you grew more as a captain through having to do it yourself earlier.'

Germon considers the best New Zealand captain he has seen, in one-day cricket, is Geoff Howarth, who 'led the way'. 'He coached me when I was a youth captain, and I learnt a lot from him in terms of angles of fielders. He was really unflappable on the park and had a pretty good one-day record.

'In test matches I think Martin Crowe was an outstanding captain technically. He was right up there, I would say in terms of tactics he was probably the best. Jeff Crowe was a very good captain as well.'

Asked if he has regrets about his term as test captain, Germon reflects, 'I just loved it all. Captaining in test matches was brilliant, to play against the best countries and try and get the best out of our team. I made my debut in India, it was a tremendous occurrence, and we lost in three days I think, just walking out with Azza [Mohammed Azharuddin]. I don't know if he was collecting any money in those days, obviously not to lose, that was a real highlight. But every time I went out to captain the side, in a test match it was great because I think I fully realised that not many had done it. It was a huge honour to do it and I enjoyed playing them.'

Today he would rather try and achieve outside cricket, saying, 'I've done a fair bit in cricket and I'm still doing a wee bit, but I think it's important to try and achieve elsewhere. I think a lot of cricketers haven't got anything else, so that's when they tend to go and end up in a commentary box.'

Of his successor, Stephen Fleming, he says, 'Flem's a good batsman. I think that if they were going to drop him they would have done it two years ago after the Australia tour, when he was struggling. I think he's there for as long as he wants to be there. But it's like any position in sport in New Zealand; it's a high profile position, you're there to be assessed and spoken about, that's all part and parcel of it. If you don't like it you get out I suppose.'

While Germon has some regrets and unfulfilled ambitions, he is not bitter at his treatment by the selectors.

'I would have liked to have played more for New Zealand and I would have liked to have toured England and Australia, which I was never able to do. I would have liked to have been part of a side that we turned around, which I never really got the chance to do. So in that sense my ambitions or goals weren't satisfied but in terms of representing my country and playing for New Zealand they were, so you can't ask for anything higher than that, and captaining your national side as well.'

Germon says his present position as director of development at St Andrew's College is 'far tougher' than being a test match captain. 'A cricketer's job, you really only have to focus on yourself and making sure that you do as well as you can and people tell you what to do — it can be quite one dimensional when you're a cricketer.'

His comments on his future role with Otago suggest the old Germon spirit is still in existence. He has come back to meet 'the challenge of trying to be part of a team that helped the Otago side and association achieve some success. I think I felt when I got out that I did have something to contribute, whether it was through coaching or something else. So it's really just the challenge of getting back into it, of trying to help Otago put some processes into place, maybe not for success this year but to have some processes to fall back on for future years.'

24. STEPHEN FLEMING

You are at your best when you are under pressure

Stephen Fleming became New Zealand's most successful test captain in September 2000. Given the job in 1997 aged 23 years and 319 days, Fleming was New Zealand's youngest test captain, following John Parker 20 years earlier. After being stand-in captain the previous month Fleming began his reign officially on 4 March 1997 when selectors Ross Dykes, Rick Pickard and David Trist dropped Lee Germon from the national side.

'Lee was very good and wished me all the best,' Fleming says of his club, provincial and national colleague. This ugly moment in New Zealand cricket history 'didn't really affect me so much [although] when you had history like that you don't like seeing your team-mate being replaced. It was a difficult situation, more so probably from Lee's point of view. They're hard situations to deal with and he did it with a lot of dignity.'

The way in which Fleming was able to detach himself from the situation emotionally reflects some of the reasons why the young Cantabrian has been able to take the challenges of leading the country at cricket in his stride.

By 2002, at just 29, Fleming had led the Black Caps through six testing summers and scored series wins against India, England, the West Indies, Sri Lanka, Bangladesh and Zimbabwe. He is currently New Zealand's most successful captain, with 17 wins from 47 tests. In building this record he has led his side to historic maiden test victories at Lord's and the Oval.

The 1981/82 season saw the first mention of the slim schoolboy, S. Fleming, who won the award for the best bowler in the Sydenham C grade team. Billy Patrick, New Zealand's captain from 1925 to 1926, was another who played for Sydenham, representing the working class Christchurch suburb's club a record 189 times. Lee Germon, who captained his country 70 years later, found the club provided 'an environment which creates warmth, humour, enjoyment and friendship'. Fleming concurs: 'It was nice to be involved in a club where there was a group who were involved with the family and were always very supportive.' The lanky, black-haired youngster's formative years with Sydenham were typified by contact with club stalwarts such as renowned characters Dave Gallop and Brian Salt, although, interestingly, he cites his mother Pauline as the person who had most influence on his cricket development.

Fleming came from a single-parent family and was forced to grow up quickly, hence his early maturity as a sportsman. 'He had very good discipline from his mother,' said early coach Bob Carter. 'She brought him up right and she is a level-headed person herself. She encouraged him to play a lot of sports and was a member of the Sydenham club. She actually ran one of the boys' teams and I think her level-headedness has helped him become a captain of New Zealand.'

Within the small district of Christchurch where Fleming was brought up is a school that has had eight former All Blacks as pupils, including double international Charlie Oliver, as well as 1945–51 test captain Walter Hadlee, John D'Arcy, Bill Cunningham and Alby Duckmanton.

Stephen Fleming at Middlesex in 2001.
Middlesex Cricket Club

Fleming also attended Waltham School before going to Cashmere High School, then to Christchurch Teachers Training College and away from the blue-collar neighbourhood he was brought up in.

'I felt very confident because a lot of the Canterbury players were in the club side,' Fleming says when recalling his provincial debut in 1991/92. Germon led Canterbury from 1990/91 to 1997/98, and Darrin Murray, Blair Hartland and Richard Petrie were all internationals between five and seven years Fleming's senior. All four were born in Christchurch between 1966 and 1968, and were current players with Sydenham and Canterbury.

However, more important to Fleming was Bob Carter, a weather-beaten English professional who spent his winters playing for Sydenham, making 69 appearances as a medium-paced all-rounder. Carter also played nine first-class games for Canterbury between 1981 and 1985, and later coached

NEW ZEALAND TEST CRICKET CAPTAINS

Nineteen-year-old Stephen Fleming celebrates his appointment as captain of the New Zealand Youth team for the forthcoming tests against Australia Youth with his maiden first-class century, 118 not out against Wellington at Lancaster Park.
Christchurch Star

Canterbury, Wellington and Northamptonshire. Fleming particularly valued the generosity of praise Carter gave him as a teenager.

Carter believes Fleming's school coaches at Cashmere High gave him his solid technical grounding, but that Fleming was largely self-taught and developed his own technique.

'He'd been brought up with cricket, watching all day every Saturday. As a captain he was pushed towards the role as he was always a tall lad and a good player who was the dominating character in his team.' In 1993 Carter took Fleming back to Northamptonshire as part of an exchange scheme, as he had Murray, Hartland and four more Canterbury players, to gain valuable experience in the second team.

In 1990/91 Fleming was selected to tour with the Young New Zealand team under Llorne Howell and scored consistently. In India in 1991/92, however, he proved more valuable as a first change bowler.

The relative ease of Fleming's advance showed that Christchurch cricket had come a long way from the game that 1940s Sydenham player Alan Burgess described. 'You had to be twice as good back then to get into the Canterbury team,' he said, referring to the perceived influence of clubs of a higher social class at that time.

Fleming says, 'I had an understanding of what I wanted to do. The way you play, to dominate that way and go out from the front, to compete on terms in that sort of environment with good players around me, I learnt pretty quickly to stand up for myself. I was always pretty confident.' Assured, undemonstrative and unshakable, Fleming's course was set for the top.

'I performed at the right times for Canterbury B,' he said. 'There were a couple of openings I was able to take. It's all about timing, taking opportunity when it comes. You get certain opportunities and you have to grab them straight away or you have to wait a bit longer,' Fleming says of his breakthrough into big cricket.

The left-handed number three batsman had played 19 first-class matches for Canterbury when he was first picked for New Zealand at the end of the 1993/94 season. His twentieth game came in March 1997, when he made 66 in the record score of 777 in the Shell Cup final against Otago. By then he had played 27 tests and 65 one-day internationals. This record demonstrates not only the diminishing role of the domestic game for international players, but also Fleming's speed of learning, and the lack of matches he had in which to prepare himself for the biggest role in New Zealand cricket.

Fleming believes the lack of time in the middle was more of an issue than his dearth of captaincy experience when he was first appointed national skipper. He has never captained Canterbury, although he has led the Southern Conference team. By the time he left Canterbury for Wellington at the end of the 1999/2000 season Fleming had played 51 tests but just 25 first-class matches for Canterbury, including only six in the previous seven seasons. This did not give him a lot of time to improve his technique outside of the highest level.

In 1996/97 New Zealand had just lost the home series against England by two games to nil, but had won the last two ODIs to square that series 2-2. Fleming scored his first test century, going on to 129 off 254 balls during the first test in Auckland. However, it took a record last-wicket stand for New Zealand against England of 106 between Nathan Astle (102 not out) and Danny Morrison (14 not out off 133 balls) to prevent an England victory. It was to be the last test for Morrison, and after an innings and 68-run defeat in the next test in Wellington, Germon's international career was also over. England captain Mike Atherton had an outstanding match with scores of 94 not out and 118.

Fleming was caught and bowled by Andrew Caddick, the former Sydenham and New Zealand Under-20 player, for one in the first innings. In the second innings he went the same way for a duck, but had no time to correct this problem.

Germon missed the last test because of a groin injury and Fleming filled in, scoring 62 and 11 in a four-wicket loss, after New Zealand had held a 118-run first innings lead.

The disappointment of allowing England to score their second highest fourth innings total to win a test was offset by an innings victory in the first test, at Carisbrook, against 1996/97's other visitors, Sri Lanka. By this time Germon had recovered from his strain, but had been dropped for ever as both captain and player. When Steve Rixon replaced Turner as coach Germon's days were numbered if results did not improve; they didn't, but under Fleming things were soon looking up.

Bryan Young's 267 not out against Sri Lanka (the second highest in a test after Martin Crowe's 299 against the same opposition) set up a heartening win for Fleming and New Zealand, with swing bowler Simon Doull recording match figures of 8/140. Fleming made 51 in 59 balls to add 140 for the second wicket with Young, sending New Zealand towards its second highest total in tests of 586/7 declared. The record was set during Crowe's record score at

Wellington in 1990/91, when New Zealand made 671/4. One week later New Zealand won their second test victory in succession for the first time since February 1985, when Howarth's team beat Pakistan for the second time in two weeks.

Now the heady days of the 1980s had returned. Chris Cairns had replaced his father Lance, Fleming had usurped Howarth and was showing the same cool demeanour, and 18-year-old Daniel Vettori, with match figures of 9/130, was simply a new proposition altogether.

In September 1997 Fleming took his team to Zimbabwe, with hopes high for continued success. His 181 runs in four innings placed him second in the averages, but both tests were drawn. In the second test at Bulawayo, the exciting young team finished 11 runs short with eight wickets down after Fleming was run out for 75 with victory in sight.

In November that year New Zealand toured Australia. The team's optimism was brought crashing down as they lost five of the six first-class games and the first test at Brisbane by 186 runs. Fleming had made 91 as New Zealand trailed by just 24 after the first innings, but having been set 319 to win in 93 overs, New Zealand collapsed to 132 all out in the second innings.

The second test was worse, with Fleming making ten and four in an innings and 70-run loss at Perth. Respect was regained at Hobart, when having been set 288 to win in 61 overs New Zealand boldly went for the runs. Fleming promoted Nathan Astle and Chris Cairns up the order. However, Fleming himself was stumped off Shane Warne for a duck and the last pair, Simon Doull and Shayne O'Connor, had to hold on for 38 minutes to draw the match.

Zimbabwe visited in the New Year of 1998, losing the first test at Wellington by ten wickets. It was New Zealand's first test win at the Basin Reserve since 1989/90, when John Wright's team beat Australia. Craig McMillan's maiden test century, along with contributions from Dion Nash, Daniel Vettori, Nathan Astle, Chris Cairns and Adam Parore, showed where the strength of the team lay.

A fourth successive home test win for Fleming followed at Auckland. Again, also for a fourth time in a row, the Kiwis won in four days or less, this time by an innings and 13 runs. Matthew Horne and Nathan Astle's fourth wicket record of 243, and Doull's 8/85 in the match, proved to be key factors as Zimbabwe proved to be lesser opposition away than at home.

New Zealand also won the ODI series, by 4-0, but on a quick trip in February 1998 Australia took the first two one-dayers. However, Fleming's 111

Fleming in 1992, as a teenage hopeful.
Christchurch Star

not out won the match at Napier and the New Zealanders went on to draw the series.

The New Zealand team then toured to Sharjah and Sri Lanka, where Fleming had his best test performance, scoring 78 and 174 not out in the 167-run win. Fleming's highest first-class innings was made in 333 balls with one six and 16 fours. He and McMillan hit 240 for the fourth wicket in the second innings at Colombo, then Paul Wiseman and Daniel Vettori shared eight second-innings wickets as New Zealand's spinners unexpectedly out-bowled Sri Lanka's.

However, the team was thrashed in the final two tests of the 1997/98 season, failing to reach 200 in four successive innings against Sri Lankan spinners Muttiah Muralitharan, Niroshan Bandaratilake and Aravinda De Silva. This spoilt Fleming's great year, although he finished top batsman with 698 runs from his ten tests as leader. A win/loss record of three to four was not as good as it sounded, as two of the wins came against test small-fry Zimbabwe. Overall Fleming had five test wins and five losses in his first 13 tests in charge, which already made him New Zealand's second most successful skipper, equal with Jeremy Coney. New Zealand had played 57 matches in 1997/98, with Fleming captain in 55 of them.

By 2001, Fleming would be number one, unchallenged as New Zealand's most successful cricket captain.

In the meantime, a 1998 Commonwealth bronze medal (Fleming topped the averages in Kuala Lumpur) and a one-day tournament in Bangladesh preceded India's 1998/99 visit. The first test, at Dunedin, was abandoned without a ball being bowled. New Zealand won by four wickets at the Basin Reserve, with Cairns and McMillan adding 137 for the fifth wicket as New Zealand chased a target of 213 for what turned out to be a decisive victory in the series.

A groin injury prevented Fleming facing South Africa in the next three tests, with Dion Nash unsuccessfully stepping in. If anything, Nash's relief job strengthened Fleming's hold on the captaincy, as it proved there was no other candidate who was better suited to the job.

Sixteen test matches had brought six wins and five losses before the World Cup in England. A good showing was important for Fleming's credibility as captain, as well as for the New Zealand public in the showpiece event of world cricket. New Zealand reached the semi-finals for the fourth time in seven tournaments.

The test series that followed became Fleming's greatest triumph as a leader. New Zealand won the second and fourth tests against England, and the series 2-1. Coney's team in 1986 was the only other side to win a series in England.

The first test, held at Edgbaston, was lost by seven wickets, thanks to England nightwatchman Alex Tudor's freakish 99 not out. The second test brought an historic first test win at Lord's, after 13 attempts going back to 1931. Fleming was fittingly at the wicket when the winning runs were scored late on the fourth day after a whole team effort had kept New Zealand on top throughout. In contrast to Fleming's joy, injured England captain Nasser Hussain had to watch idly as his team floundered in their second innings. New Zealand needed just 58 to win as no England batsman passed 50.

The third test at Manchester was a rainy draw, but when Fleming caught Dean Headley off Chris Harris he equalled Martin Crowe's New Zealand test record of 71 catches.

The fourth test was another New Zealand triumph. In the first innings Fleming's epic 332-minute 66 not out, and Cairns' second-innings 93-ball 80, helped leave England needing 245 to win the series. Fleming hit just three fours in his stay, during which he became the seventh New Zealander to pass 1000 runs as captain. Cairns, Nash, Shayne O'Connor and Vettori took the last eight England wickets for 39 and New Zealand scored their maiden test win at the Oval. It was the first time New Zealand had won two tests in a series in England. Coach Steve Rixon and manager John Graham, who had brought to the team modern methods of training, motivation and some discipline, both retired at the end of the tour with New Zealand cricket at its highest point since 1990.

New coach David Trist and manager Jeff Crowe accompanied New Zealand to India in September 1998, but the series was lost 1-0, with Anil Kumble taking ten wickets in the second test in Kanpur, which India won by eight wickets. Fleming topped the test averages with 261 runs at 52.20, but again scored no centuries, although no other New Zealand batsman made a score more than new Canterbury captain Gary Stead's 78 in the third and final test in Ahmedabad, where Sachin Tendulkar hit a maiden test double century.

The West Indies arrived before Christmas and Fleming's team was quick to humiliate the fading stars of the eighties and early nineties. On the final day at Hamilton Cairns took 7/27, dismissing the tourists for 97, after Adrian Griffith and Sherwin Campbell had put on 276 for the first wicket in the first innings. Cairns also scored a swift 66, and took 3/73 in the first innings which, along with Fleming's 189-ball 66, set up a nine-wicket win.

Mathew Sinclair, on his test debut, made 214 in the next test, held at Wellington. Fleming helped him add 164 for the third wicket. Cairns and Nash ensured an innings win against the fragile West Indians for the first time by a New Zealand team. The new world order in test cricket saw Australia firmly at the top, followed by South Africa, India, then Sri Lanka, New Zealand and Pakistan, with the West Indies and England on the decline and Zimbabwe at the bottom.

Australia made a late season tour, and won the test series 3-0, outclassing the New Zealanders after some early competitiveness. Shane Warne, the Australian leg spinner, acknowledged New Zealand's emerging status beyond the category of easy beats.

In a chapter on captaincy in his 2001 autobiography, *My Autobiography*, Warne wrote: 'One man I rate extremely highly is Stephen Fleming of New Zealand. The side has had all sorts of problems bonding and suffered run-ins with coaches down the years, but Fleming has helped bring them together and pull in the same direction.

'Like a good captain he gels the team. Until he took charge we always felt they were content simply to compete against us. Under Fleming they have developed a more ruthless streak, set their sights that bit higher and are genuinely annoyed if they don't win.'

Fleming returned the compliment, writing, 'The thing with the Aussies is they have a very strong belief in their ability. In the last test series [1999/2000] there were times when we had the advantage, but we just didn't have the belief to push on.'

While his stature on and off the field grew, Fleming's batting form had dipped, and there was comment on his lack of centuries. In eight matches during 1999/2000 his top score was 73, although he averaged 40. As a captain in series New Zealand had won, Fleming had played 14 matches, scoring 575 runs at 30.26, with five 50s and a top sore of 67. In drawn series he had played six matches, scoring 432 runs at 48.00, with five more 50s and a top score of 86. In lost series Fleming had played 16 matches, scoring 1125 runs at 38.79, with a top score of 174 not out, plus nine 50s. These statistics indicate that Fleming is a battler in a crisis, and responds well when the pressure is on him to concentrate.

'You are at your best when you are under pressure,' he says in his characteristic detached manner. 'It's been like that all the way through my career. When the pressure's not on so much you don't do so well and that's probably where I've missed out a little bit. I like having it that way. It's not always a nice feeling, but I enjoy responding.' Fleming says that the stresses of playing at this level 'make me play better, make me concentrate better, and I've got to replicate that every time I bat'.

Despite misgivings that the captaincy was affecting his batting, Fleming now had ten wins as captain, along with ten losses from his 27 matches in charge.

At the end of 2000 Fleming's team went back to South Africa, six years after the debacle of 1994/95. First they won the ICC Trophy in Nairobi, a maiden international tournament victory, and collected two more wins against Zimbabwe, who the team had also beaten twice at home in 1997/98. His wins equalled, then passed, Geoff Howarth's record of test victories as a New Zealand captain.

After the second win, Fleming's twelfth as captain, he said, 'To get the record today, on a personal note, is something that makes me very proud and is a tribute to the team. For the whole series we targeted a 2-0 result and I would have been disappointed with anything else.'

Now ruthless at beating lesser opposition, New Zealand moved on to South Africa, the second strongest side in the world and scene of Fleming's disgrace five years earlier when he was one of several players who smoked cannabis at a team function.

The first two tests were lost. In his tour diary *Cricketing Safari*, written with Nathan Astle, Fleming was candid regarding his frustrating lack of big scores in tests. 'Bugger! Dismissed for 99. I am absolutely devastated after playing one of my most controlled test innings,' he wrote, noting that he was given out when caught off the arm. Moreover, the statistical barrier of 100 was becoming a barrier to winning and saving tests (as in the first test at Bloemfontein when he made the 99). 'Anxiety and pressure are huge components of test stress, and learning to manage these at a level that enables you to operate is the key to consistency,' was Fleming's response to imminent defeat at Port Elizabeth in the second test. The third was drawn.

Stephen Fleming after making 56 in the first innings against Pakistan at Lancaster Park. Wasim Akram, 'outstanding for strength and economy', was a thorn in New Zealand's side for 15 years.
Christchurch Star

'My captaincy will be an issue on my return, and quite rightly so,' Fleming wrote in his end of tour summary. 'Teams are judged by their results and those in charge carry the weight of the team's performances. There have been great developments off the paddock but they amount to nothing until they bear fruit. My style has me reviewing and replaying consistently, looking to improve everything we do. A lot of this occurs directly after a match or a day's play.

'Critics believe I am not emotional enough: that when times are tough I don't provide any inspiration through my body language. I respect others' opinions, but don't believe by flapping my arms around and becoming more expressive I am going to become a better captain. Perhaps I should just wait 30 seconds before talking to a bowler so that when the TV comes back on, people will see me communicating.'

The media intensity continued during a three-test series against Pakistan. Coach Trist was withdrawing from the role of spokesperson at press conferences and Fleming was willingly taking on this extra responsibility. Nevertheless, the New Zealand team lost heavily in the second test at Wellington, and was unable to defeat Zimbabwe in the Boxing Day test.

Suddenly a huge 185-run win in the last test of the summer at Hamilton changed things around, and with exciting successes in the one-day series and Craig McMillan's test record of 26 runs in an over, Fleming regained favour with the media.

Chairman of selectors Sir Richard Hadlee affirmed Fleming's aptitude for the position. 'He's got the job for the next ten years if he wants it,' Hadlee said in March 2001. There could be no greater testament to the esteem in which Fleming is held by those who count.

For the 2000/01 season the golf-loving Fleming had moved to Wellington, where his girlfriend Kelly Payne lived, and in April 2001 he took up another challenge when he followed the long line of Kiwis in English county cricket.

He went to score runs, saying, 'The more I go past three figures the more I understand the process.' He had what he termed a 'reasonable season', with a broken finger and a trip to Sri Lanka shortening it, but the aborted tour of Pakistan lengthened his stay at the end. 'I am always looking to get better, whether it be captaincy, batting or life in general,' he wrote. 'Middlesex was too good an opportunity to miss.'

A column written for website CricInfo is revealing at times. Under the heading 'Flem's English Crusade' he noted, 'Without the leadership pressures my concentration is not as intense — I hate nothing more than dropping a catch.

'A lot of it is concentration and it's something I have worked very hard on controlling, especially when I'm captain of the side.'

Although Fleming has stepped in for Middlesex captain Angus Fraser occasionally in England, he was not captain on the August day at Lord's when he missed Warwickshire's Mark Wagh on 92 at slip. Wagh went on to make 315, only the fourth triple century scored at Lord's. Perhaps Fleming is correct in linking the captaincy with increased concentration.

The professionalism that English cricket had traditionally imbued in Kiwi players, from Lowry to Nash, and including Ian Cromb, Glenn Turner, Geoff Howarth and John Wright, was something Fleming had already picked up from early coach Bob Carter. No longer did Kiwis need to go to England to learn their cricket. Nor did they need English coaches. After Trist retired Denis Aberhart, another safe figure as a former provincial coach of Canterbury (between 1992/93 and 1996/97), took over the national job.

'Contrary to media belief I look forward to working with Abbo, and sharing ideas as we continue our work towards the next World Cup,' Fleming wrote when Aberhart, like Fleming a trained teacher, was appointed in July 2001. Aberhart's appointment allowed Fleming the leeway to develop his role and showed that New Zealand Cricket's administrators had confidence in the mature captain.

However, despite Fleming's success overseas, and his overall record as a test captain, he was still watchful of the media at home. He has commented on two areas of modern cricket that arouse him — poor pitches and match fixing. Playing Pakistan at Hamilton in 2000/01, Fleming's men levelled the series — 'A great game in conditions that suited us better than the first two tests that were played,' he said. But the Condon report on match fixing suggested to Fleming that 'when we do play well, and beat more favoured opposition, people see it as suspect'. In September 1999 a representative of an Asian betting syndicate had approached Fleming at the team's hotel prior to the third test against South Africa. Martin Crowe was also implicated and exonerated in the series of scandals that cost test captains Mohammed Azharuddhin and Hansie Cronje their jobs and their reputations.

Regarding pitches, Fleming echoed John Reid's 1965 view, describing English wickets, especially one-day surfaces, as 'diabolical'. However, an unusually outspoken Fleming also wrote, 'What on earth were we doing playing on the wicket that we did in the first test at Auckland [against Pakistan in 2000/01] — a portable pitch that had never been used before? I'm a strong believer in playing to your strengths when at home.'

The *New Zealand Herald* reported that Fleming 'gave little sign that he recognised the enormity of the catastrophe' at the collapse on the fifth day of this match that saw nine wickets crash for 26 runs. Phrases such as 'demeanour of a man under pressure', 'stubborn disregard for reality', were used, although the key was perhaps 'no natural successor'.

The team had matured under Fleming, coming a long way from the Young Guns of the early nineties when Cairns, Nash and Parore first showed their gifts. So how did the laid-back, reserved Fleming harness the talents of these players? At the beginning it was undoubtedly coach Steve Rixon and manager (and former Auckland Grammar School headmaster) John Graham who helped Fleming into the role.

In person Fleming is tough and has the fierceness of a schoolmaster under his exterior politeness. When he's had enough of an interview he takes control and ends the questioning. His decisiveness has harnessed the explosive talents of the players who make things happen in the team, but who underperformed under Germon and Turner.

The drawn series against Australia in November and December 2001 was generally seen as a triumph for New Zealand and Fleming. He broke a run of 46 test innings without a century at Perth, in the course of which he added 199 for the second wicket with new cap Lou Vincent. The 22-year-old Vincent praised Fleming for getting him through the day to become the sixth New Zealander to make a century on test debut. 'He's an inspiring leader; he kept me cool and composed at times in the game when the timing, the head and the feet were all over the place.'

Drawing against the world champions was followed by two easy victories against Bangladesh. In all the year 2001 brought three test wins, four draws and a single loss, to Pakistan.

The increased responsibility that has been placed on Fleming has brought out the best in his seemingly nerveless character. 'I like to think that my preparation is such that I'm feeling good. You don't need to get wound up to make yourself a better performer,' he has said. 'David Trist's man-management style leaves it up to the captain more than anything.'

If anything, Trist's successor Denis Aberhart has taken the role of coach even nearer to that of facilitator than before. His methods of 'working behind the scenes' are, according to Fleming, 'very much what I am into. They promote individual responsibility.'

To the suggestion that the Australian media were high in their praise of his captaincy and on-field leadership, perhaps stemming from the time he took a strong hand in the team organisation during the 2000/01 season, Fleming replies, 'If I seemed more outgoing on the field it was because the players were maturing together. We had all done our homework on the Australians; we all had a good understanding of what we had to do. I do not think there was really a direction change, more a matter of a group of players maturing together.'

Chris Cairns, so often New Zealand's match-winner during Fleming's leadership, wrote after returning from the tour of Australia: 'On this tour I also thought it would be the making of Fleming if he could clock up one of those elusive centuries the media keeps reminding him about. I'm sure it plays on his mind but to get that 100 in Perth against Australia has lifted Flem to another level.... Flem is now the country's leading sports captain and will be for some time. He has mana and will give New Zealand cricket some great direction in the future.'

At Bridgetown in June 2002, Fleming's 130 won him a rare Man of the Match award, and, more importantly, New Zealand's first test victory in the West Indies. With a test away average of almost 40, ten runs an innings more than at home, Fleming has shown he bats best not only in adversity but also when abroad. 'I enjoy the space you get when on tour,' he told the NZPA. 'My record suggests I play better away from home ... you don't hear the criticism ... your mind's a lot clearer and you just go about your work.'

This involved picking the team up after a bomb blast ended the 2001/02 tour to Pakistan, and led New Zealand's greatest skipper to re-evaluate his life. 'You don't realise how much these guys mean to you; the relationships you develop are pretty special.'

The role of New Zealand test captain has indeed changed from when Tom Lowry led his intrepid side onto Lancaster Park on that auspicious date in Kiwi cricket history — 10 January 1930

25. DION NASH 27 February 1999 – 22 March 1999

The belligerent generation

Dion Nash became New Zealand's replacement for Stephen Fleming as captain after Fleming injured his groin while fielding in a one-day international against India at Taupo in January 1999.

New Zealand had just won the three-match test series 1-0, and beat India by five wickets in this, the first one-day international of a drawn five-match series. The 27-year-old Nash, in the absence of more suitable candidates who did not already carry a large all-round workload, won the appointment as captain and kept the job for the rest of the season.

The next crucial injury to beset New Zealand came in the first ODI against the second visitors of the summer, South Africa. Key all-rounder Chris Cairns injured himself setting off for a run and was run out. The staunch Nash, without his best batsman and bowler, saw his team win the series 2-1, but his own form was worrying.

Having gained experience in England with Middlesex in 1995 and 1996, Nash became one of the long line of Kiwis to follow that path to test captaincy. His home ground in England, Lord's, was the scene of his greatest test performance, taking 11/169 and scoring 56 in one of the best all-round performances produced by a New Zealander. However, the intensity of English cricket had wrecked Nash's fitness, and he bowled just ten first-class overs for his county in 1996 before returning home injured.

An admirer of Dennis Lillee and Dean Jones, Nash displayed the same competitive instincts as his heroes from an early age at Dargaville High School. Later, Nash and New Zealand wicket-keeper Adam Parore gained reputations for their sledging on the pitch. After school Nash played for Northern Districts, but moved to Otago after becoming an undergraduate in Dunedin.

Strongly built and youthfully exuberant, Nash had made a name internationally in 1990/91, opening the batting and bowling for Young New

Dion Nash

Zealand. The next step in his career came in 1991/92 with a tour to India with New Zealand Youth. Such was Nash's success that he was fast-tracked into the New Zealand test team to play Zimbabwe in 1992. In India Nash had impressed with a one-day international century, as well as figures of 5/44 in the second 'test' at Bombay. Nash replaced Simon Doull in the second test in Zimbabwe, an easy victory for the Kiwis. This was the first test to be interrupted by a one-day international. The feisty all-rounder, still two weeks short of his twenty-first birthday, took the important wickets of Andy Flower and Kevin Arnott when given the responsibility of opening the bowling with Murphy Su'a.

Nash had shone as one of the first graduates of the Cricket Academy winter programme, and this led to the chance in Zimbabwe. This system of development had superseded the Brabin and Rothmans age-group teams that produced many players, such as Richard Hadlee, from the fifties to the seventies. But it took until 1994 for Nash to get a consistent international run, and he had just six wickets at 62.5 and a top score of 19 before his second full tour, to England in 1994.

Dion Nash in November 1992.
Christchurch Star

At 22 years of age, Nash became an overnight success when he went on a record-breaking all-round rampage. His first innings 6/76 was a record for a New Zealander at Lord's, and followed his test best 56. Leading by 195 runs after the first innings, Ken Rutherford set England 407 to win after declaring on 211/5. Nash removed the top order, including Graham Gooch lbw for a duck, but his 5/93, which made him the first New Zealand bowler to take 11 wickets in a test against England, was not enough to force the draw. Nash's all-round performance was the first ten wickets/50 runs double seen in a test at Lord's.

With his career kick-started, the ultra-competitive Nash went from strength to strength, establishing himself as a key player in New Zealand's improving form under Stephen Fleming's captaincy.

New Zealand Test Cricket Captains

In February 1998 Nash was cautioned after a collision with Australian captain Steve Waugh during a one-day international when Waugh had to retire hurt, although his 'no compromise' attitude appealed to some sections of the crowd.

At 27, Nash became New Zealand's twenty-fifth test captain against a strong South African side on their fifth visit to New Zealand (and just their second since 1963/64).

A feature of the two high-scoring draws was a South African record of 275 not out at Eden Park by Daryl Cullinan, which was replied to by Geoff Allott's first-class record 101-minute duck.

New Zealand took just one wicket (to Daniel Vettori) in the rain-affected draw at Christchurch, but lost the last test by eight wickets at Wellington. Nash put in South Africa, who made 621/5 declared in the first 200 overs. Cullinan, dismissed for 152, had made 427 unbeaten runs in the series. Nash took his first test wicket as captain (Jacques Kallis) after 12 days of trying, but New Zealand were outplayed and could set South Africa just 16 to win. Fleming returned as captain for the fourth one-day international three days later.

Nash also captained the Northern Conference in 1997/98 and later led Auckland.

Angus Fraser, Nash's former Middlesex team-mate, was surprised to find Nash was captaining New Zealand. According to Fraser, Nash told him, 'It was circumstance more than anything else, but it was a challenge I enjoyed and one that was a good experience.'

Nash's desire to star at Lord's backfired when the ruptured disc he sustained at Middlesex plagued him. Fleming welcomed Nash back on another, perhaps final comeback in 2001, writing, 'We have sorely missed his attitude and ability to make things happen.' Nash, Adam Parore, Chris Cairns, Chris Harris and Stephen Fleming were the only players remaining from New Zealand international cricket's difficult years of the early nineties.

The belligerent all-rounder did return once more, but his appearance in Australia in 2001/02 was short-lived before further injury brought him home. Some promising form for Auckland ended with a three-week ban that resulted from a breach of the code of conduct.

In some ways Nash's career echoed that of the mercurial all-rounder of the 1960s and 1970s, Bruce Taylor. Both burst onto the scene as 21-year-olds after stand-out age group performances. Nash had played four first-class games and

Taylor just three before making a test debut. Replacing injured players, the bowling all-rounders had regular arresting days with either bat or ball, often winning matches single-handedly. Nash and Taylor then captained their provinces (Auckland and Wellington respectively) before back injuries forced them out of the game. Perhaps because of his Middlesex exertions Nash's breakdown came earlier than Taylor's, who played his last test at 31. Both later became renowned for their language on the pitch, but they were also renowned as cricketers who could make things happen.

With a record that shows him to be one of New Zealand's greatest all-rounders, Nash proved a magnificent competitor for his country throughout the 1990s.

Nash decided to retire in May 2002 after several unsuccessful comebacks from injury. 'I'm really happy with it. I've known for a couple of months that it might be the case, but I wanted to cover all my bases and make sure I made the decision when I was feeling fitter,' he told CricInfo. For the easily stimulated Nash, the motivation to continue had gone. 'Getting over the injuries has taken so much energy, both physical and mental,' he said.

Nash recalls the 1999 England tour as his finest: 'We came out of that tour as grown men. I have been very lucky. Cricket has been a fantastic vehicle for me to grow as a human being and to display the skills I have.'

ABBREVIATIONS

Y	=	years
D	=	days
MAT	=	matches
I	=	innings
NO	=	not out
R	=	runs
HS	=	highest score
AVE	=	average
CT	=	catches
ST	=	stumpings
O	=	overs
M	=	maidens
W	=	wickets
BBI	=	best bowling innings
SR	=	strike rate
ECON	=	economy rate
5W	=	5-wicket innings
10W	=	10-wicket innings
BAT AV.	=	batting average
BOWL AV.	=	bowling average
DNB	=	did not bat
C	=	caught
*	=	not out

STATISTICS

1. Thomas Coleman Lowry

Right-hand bat, right-arm slow medium bowler, wicket-keeper

BORN:	17 February 1898, Fernhill, Napier
DIED:	20 July 1976, Okawa, Hastings (aged 78)
TEAMS:	Auckland, Cambridge University, Somerset, Wellington, New Zealand
TEST DEBUT:	New Zealand v England at Christchurch, 1st test, 1929/30
LAST TEST:	New Zealand v England at Manchester, 3rd test, 1931

Test career, 1929/30–1931 (31 y 327 d to 33 y 182 d)

BATTING AND FIELDING

MAT	I	NO	R	HS	AVE	100	50	CT	ST
7	8	0	223	80	27.87	0	2	8	0

BOWLING

O	M	R	W	AVE	BBI	5W	10W	SR	ECON
2	1	5	0	-	-	0	0	-	2.50

First-class career, 1919–1932/33

BATTING AND FIELDING

MAT	I	NO	R	HS	AVE	100	50	CT	ST
198	322	20	9421	181	31.19	18	0	188	49

BOWLING

R	W	AVE	BBI	5W	10W
1323	49	27.00	4-14	0	0

Tests as captain

MAT	R	HS	BAT AV.	100	50	W	BBI	BOWL AV.	5W	CT	ST
7	223	80	27.87	0	2	0	-	-	0	8	0

1st test v Eng in NZ, 1929/30 at Christchurch, lost by 8 wickets	0, 40 c2
2nd test v Eng in NZ, 1929/30 at Wellington, drawn	6, DNB c4
3rd test v Eng in NZ, 1929/30 at Auckland, drawn	DNB
4th test v Eng in NZ, 1929/30 at Auckland, drawn	80
1st test v Eng in Eng, 1931 at Lord's, drawn	1, 34 c2
2nd test v Eng in Eng, 1931 at the Oval, lost by innings and 26 runs	62, 0
3rd test v Eng in Eng, 1931 at Manchester, drawn	

2. Milford Laurenson Page
Right-hand bat, right-arm medium bowler

BORN:	8 May 1902, Lyttelton, New Zealand
DIED:	13 February 1987, Christchurch (aged 84)
TEAMS:	Canterbury, New Zealand
TEST DEBUT:	New Zealand v England at Christchurch, 1st test, 1929/30
LAST TEST:	New Zealand v England at the Oval, 3rd test, 1937

Test career, 1929/30–1937 (27 y 247 d to 35 y 101 d)

BATTING AND FIELDING

MAT	I	NO	R	HS	AVE	100	50	CT	ST
14	20	0	492	104	24.60	1	2	6	0

BOWLING

O	M	R	W	AVE	BBI	5W	10W	SR	ECON
63.1	11	231	5	46.20	2-21	0	0	75.8	3.65

First-class career, 1920/21–1942/43

BATTING AND FIELDING

MAT	I	NO	R	HS	AVE	100	50	CT	ST
132	213	17	5857	206	29.88	9	32	117	0

BOWLING

R	W	AVE	BBI	5W	10W
2365	73	32.39	4-10	0	0

Tests as captain

MAT	R	HS	BAT AV.	100	50	W	BBI	BOWL AV.	5W	CT	ST
7	204	53	18.54	0	1	3	2/21	50.00	0	4	0

1st test v SA in NZ, 1931/32 at Christchurch, lost by an innings and 112 runs	22, 0 0/27 c2
2nd test v SA in NZ, 1931/32 at Wellington, lost by 8 wickets	7, 23 1/30, 0/14 c1
1st test v Eng in NZ, 1932/33 at Christchurch, drawn	22, DNB 2/21
2nd test v Eng in NZ, 1932/33 at Auckland, drawn	20, DNB 0/30 c1
1st test v Eng in Eng, 1937 at Lord's, drawn	9, 13 0/12
2nd test v Eng in Eng, 1937 at Manchester, lost by 130 runs	33, 2 0/16
3rd test v Eng in Eng, 1937 at the Oval, drawn	53, DNB (absent)

3. Walter Arnold Hadlee
Right-hand bat, right-arm medium bowler

BORN:	4 June 1915, Lincoln, Canterbury
TEAMS:	Canterbury, Otago, New Zealand
TEST DEBUT:	New Zealand v England at Lord's, 1st test, 1937
LAST TEST:	New Zealand v England at Wellington, 2nd test, 1950/51

Test career, 1937–1950/51 (22 y 22 d to 35 y 297 d)

BATTING AND FIELDING

MAT	I	NO	R	HS	AVE	100	50	CT	ST
11	19	1	543	116	30.16	1	2	6	0

BOWLING

O	M	R	W	AVE	BBI	5W	10W	SR	ECON
-	-	-	-	-	-	-	-	-	-

First-class career, 1933/34–1951/52

BATTING AND FIELDING

MAT	I	NO	R	HS	AVE	100	50	CT	ST
117	203	17	7523	198	40.44	18	31	70	0

BOWLING

R	W	AVE	BBI	5W	10W
293	6	48.83	3-14	0	0

Tests as captain

MAT	R	HS	BAT AV.	100	50	W	BBI	BOWL AV.	5W	CT	ST
8	392	116	32.66	1	1	-	-	-	-	5	0

Only test v Aus in NZ, 1945/46 at Wellington, lost by an innings and 103 runs	6, 3 c2
Only test v Eng in NZ, 1946/47 at Christchurch, drawn	116, (no second innings)
1st test v Eng in Eng, 1949 at Leeds, drawn	34, 13*
2nd test v Eng in Eng, 1949 at Lord's, drawn	43, c1
3rd test v Eng in Eng, 1949 at Manchester, drawn	34, 22
4th test v Eng in Eng, 1949 at the Oval, drawn	25, 22 c1
1st test v Eng in NZ, 1950/51 at Christchurch, drawn	50, DNB
2nd test v Eng in NZ, 1950/51 at Wellington, lost by 6 wickets	15, 9 c1

4. Bert Sutcliffe
Left-hand bat, slow left-arm orthodox bowler

BORN:	17 November 1923, Ponsonby, Auckland
DIED:	20 April 2001, Auckland (aged 77)
TEAMS:	Auckland, Otago, Northern Districts, New Zealand
TEST DEBUT:	New Zealand v England at Christchurch, only test, 1946/47
LAST TEST:	New Zealand v England at Birmingham, 1st test, 1965

Test career, 1946/47–1965 (23 y 124 d to 41 y 196 d)

BATTING AND FIELDING

MAT	I	NO	R	HS	AVE	100	50	CT	ST
42	76	8	2727	230*	40.10	5	15	20	0

BOWLING

BALLS	M	R	W	AVE	BBI	5W	10W	SR	ECON
538	10	344	4	86.00	2-38	0	0	134.5	3.83

First-class career, 1941/42–1965/66

BATTING AND FIELDING

MAT	I	NO	R	HS	AVE	100	50	CT	ST
233	407	39	17447	385	47.41	44	83	160	1

BOWLING

R	W	AVE	BBI	5W	10W
3273	86	38.05	5-19	2	0

Tests as captain

MAT	R	HS	BAT AV.	100	50	W	BBI	BOWL AV.	5W	CT	ST
4	216	52	30.85	0	1	-	-	-	-	6	0

1st test v WI in NZ, 1951/52 at Christchurch, lost by 5 wickets	45, 36 c1
2nd test v WI in NZ, 1951/52 at Auckland, drawn	20, 2* c1
4th test v SA in SA, 1953/54 at Johannesburg, lost by 9 wickets	0, 23 c2
5th test v SA in SA, 1953/54 at Port Elizabeth, lost by 5 wickets	38, 52 c2

5. Walter Mervyn Wallace
Right-hand bat, right-arm off break bowler

BORN: 19 December 1916, Grey Lynn, Auckland
TEAMS: Auckland, New Zealand
TEST DEBUT: New Zealand v England at Lord's, 1st test, 1937
LAST TEST: New Zealand v South Africa at Auckland, 2nd test, 1952/53

Test career, 1937–1952/53 (20 y 189 d to 36 y 88 d)

BATTING AND FIELDING

MAT	I	NO	R	HS	AVE	100	50	CT	ST
13	21	0	439	66	20.90	0	5	5	0

BOWLING

O	M	R	W	AVE	BBI	5W	10W	SR	ECON
1	0	5	0	-	-	0	0	-	5.00

First-class career, 1933/34–1960/61

BATTING AND FIELDING

MAT	I	NO	R	HS	AVE	100	50	CT	ST
121	192	17	7757	211	44.32	17	43	68	0

BOWLING

R	W	AVE	BBI	5W	10W
18	0	-	-	0	0

Tests as captain

MAT	R	HS	BAT AV.	100	50	W	BBI	BOWL AV.	5W	CT	ST
2	29	23	9.66	0	0	-	-	-	-	0	0

1st test v SA in NZ, 1952/53 at Wellington, lost by an innings and 180 runs   4, 2
2nd test v SA in NZ, 1952/53 at Auckland, drawn   23, DNB

6. Geoffrey Osbourne Rabone
Right-hand bat, leg break, right-arm off break bowler

BORN:	6 November 1921, Gore, Otago
TEAMS:	Wellington, Auckland, New Zealand
TEST DEBUT:	New Zealand v England at Leeds, 1st test, 1949
LAST TEST:	New Zealand v England at Auckland, 2nd test, 1954/55

Test career, 1949–1954/55 (27 y 217 d to 33 y 142 d)

BATTING AND FIELDING

MAT	I	NO	R	HS	AVE	100	50	CT	ST
12	20	2	562	107	31.22	1	2	5	0

BOWLING

BALLS	M	R	W	AVE	BBI	5W	10W	SR	ECON
1385	48	635	16	39.68	6-68	1	0	86.5	2.75

First-class career, 1945/46–1960/61

BATTING AND FIELDING

MAT	I	NO	R	HS	AVE	100	50	CT	ST
82	135	14	3425	125	28.30	3	19	76	0

BOWLING

R	W	AVE	BBI	5W	10W
4835	173	27.94	8-66	0	0

Tests as captain

MAT	R	HS	BAT AV.	100	50	W	BBI	BOWL AV.	5W	CT	ST
5	315	107	35.00	1	2	8	6/68	16.87	1	1	0

1st test v SA in SA, 1953/54 at Durban, lost by an innings and 58 runs	107, 68 1/31
2nd test v SA in SA, 1953/54 at Johannesburg, lost by 132 runs	1, 22 0/16
3rd test v SA in SA,1953/54 at Cape Town, drawn	56, 6/68, 1/16
1st test v Eng in NZ, 1954/55 at Dunedin, lost by 8 wickets	18, 7
2nd test v Eng in NZ, 1954/55 at Auckland, lost by an innings and 20 runs	29, 7 0/4 c1

7. Henry Butler Cave
Right-hand bat, right-arm medium bowler

BORN:	10 October 1922, Wanganui
DIED:	15 September 1989, Wanganui (aged 66)
TEAMS:	Wellington, Central Districts, New Zealand
TEST DEBUT:	New Zealand v England at Leeds, 1st test, 1949
LAST TEST:	New Zealand v England at Leeds, 3rd test, 1958

Test career, 1949–58 (26 y 244 d to 35 y 271 d)

BATTING AND FIELDING

MAT	I	NO	R	HS	AVE	100	50	CT	ST
19	31	5	229	22*	8.80	0	0	8	0

BOWLING

O	M	R	W	AVE	BBI	5W	10W	SR	ECON
679	242	1467	34	43.14	4-21	0	0	119.8	2.16

First-class career, 1945/46–1958/59

BATTING AND FIELDING

MAT	I	NO	R	HS	AVE	100	50	CT	ST
117	175	39	2187	118	16.08	2	3	70	0

BOWLING

R	W	AVE	BBI	5W	10W
8664	362	23.93	7-31	13	1

Tests as captain

MAT	R	HS	BAT AV.	100	50	W	BBI	BOWL AV.	5W	CT	ST
9	139	22*	11.58	0	0	15	3/45	44.66	0	4	0

1st test v Pak in Pak, 1955/56 at Karachi, lost by an innings and 1 run   0, 21 3/56 c1
2nd test v Pak in Pak, 1955/56 at Lahore, lost by 4 wickets   14, 17 0/84, 0/26 c2
3rd test v Pak in Pak, 1955/56 at Dacca, drawn   0, DNB 3/45
1st test v Ind in Ind, 1955/56 at Hyderabad, drawn   14, DNB 0/59
2nd test v Ind in Ind, 1955/56 at Bombay, lost by an innings and 27 runs   12, 21 3/77
3rd test v Ind in Ind, 1955/56 at Delhi, drawn   DNB 1/68
4th test v Ind in Ind, 1955/56 at Calcutta, drawn   5, 4* 1/29, 2/85
5th test v Ind in Ind, 1955/56 at Madras, lost by an innings and 109 runs   9, 22* 0/94 c1
1st test v WI in NZ, 1955/56 at Dunedin, lost by an innings and 71 runs   0, 0 2/47

8. John Richard Reid
Right-hand bat, right-arm off break, right-arm fast medium bowler, wicket-keeper

BORN:	3 June 1928, Auckland
TEAMS:	Wellington, Otago, New Zealand
TEST DEBUT:	New Zealand v England at Manchester, 3rd test, 1949
LAST TEST:	New Zealand v England at Leeds, 3rd test, 1965

Test career, 1949–65 (21 y 50 d to 37 y 40 d)

BATTING AND FIELDING

MAT	I	NO	R	HS	AVE	100	50	CT	ST
58	108	5	3428	142	33.28	6	22	43	1

BOWLING

BALLS	M	R	W	AVE	BBI	5W	10W	SR	ECON
7725	444	2835	85	33.35	6-60	1	0	90.8	2.20

First-class career, 1947/48–1964/65

BATTING AND FIELDING

MAT	I	NO	R	HS	AVE	100	50	CT	ST
246	418	28	16,128	296	41.35	39	-	240	7

BOWLING

R	W	AVE	BBI	5W	10W
10,535	466	22.60	7-20	15	1

Tests as captain

MAT	R	HS	BAT AV.	100	50	W	BBI	BOWL AV.	5W	CT	ST
34	2129	142	34.33	3	14	54	6-60	30.12	1	22	1

2nd test v WI in NZ, 1955/56 at Christchurch, lost by an innings and 64 runs	28, 40 3/68 c1
3rd test v WI in NZ, 1955/56 at Wellington, lost by 9 wickets	1, 5 3/85
4th test v WI in NZ, 1955/56 at Auckland, won by 190 runs	84, 12 1/48, 0/14
1st test v Eng in Eng, 1958 at Birmingham, lost by 205 runs	7, 13 0/16, 0/18 c2
2nd test v Eng in Eng, 1958 at Lord's, lost by an innings and 148 runs	6, 5 1/41
3rd test v Eng in Eng, 1958 at Leeds, lost by an innings and 71 runs	3, 13 0/54 c1
4th test v Eng in Eng, 1958 at Manchester, lost by an innings and 13 runs	14, 8 3/47 st1
5th test v Eng in Eng, 1958 at the Oval, drawn	27, 51* 2/11 c1
1st test v Eng in NZ, 1958/59 at Christchurch, lost by an innings and 99 runs	40, 1 3/34
2nd test v Eng in NZ, 1958/59 at Auckland, drawn	3, 0/19
1st test v SA in SA, 1961/62 at Durban, lost by 30 runs	13, 16 0/38
2nd test v SA in SA, 1961/62 at Johannesburg, drawn	39, 75* 0/33 c1
3rd test v SA in SA, 1961/62 at Cape Town, won by 72 runs	92, 14 2/21 c2

4th test v SA in SA, 1961/62 at Johannesburg, lost by an innings and 51 runs	60, 142 3/55
5th test v SA in SA, 1961/62 at Port Elizabeth, won by 40 runs	26, 69 2/26, 4/44
1st test v Eng in NZ, 1962/63 at Auckland, lost by an innings and 215 runs	59, 21* 0/67 c1
2nd test v Eng in NZ, 1962/63 at Wellington, lost by an innings and 47 runs	0, 9 1/73
3rd test v Eng in NZ, 1962/63 at Christchurch, lost by 7 wickets	74, 100 1/31 c2
1st test v SA in NZ, 1963/64 at Wellington, drawn	16, 12 2/47, 1/55
2nd test v SA in NZ, 1963/64 at Dunedin, drawn	2, 2 6/60
3rd test v SA in NZ, 1963/64 at Auckland, drawn	19, 37 3/77, 0/39
1st test v Pak in NZ, 1964/65 at Wellington, drawn	97, 14 0/24, 0/16 c1
2nd test v Pak in NZ, 1964/65 at Auckland, drawn	52, 11 0/26, 2/52
3rd test v Pak in NZ, 1964/65 at Christchurch, drawn	27, 28 1/24 c1
1st test v Ind in Ind, 1964/65 at Madras, drawn	42, DNB 1/70 c1
2nd test v Ind in Ind, 1964/65 at Calcutta, drawn	82, 11 0/5
3rd test v Ind in Ind, 1964/65 at Bombay, drawn	22, 10 0/8 c1
4th test v Ind in Ind, 1964/65 at Delhi, lost by 7 wickets	9, 22 1/89, 1/3
1st test v Pak in Pak, 1964/65 at Rawalpindi, lost by an innings and 64 runs	4, 0 3/80
2nd test v Pak in Pak, 1964/65 at Lahore, drawn	88, 0/21 c2
3rd test v Pak in Pak, 1964/65 at Karachi, lost by 8 wickets	128, 76 1/28, 1/6
1st test v Eng in Eng, 1965 at Birmingham, lost by 9 wickets	2, 44 1/43, 0/7
2nd test v Eng in Eng, 1965 at Lord's, lost by 7 wickets	21, 22 0/4
3rd test v Eng in Eng, 1965 at Leeds, lost by an innings and 187 runs	54, 5

9. Murray Ernest Chapple
Right-hand bat, left-arm medium bowler

BORN:	25 July 1930, Christchurch
DIED:	31 July 1985, Hamilton (aged 55)
TEAMS:	Canterbury, Central Districts, New Zealand
TEST DEBUT:	New Zealand v South Africa at Auckland, 2nd test, 1952/53
LAST TEST:	New Zealand v England at Christchurch, 1st test, 1965/66

Test career, 1952/53–1965/66 (22 y 231 d to 35 y 219 d)

BATTING AND FIELDING

MAT	I	NO	R	HS	AVE	100	50	CT	ST
14	27	1	497	76	19.11	0	3	10	0

BOWLING

BALLS	M	R	W	AVE	BBI	5W	10W	SR	ECON
248	17	84	1	84.00	1-24	0	0	248.0	2.03

First-class career, 1949/50–1971/72

BATTING AND FIELDING

MAT	I	NO	R	HS	AVE	100	50	CT	ST
119	201	16	5344	165	28.88	4	31	67	0

BOWLING

R	W	AVE	BBI	5W	10W
3559	142	25.06	5-24	4	0

Tests as captain

MAT	R	HS	BAT AV.	100	50	W	BBI	BOWL AV.	5W	CT	ST
1	15	15	7.50	0	0	1	1/24	24.00	0	1	0

1st test v Eng in NZ, 1965/66 at Christchurch, drawn	15, 0 1/24

10. Barry Whitley Sinclair
Right-hand bat, right-arm bowler

BORN:	23 October 1936, Wellington
TEAMS:	Wellington, New Zealand
TEST DEBUT:	New Zealand v England at Auckland, 1st test, 1962/63
LAST TEST:	New Zealand v India at Auckland, 4th test, 1967/68

Test career, 1962/63–1967/68 (26 y 123 d to 31 y 141 d)

BATTING AND FIELDING

MAT	I	NO	R	HS	AVE	100	50	CT	ST
21	40	1	1148	138	29.43	3	3	8	0

BOWLING

O	M	R	W	AVE	BBI	5W	10W	SR	ECON
10	3	32	2	16.00	2-32	0	0	30.0	3.20

First-class career, 1955/56–1970/71

BATTING AND FIELDING

MAT	I	NO	R	HS	AVE	100	50	CT	ST
118	204	18	6114	148	32.87	6	38	45	0

BOWLING

R	W	AVE	BBI	5W	10W
86	2	43.00	2-32	0	0

List A limited overs, 1969/70–1971/72

MAT	I	NO	R	HS	AVE	100	50	CT	ST
5	5	1	118	48	29.50	0	0	0	0

Tests as captain

MAT	R	HS	BAT AV.	100	50	W	BBI	BOWL AV.	5W	CT	ST
3	203	114	33.83	1	0	-	-	-	-	2	0

2nd test v Eng in NZ, 1965/66 at Dunedin, drawn	33, 39 c1
3rd test v Eng in NZ, 1965/66 at Auckland, drawn	114, 9
1st test v Ind in NZ, 1967/68 at Dunedin, lost by 5 wickets	0, 8

11. Graham Thorne Dowling
Right-hand bat, right-arm medium bowler

BORN:	4 March 1937, Christchurch
TEAMS:	Canterbury, New Zealand
TEST DEBUT:	New Zealand v South Africa at Johannesburg, 2nd test, 1961/62
LAST TEST:	New Zealand v West Indies at Port of Spain, 2nd test, 1971/72

Test career, 1961/62–1971/72 (24 y 297 d to 35 y 10 d)

BATTING AND FIELDING

MAT	I	NO	R	HS	AVE	100	50	CT	ST
39	77	3	2306	239	31.16	3	11	23	0

BOWLING

O	M	R	W	AVE	BBI	5W	10W	SR	ECON
6	2	19	1	19.00	1-19	0	0	36.0	3.16

First-class career, 1958/59–1971/72

BATTING AND FIELDING

MAT	I	NO	R	HS	AVE	100	50	CT	ST
158	282	13	9399	239	34.94	16	-	111	0

BOWLING

R	W	AVE	BBI	5W	10W
378	9	42.00	3-100	0	0

List A limited overs, 1969/70–1971/72

BATTING AND FIELDING

MAT	I	NO	R	HS	AVE	100	50	CT	ST
5	5	0	163	87	32.60	0	1	2	0

BOWLING

BALLS	R	W	AVE	BBI	4W	5W	SR	ECON
32	16	0	-	-	0	0	-	3.00

Tests as captain

MAT	R	HS	BAT AV.	100	50	W	BBI	BOWL AV.	5W	CT	ST
19	1158	239	32.16	1	5	-	-	-	-	12	0

2nd test v Ind in NZ, 1967/68 at Christchurch, won by 6 wickets	239, 5
3rd test v Ind in NZ, 1967/68 at Wellington, lost by 8 wickets	15, 14 c1
4th test v Ind in NZ, 1967/68 at Auckland, lost by 272 runs	8, 37 c1
1st test v WI in NZ, 1968/69 at Auckland, lost by 5 wickets	18, 71 c1
2nd test v WI in NZ, 1968/69 at Wellington, won by six wickets	21, 23
3rd test v WI in NZ, 1968/69 at Christchurch, drawn	23, 76
1st test v Eng in Eng, 1969 at Lord's, lost by 230 runs	41, 4
2nd test v Eng in Eng, 1969 at Nottingham, drawn	18, 22
3rd test v Eng in Eng, 1969 at the Oval, lost by 8 wickets	14, 30
1st test v Ind in Ind, 1969/70 at Bombay, lost by 60 runs	32, 36*

2nd test v Ind in Ind, 1969/70 at Nagpur, won by 167 runs	69, 18 c1
3rd test v Ind in Ind, 1969/70 at Hyderabad, drawn	42, 60 c2
1st test v Pak in Pak, 1969/70 at Karachi, drawn	40, 3 c2
2nd test v Pak in Pak, 1969/70 at Lahore, won by 5 wickets	10, 9 c1
3rd test v Pak in Pak, 1969/70 at Dacca, drawn	15, 2 c1
1st test v Eng in NZ, 1970/71 at Christchurch, lost by 8 wickets	13, 1
2nd test v Eng in NZ, 1970/71 at Auckland, drawn	53, 31* c1
1st test v WI in WI, 1971/72 at Kingston, drawn	4, 23 c1
2nd test v WI in WI, 1971/72 at Port of Spain, drawn	8, 10

12. Bevan Ernest Congdon
Right-hand bat, right-arm medium bowler

BORN:	11 February 1938, Motueka, Nelson
TEAMS:	Central Districts, Wellington, Otago, Canterbury, New Zealand
TEST DEBUT:	New Zealand v Pakistan at Wellington, 1st test, 1964/65
LAST TEST:	New Zealand v England at Lord's, 3rd test, 1978
ODI DEBUT:	New Zealand v Pakistan at Christchurch one-off ODI, 1972/73
LAST ODI:	New Zealand v England at Manchester, Prudential Trophy, 1978

Test career, 1964/65–1978 (26 y 346 d to 40 y 198 d)
BATTING AND FIELDING

MAT	I	NO	R	HS	AVE	100	50	CT	ST
61	114	7	3448	176	32.22	7	19	44	0

BOWLING

BALLS	M	R	W	AVE	BBI	5W	10W	SR	ECON
5620	197	2154	59	36.50	5-65	1	0	95.2	2.29

One-day internationals, 1972/73–1978
BATTING AND FIELDING

MAT	I	NO	R	HS	AVE	SR	100	50	CT	ST
11	9	3	338	101	56.33	71.61	1	2	0	0

BOWLING

BALLS	M	R	W	AVE	BBI	4W	5W	SR	ECON
437	8	287	7	41.00	2-17	0	0	62.4	3.94

First-class career, 1960/61–1977/78
BATTING AND FIELDING

MAT	I	NO	R	HS	AVE	100	50	CT	ST
241	416	40	13,101	202*	34.84	23	68	201	0

BOWLING

R	W	AVE	BBI	5W	10W
6125	204	30.02	6-42	4	0

List A limited overs, 1969/70–1978
BATTING AND FIELDING

MAT	I	NO	R	HS	AVE	100	50	CT	ST
40	37	6	1269	101	40.93	1	10	12	0

BOWLING

BALLS	R	W	AVE	BBI	4W	5W	SR	ECON
1895	1087	41	26.51	4-33	1	0	46.2	3.44

Tests as captain

MAT	R	HS	BAT AV.	100	50	W	BBI	BOWL AV.	5W	CT	ST
17	1067	176	41.03	4	3	33	4/46	35.75	0	11	0

3rd test v WI in WI, 1971/72 at Bridgetown, drawn	126, 2/26, 2/66
4th test v WI in WI, 1971/72 at Georgetown, drawn	61*, 2/86
5th test v WI in WI, 1971/72 at Port of Spain, drawn	11, 58 1/73, 0/39 c1
1st test v Pak in NZ, 1972/73 at Wellington, drawn	19, 0 0/16, 0/40 c3
2nd test v Pak in NZ, 1972/73 at Dunedin, lost by an innings and 166 runs	35, 7 1/72
3rd test v Pak in NZ, 1972/73 at Auckland, drawn	24, 6* 2/48, 2/44
1st test v Eng in Eng, 1973 at Nottingham, lost by 38 runs	9, 176 1/12, 0/28
2nd test v Eng in Eng, 1973 at Lord's, drawn	175, 0/7, 0/22 c2
3rd test v Eng in Eng, 1973 at Leeds, lost by an innings and 1 run	0, 2 2/54
1st test v Aus in Aus, 1973/74 at Melbourne, lost by an innings and 25 runs	31, 14 2/31
2nd test v Aus in Aus, 1973/74 at Sydney, drawn	4, 17 1/29
3rd test v Aus in Aus, 1973/74 at Adelaide, lost by an innings and 57 runs	13, 71* 1/60 c1
1st test v Aus in NZ, 1973/74 at Wellington, drawn	132, 1/54, 3/60
2nd test v Aus in NZ, 1973/74 at Christchurch, won by 5 wickets	8, 2 3/33, 0/26 c2
3rd test v Aus in NZ, 1973/74 at Auckland, lost by 297 runs	4, 4 4/46, 1/66 c1
1st test v Eng in NZ, 1974/75 at Auckland, lost by an innings and 83 runs	2, 18 2/115 c1
2nd test v Eng in NZ, 1974/75 at Christchurch, drawn	38 0/27

13. Glenn Maitland Turner
Right-hand bat, right-arm off break bowler

BORN:	26 May 1947, Dunedin
TEAMS:	Otago, Worcestershire, Northern Districts, New Zealand
TEST DEBUT:	New Zealand v West Indies at Auckland, 1st test, 1968/69
LAST TEST:	New Zealand v Sri Lanka at Wellington, 2nd test, 1982/83
ODI DEBUT:	New Zealand v Pakistan at Christchurch, one-off ODI, 1972/73
LAST ODI:	New Zealand v Pakistan at Nottingham, World Cup, 1983

Test career, 1968/69–1982/83 (22 y 277 d to 35 y 293 d)

BATTING AND FIELDING

MAT	I	NO	R	HS	AVE	100	50	CT	ST
41	73	6	2991	259	44.64	7	14	42	0

BOWLING

O	M	R	W	AVE	BBI	5W	10W	SR	ECON
2	1	5	0	-	-	0	0	-	2.50

One-day internationals, 1972/73–1983

BATTING AND FIELDING

MAT	I	NO	R	HS	AVE	SR	100	50	CT	ST
41	40	6	1598	171*	47.00	67.76	3	9	13	0

BOWLING

O	M	R	W	AVE	BBI	4W	5W	SR	ECON
1	1	0	0	-	-	0	0	-	0.00

First-class career, 1964/65–1982/83

BATTING AND FIELDING

MAT	I	NO	R	HS	AVE	100	50	CT	ST
455	792	101	34,346	311*	49.70	103	-	410	0

BOWLING

R	W	AVE	BBI	5W	10W
189	5	37.80	3-18	0	0

List A limited overs, 1969–83

BATTING AND FIELDING

MAT	I	NO	R	HS	AVE	100	50	CT	ST
313	308	22	10,784	171*	37.70	14	66	125	0

BOWLING

BALLS	R	W	AVE	BBI	4W	5W	SR	ECON
196	152	9	16.88	2-4	0	0	21.7	4.65

Tests as captain

MAT	R	HS	BAT AV.	100	50	W	BBI	BOWL AV.	5W	CT	ST
10	616	117	34.22	2	2	-	-	-	-	13	0

1st test v Ind in NZ, 1975/76 at Auckland, lost by 8 wickets   23, 13 c3
2nd test v Ind in NZ, 1975/76 at Christchurch, drawn   117, c1
3rd test v Ind in NZ, 1975/76 at Wellington, won by an innings and 33 runs   64, c2
1st test v Pak in Pak, 1976/77 at Lahore, lost by 6 wickets   8, 1 c1
2nd test v Pak in Pak, 1976/77 at Hyderabad, lost by 10 wickets   49, 2 c2
1st test v Ind in Ind, 1976/77 at Bombay, lost by 162 runs   65, 6 c1
2nd test v Ind in Ind, 1976/77 at Kanpur, drawn   113, 35 c1
3rd test v Ind in Ind, 1976/77 at Madras, lost by 216 runs   37, 5
1st test v Aus in NZ, 1976/77 at Christchurch, drawn   15, 36 c1
2nd test v Aus in NZ, 1976/77 at Auckland, lost by 10 wickets   4, 23 c1

14. John Morton Parker
Right-hand bat, leg break googly bowler, wicket-keeper

BORN:	21 February 1951, Dannevirke
TEAMS:	Worcestershire, Northern Districts, New Zealand
TEST DEBUT:	New Zealand v Pakistan at Wellington, 1st test, 1972/73
LAST TEST:	New Zealand v Australia at Melbourne, 3rd test, 1980/81
ODI DEBUT:	New Zealand v Australia at Christchurch, 2nd ODI, 1973/74
LAST ODI:	New Zealand v Australia at Sydney, World Series Cup, 1980/81

Test career, 1972/73–1980/81 (21 y 347 d to 29 y 313 d)

BATTING AND FIELDING

MAT	I	NO	R	HS	AVE	100	50	CT	ST
36	63	2	1498	121	24.55	3	5	30	0

BOWLING

BALLS	M	R	W	AVE	BBI	5W	10W	SR	ECON
40	2	24	1	24.00	1-24	0	0	40.0	3.60

One-day internationals, 1973/74–1980/81

BATTING AND FIELDING

MAT	I	NO	R	HS	AVE	SR	100	50	CT	ST
24	20	0	248	66	12.40	60.48	0	1	11	1

BOWLING

BALLS	M	R	W	AVE	BBI	4W	5W	SR	ECON
16	0	10	1	10.00	1-10	0	0	16.0	3.75

First-class career, 1971–1983/84

BATTING AND FIELDING

MAT	I	NO	R	HS	AVE	100	50	CT	ST
207	362	39	11,254	195	34.84	21	53	177	5

BOWLING

R	W	AVE	BBI	5W	10W
681	14	48.64	3-26	0	0

List A limited overs, 1972–1983/84

BATTING AND FIELDING

MAT	I	NO	R	HS	AVE	100	50	CT	ST
113	106	8	2121	107	21.64	1	9	45	2

BOWLING

BALLS	R	W	AVE	BBI	4W	5W	SR	ECON
20	12	1	12.00	1-10	0	0	20.0	3.60

Statistics

Tests as captain

MAT	R	HS	BAT AV.	100	50	W	BBI	BOWL AV.	5W	CT	ST
1	40	24	20.00	0	0	-	-	-	-	0	0

3rd test v Pak in Pak, 1976/77 at Karachi, drawn   24, 16

15. Mark Gordon Burgess
Right-hand bat, right-arm off break bowler

BORN:	17 July 1944, Auckland
TEAMS:	Auckland, New Zealand
TEST DEBUT:	New Zealand v India at Dunedin, 1st test, 1967/68
LAST TEST:	New Zealand v Australia at Melbourne, 3rd test, 1980/81
ODI DEBUT:	New Zealand v Pakistan at Christchurch, one-off ODI, 1972/73
LAST ODI:	New Zealand v Australia at Sydney, World Series Cup, 1980/81

Test career, 1967/68–1980/81 (23 y 213 d to 36 y 166 d)

BATTING AND FIELDING

MAT	I	NO	R	HS	AVE	100	50	CT	ST
50	92	6	2684	119*	31.20	5	14	34	0

BOWLING

BALLS	M	R	W	AVE	BBI	5W	10W	SR	ECON
498	27	212	6	35.33	3-23	0	0	83.0	2.55

One-day internationals, 1972/73–1980/81

BATTING AND FIELDING

MAT	I	NO	R	HS	AVE	SR	100	50	CT	ST
26	20	0	336	47	16.80	65.24	0	0	8	0

BOWLING

BALLS	M	R	W	AVE	BBI	4W	5W	SR	ECON
74	0	69	1	69.00	1-10	0	0	74.0	5.59

First-class career, 1963/64–1979/80

BATTING AND FIELDING

MAT	I	NO	R	HS	AVE	100	50	CT	ST
192	322	35	10,281	146	35.82	20	-	152	0

BOWLING

R	W	AVE	BBI	5W	10W
1148	30	38.26	3-23	0	0

List A limited overs, 1969/70–1980/81

BATTING AND FIELDING

MAT	I	NO	R	HS	AVE	100	50	CT	ST
42	36	2	603	47	17.73	0	0	12	0

BOWLING

BALLS	R	W	AVE	BBI	4W	5W	SR	ECON
217	153	4	38.25	2-28	0	0	54.2	4.23

Tests as captain

MAT	R	HS	BAT AV.	100	50	W	BBI	BOWL AV.	5W	CT	ST
10	449	71	24.94	0	3	-	-	-	-	8	-

1st test v Eng in NZ, 1977/78 at Wellington, won by 72 runs	9, 6 c2
2nd test v Eng in NZ, 1977/78 at Christchurch, lost by 174 runs	29, 6* c2
3rd test v Eng in NZ, 1977/78 at Auckland, drawn	50, 17 c2
1st test v Eng in Eng, 1978 at the Oval, lost by 7 wickets	34, 7
2nd test v Eng in Eng, 1978 at Nottingham, lost by an innings and 119 runs	5, 7 c1
3rd test v Eng in Eng, 1978 at Lord's, lost by 7 wickets	68, 14
1st test v Pak in NZ, 1978/79 at Christchurch, lost by 128 runs	16, 6 c1
2nd test v Pak in NZ, 1978/79 at Napier, drawn	40
3rd test v Pak in NZ, 1978/79 at Auckland, drawn	3, 71
2nd test v Aus in Aus, 1980/81 at Perth, lost by 8 wickets	43, 18

16. Geoffrey Philip Howarth
Right-hand bat, right-arm off break bowler

BORN:	29 March 1951, Auckland
TEAMS:	Surrey, Auckland, Northern Districts, New Zealand
TEST DEBUT:	New Zealand v England at Auckland, 1st test, 1974/75
LAST TEST:	New Zealand v West Indies at Kingston, 4th test, 1984/85
ODI DEBUT:	New Zealand v England at Dunedin, 1st ODI, 1974/75
LAST ODI:	New Zealand v West Indies at Bridgetown, 5th ODI, 1984/85

Test career, 1974/75–1984/85 (23 y 328 d to 34 y 40 d)

BATTING AND FIELDING

MAT	I	NO	R	HS	AVE	100	50	CT	ST
47	83	5	2531	147	32.44	6	11	29	0

BOWLING

BALLS	M	R	W	AVE	BBI	5W	10W	SR	ECON
614	20	271	3	90.33	1-13	0	0	204.6	2.64

One-day internationals, 1974/75–1984/85

BATTING AND FIELDING

MAT	I	NO	R	HS	AVE	SR	100	50	CT	ST
70	65	5	1384	76	23.06	59.73	0	6	16	0

BOWLING

BALLS	M	R	W	AVE	BBI	4W	5W	SR	ECON
15	0	68	3	22.66	1-4	0	0	30.0	4.53

First-class career, 1971–1985/86

BATTING AND FIELDING

MAT	I	NO	R	HS	AVE	100	50	CT	ST
338	584	42	17,294	183	31.90	32	-	229	0

BOWLING

R	W	AVE	BBI	5W	10W
3593	112	32.08	5-32	1	0

List A limited overs, 1971–1985/86

BATTING AND FIELDING

MAT	I	NO	R	HS	AVE	100	50	CT	ST
279	263	12	6016	122	23.96	2	29	76	0

BOWLING

BALLS	R	W	AVE	BBI	4W	5W	SR	ECON
682	487	24	20.29	4-16	1	0	28.4	4.28

Tests as captain

MAT	R	HS	BAT AV.	100	50	W	BBI	BOWL AV.	5W	CT	ST
30	1491	147	30.42	2	8	1	1/32	104.00	0	21	0

1st test v WI in NZ, 1979/80 at Dunedin, won by 1 wicket	33, 11 c1
2nd test v WI in NZ, 1979/80 at Christchurch, drawn	147, 1/32 c1
3rd test v WI in NZ, 1979/80 at Auckland, drawn	47, 1 c1
1st test v Aus in Aus, 1980/81 at Brisbane, lost by 10 wickets	65, 4
3rd test v Aus in Aus, 1980/81 at Melbourne, drawn	65, 20
1st test v Ind in NZ, 1980/81 at Wellington, won by 62 runs	137*, 7
2nd test v Ind in NZ, 1980/81 at Christchurch, drawn	26, 0/2 c1
3rd test v Ind in NZ, 1980/81 at Auckland, drawn	0, 2 c1
1st test v Aus in NZ, 1981/82 at Wellington, drawn	58*
2nd test v Aus in NZ, 1981/82 at Auckland, won by 5 wickets	56, 19 0/8, 0/4 c1
3rd test v Aus in NZ, 1981/82 at Christchurch, lost by 8 wickets	9, 41
1st test v SL in NZ, 1982/83 at Christchurch, won by an innings and 25 runs	0, c1
2nd test v SL in NZ, 1982/83 at Wellington, won by 6 wickets	36, 1
1st test v Eng in Eng, 1983 at the Oval, lost by 189 runs	4, 67 c2
2nd test v Eng in Eng, 1983 at Leeds, won by 5 wickets	13, 20 c2
3rd test v Eng in Eng, 1983 at Lord's, lost by 127 runs	25, 0
4th test v Eng in Eng, 1983 at Nottingham, lost by 165 runs	36, 24 c3
1st test v Eng in NZ, 1983/84 at Wellington, drawn	15, 34 c1
2nd test v Eng in NZ, 1983/84 at Christchurch, won by an innings and 132 runs	9, c2
3rd test v Eng in NZ, 1983/84 at Auckland, drawn	35, DNB
1st test v SL in SL, 1983/84 at Kandy, won by 165 runs	62, 60 c2
2nd test v SL in SL, 1983/84 at Colombo, drawn	24, 10
3rd test v SL in SL, 1983/84 at Colombo, won by an innings and 61 runs	7
1st test v Pak in NZ, 1984/85 at Wellington, drawn	33, 17
2nd test v Pak in NZ, 1984/85 at Auckland, won by an innings and 99 runs	13
3rd test v Pak in NZ, 1984/85 at Dunedin, won by 2 wickets	23, 17
1st test v WI in WI, 1984/85 at Port of Spain, drawn	45, 14 c1
2nd test v WI in WI, 1984/85 at Georgetown, drawn	4, c1
3rd test v WI in WI, 1984/85 at Bridgetown, lost by 10 wickets	1, 5
4th test v WI in WI, 1984/85 at Kingston, lost by 10 wickets	5, 84

17. Jeremy Vernon Coney
Right-hand bat, right-arm medium bowler

BORN:	21 June 1952, Wellington
TEAMS:	Wellington, New Zealand
TEST DEBUT:	New Zealand v Australia at Sydney, 2nd test, 1973/74
LAST TEST:	New Zealand v West Indies at Christchurch, 3rd test, 1986/87
ODI DEBUT:	New Zealand v Sri Lanka at Nottingham, World Cup, 1979
LAST ODI:	New Zealand v West Indies at Christchurch, 4th ODI, 1986/87

Test career, 1973/74–1986/87 (21 y 198 d to 34 y 267 d)

BATTING AND FIELDING

MAT	I	NO	R	HS	AVE	100	50	CT	ST
52	85	14	2668	174*	37.57	3	16	64	0

BOWLING

BALLS	M	R	W	AVE	BBI	5W	10W	SR	ECON
2835	135	966	27	35.77	3-28	0	0	105.0	2.04

One-day internationals, 1979–1986/87

BATTING AND FIELDING

MAT	I	NO	R	HS	AVE	SR	100	50	CT	ST
88	80	19	1874	66*	30.72	64.95	0	8	40	0

BOWLING

O	M	R	W	AVE	BBI	4W	5W	SR	ECON
488.3	24	2039	54	37.75	4-46	1	0	54.2	4.17

First-class career, 1971/72–1986/87

BATTING AND FIELDING

MAT	I	NO	R	HS	AVE	100	50	CT	ST
165	272	48	7872	174*	35.14	8	47	192	0

BOWLING

R	W	AVE	BBI	5W	10W
3460	111	31.17	6-17	1	0

List A limited overs, 1972/73–1986/87

BATTING AND FIELDING

MAT	I	NO	R	HS	AVE	100	50	CT	ST
127	116	28	2763	73*	31.39	0	14	57	0

BOWLING

BALLS	R	W	AVE	BBI	4W	5W	SR	ECON
3881	2717	71	38.26	4-46	1	0	54.6	4.20

Tests as captain

MAT	R	HS	BAT AV.	100	50	W	BBI	BOWL AV.	5W	CT	ST
15	634	101*	30.19	1	3	6	3/47	47.66	0	22	0

Statistics

1st test v Pak in Pak, 1984/85 at Lahore, lost by 6 wickets	7, 26, 0/4 c2
2nd test v Pak in Pak, 1984/85 at Hyderabad, lost by 7 wickets	6, 5 0/8, 0/9 c2
3rd test v Pak in Pak, 1984/85 at Karachi, drawn	16, 0/5
1st test v Aus in Aus, 1985/86 at Brisbane, won by an innings and 41 runs	22 0/8, 0/3 c3
2nd test v Aus in Aus, 1985/86 at Sydney, lost by 4 wickets	8, 7 0/1, 0/15
3rd test v Aus in Aus, 1985/86 at Perth, won by 6 wickets	19, 16 2/43, 1/9
1st test v Aus in NZ, 1985/86 at Wellington, drawn	101* 3/47
2nd test v Aus in NZ, 1985/86 at Christchurch, drawn	98 0/28, 0/10 c3
3rd test v Aus in NZ, 1985/86 at Auckland, won by 8 wickets	93 0/18 c3
1st test v Eng in Eng, 1986 at Lord's, drawn	51 0/12
2nd test v Eng in Eng, 1986 at Nottingham, won by 8 wickets	24, 20* 0/18
3rd test v Eng in Eng, 1986 at the Oval, drawn	38 0/18
1st test v WI in NZ, 1986/87 at Wellington, drawn	3, 4 0/8
2nd test v WI in NZ, 1986/87 at Auckland, won by 10 wickets	15, 17 0/22
3rd test v WI in NZ, 1986/87 at Christchurch, won by 5 wickets	36, 2 c3

18. Jeffrey John Crowe
Right-hand bat, right-arm bowler

BORN:	14 September 1958, Auckland
TEAMS:	South Australia, Auckland, New Zealand
TEST DEBUT:	New Zealand v Sri Lanka at Christchurch, 1st test, 1982/83
LAST TEST:	New Zealand v Australia at Wellington, only test, 1989/90
ODI DEBUT:	New Zealand v Australia at Melbourne, World Series Cup, 1982/83
LAST ODI:	New Zealand v Australia at Auckland, Triangular Series, 1989/90

Test career, 1982/83–1989/90 (24 y 171 d to 31 y 186 d)
BATTING AND FIELDING

MAT	I	NO	R	HS	AVE	100	50	CT	ST
39	65	4	1601	128	26.24	3	6	41	0

BOWLING

O	M	R	W	AVE	BBI	5w	10w	SR	ECON
3	1	9	0	-	-	0	0	-	3.00

One-day internationals, 1982/83–1989/90
BATTING AND FIELDING

MAT	I	NO	R	HS	AVE	SR	100	50	CT	ST
75	71	12	1518	88*	25.72	61.80	0	7	28	0

BOWLING

O	M	R	W	AVE	BBI	4w	5w	SR	ECON
1	0	1	0	-	-	0	0	-	1.00

First-class career, 1977/78–1991/92
BATTING AND FIELDING

MAT	I	NO	R	HS	AVE	100	50	CT	ST
180	304	34	10,233	159	37.90	22	56	199	0

BOWLING

R	W	AVE	BBI	5w	10w
55	1	55.00	1-10	0	0

List A limited overs, 1979/80–1991/92
BATTING AND FIELDING

MAT	I	NO	R	HS	AVE	100	50	CT	ST
139	133	20	2974	130*	26.31	1	14	56	0

BOWLING

O	R	W	AVE	BBI	4w	5w	SR	ECON
1	1	0	-	-	0	0	-	1.00

Tests as captain

MAT	R	HS	BAT AV.	100	50	W	BBI	BOWL AV.	5w	CT	ST
6	238	120*	23.80	1	0	-	-	-	-	3	-

1st test v SL in SL, 1986/87 at Colombo, drawn	120*
1st test v Aus in Aus, 1987/88 at Brisbane, lost by 9 wickets	16, 12
2nd test v Aus in Aus, 1987/88 at Adelaide, drawn	0, 19
3rd test v Aus in Aus, 1987/88 at Melbourne, drawn	6, 25 c1
1st test v Eng in NZ, 1987/88 at Christchurch, drawn	28, 0 c1
2nd test v Eng in NZ, 1987/88 at Auckland, drawn	11, 1 c1

19. John Geoffrey Wright
Left-hand bat, right-arm medium bowler

BORN:	5 July 1954, Darfield, Canterbury
TEAMS:	Northern Districts, Derbyshire, Canterbury, Auckland, New Zealand
TEST DEBUT:	New Zealand v England at Wellington, 1st test, 1977/78
LAST TEST:	New Zealand v Australia at Auckland, 3rd test, 1992/93
ODI DEBUT:	New Zealand v England at Scarborough, Prudential Trophy, 1978
LAST ODI:	New Zealand v Sri Lanka at Colombo, 2nd ODI, 1992/93

Test career, 1977/78–1992/93 (23 y 220 d to 38 y 254 d)

BATTING AND FIELDING

MAT	I	NO	R	HS	AVE	100	50	CT	ST
82	148	7	5334	185	37.82	12	23	38	0

BOWLING

O	M	R	W	AVE	BBI	5W	10W	SR	ECON
5	1	5	0	-	-	0	0	-	1.00

One-day internationals, 1978–1992/93

BATTING AND FIELDING

MAT	I	NO	R	HS	AVE	SR	100	50	CT	ST
149	148	1	3891	101	26.46	57.35	1	24	51	0

BOWLING

O	M	R	W	AVE	BBI	4W	5W	SR	ECON
4	1	8	0	-	-	0	0	-	2.00

First-class career, 1975/76–1992/93

BATTING AND FIELDING

MAT	I	NO	R	HS	AVE	100	50	CT	ST
366	636	44	25,073	192	42.35	59	126	192	0

BOWLING

R	W	AVE	BBI	5W	10W
339	2	169.50	1-4	0	0

List A limited overs, 1976/77–1992/93

BATTING AND FIELDING

MAT	I	NO	R	HS	AVE	100	50	CT	ST
348	344	13	10,229	108	30.90	6	68	107	0

BOWLING

BALLS	R	W	AVE	BBI	4W	5W	SR	ECON
42	18	1	18.00	1-8	0	0	42.0	2.57

Tests as captain

MAT	R	HS	BAT AV.	100	50	W	BBI	BOWL AV.	5W	CT	ST
14	1070	185	48.63	3	4	-	-	-	-	8	0

3rd test v Eng in NZ, 1987/88 at Wellington, drawn	36
1st test v Ind in Ind, 1988/89 at Bangalore, lost by 172 runs	22, 58
2nd test v Ind in Ind, 1988/89 at Mumbai, won by 136 runs	33, 36 c1
3rd test v Ind in Ind, 1988/89 at Hyderabad, lost by 10 wickets	17, 62 c1
1st test v Pak in NZ, 1988/89 at Dunedin, abandoned without a ball being bowled	
2nd test v Pak in NZ, 1988/89 at Wellington, drawn	7, 19
3rd test v Pak in NZ, 1988/89 at Auckland, drawn	2, 36
Only test v Aus in Aus, 1989/90 at Perth, drawn	34, 3 c3
1st test v Ind in NZ, 1989/90 at Christchurch, won by 10 wickets	185
2nd test v Ind in NZ, 1989/90 at Napier, drawn	113* c1
3rd test v Ind in NZ, 1989/90 at Auckland, drawn	3, 74
Only test v Aus in NZ, 1989/90 at Wellington, won by 9 wickets	36, 117* c 2
1st test v Eng in Eng, 1990 at Nottingham, drawn	8, 1
2nd test v Eng in Eng, 1990 at Lord's, drawn	98
3rd test v Eng in Eng, 1990 at Birmingham, lost by 114 runs	24, 46

20. Martin David Crowe
Right-hand bat, right-arm medium bowler

BORN:	22 September 1962, Henderson, Auckland
TEAMS:	Auckland, Central Districts, Somerset, Wellington, New Zealand
TEST DEBUT:	New Zealand v Australia at Wellington, 1st test, 1981
LAST TEST:	New Zealand v India at Cuttack, 3rd test, 1995/96
ODI DEBUT:	New Zealand v Australia at Auckland, 1st ODI, 1981/82
LAST ODI:	New Zealand v India at Nagpur, 5th ODI, 1995/96

Test career 1981/82–1995/96 (19 y 157 d to 33 y 51 d)

BATTING AND FIELDING

MAT	I	NO	R	HS	AVE	100	50	CT	ST
77	131	11	5444	299	45.36	17	18	71	0

BOWLING

O	M	R	W	AVE	BBI	5W	10W	SR	ECON
229.3	52	676	14	48.28	2-25	0	0	98.3	2.94

One-day internationals, 1981/82–1995/96

BATTING AND FIELDING

MAT	I	NO	R	HS	AVE	SR	100	50	CT	ST
143	140	18	4704	107*	38.55	72.62	4	34	66	0

BOWLING

O	M	R	W	AVE	BBI	4W	5W	SR	ECON
216	21	954	29	32.89	2-9	0	0	44.6	4.41

First-class career, 1979/80–1995/96

BATTING AND FIELDING

MAT	I	NO	R	HS	AVE	100	50	CT	ST
247	412	62	19,608	299	56.02	71	80	226	0

BOWLING

R	W	AVE	BBI	5W	10W
4010	119	33.69	5-18	4	0

List A limited overs, 1979/80–1995/96

BATTING AND FIELDING

MAT	I	NO	R	HS	AVE	100	50	CT	ST
260	255	27	8728	155*	38.28	11	59	115	0

BOWLING

O	R	W	AVE	BBI	4W	5W	SR	ECON
656.4	2839	97	29.26	4-24	2	0	40.6	4.32

Tests as captain

MAT	R	HS	BAT AV.	100	50	W	BBI	BOWL AV.	5W	CT	ST
16	1466	299	54.29	4	4	1	1/22	69.00	0	13	0

Test	Score
1st test v Pak in Pak, 1990/91 at Karachi, lost by an innings and 43 runs	7, 68* 0/22 c2
2nd test v Pak in Pak, 1990/91 at Lahore, lost by 9 wickets	20, 108* c2
3rd test v Pak in Pak, 1990/91 at Faisalabad, Pak won by 65 runs	31, 10, DNB 1/22 c3
1st test v SL in NZ, 1990/91 at Wellington, drawn	30, 299 c1
2nd test v SL in NZ, 1990/91 at Hamilton, drawn	36
1st test v Eng in NZ, 1991/92 at Christchurch, lost by an innings and 4 runs	20, 48 c1
2nd test v Eng in NZ, 1991/92 at Auckland, lost by 168 runs	45, 56 c1
3rd test v Eng in NZ, 1991/92 at Wellington, drawn	30, 13*
1st test v Zim in Zim, 1992/93 at Bulawayo, drawn	42, 6, DNB 0/15 c1
2nd test v Zim in Zim, 1992/93 at Harare, won by 177 runs	140, 61
1st test v SL in SL, 1992/93 at Moratuwa, drawn	19, 11 0/10
2nd test v SL in SL, 1992/93 at Colombo, lost by nine wickets	0, 107 c1
1st test v Aus in NZ, 1992/93 at Christchurch, lost by an innings and 60 runs	15, 14 c1
2nd test v Aus in NZ, 1992/93 at Wellington, drawn	98, 3
3rd test v Aus in NZ, 1992/93 at Auckland, won by 5 wickets	31, 25
1st test v Aus in Aus, 1993/94 at Perth, drawn	42, 31*

21. Ian David Stockley Smith
Right-hand bat, wicket-keeper

BORN:	28 February 1957, Nelson
TEAMS:	Central Districts, Auckland, New Zealand
TEST DEBUT:	New Zealand v Australia at Brisbane, 1st test, 1980/81
LAST TEST:	New Zealand v England at Wellington, 3rd test, 1991/92
ODI DEBUT:	New Zealand v Australia at Sydney, World Series Cup, 1980/81
LAST ODI:	New Zealand v Pakistan at Auckland, World Cup, 1991/92

Test career, 1980/81–1991/92 (23 y 274 d to 34 y 347 d)

BATTING AND FIELDING

MAT	I	NO	R	HS	AVE	100	50	CT	ST
63	88	17	1815	173	25.56	2	6	168	8

BOWLING

O	M	R	W	AVE	BBI	5W	10W	SR	ECON
3	1	5	0	-	-	0	0	-	1.66

One-day internationals, 1980/81–1991/92

BATTING AND FIELDING

MAT	I	NO	R	HS	AVE	SR	100	50	CT	ST
98	77	16	1055	62*	17.29	99.43	0	3	81	5

BOWLING

O	M	R	W	AVE	BBI	4W	5W	SR	ECON
-	-	-	-	-	-	-	-	-	-

First-class career, 1977/78–1991/92

BATTING AND FIELDING

MAT	I	NO	R	HS	AVE	100	50	CT	ST
178	250	42	5570	173	26.77	6	24	417	36

BOWLING

R	W	AVE	BBI	5W	10W
38	0	-	-	0	0

List A limited overs, 1979/80–1991/92

BATTING AND FIELDING

MAT	I	NO	R	HS	AVE	100	50	CT	ST
153	127	22	1875	70	17.85	0	5	137	12

BOWLING

O	R	W	AVE	BBI	4W	5W	SR	ECON
8.4	23	2	11.50	2-11	0	0	26.0	2.65

Statistics

Tests as captain

Mat	R	HS	Bat av.	100	50	W	BBI	Bowl av.	5W	Ct	St
1	3	3	3.00	0	0	-	-	-	-	6	0

3rd test v SL in NZ, 1990/91 at Auckland, drawn   3 c6

22. Kenneth Robert Rutherford
Right-hand bat, right-arm medium bowler

BORN:	26 October 1965, Dunedin
TEAMS:	Otago, Transvaal, Gauteng, New Zealand
TEST DEBUT:	New Zealand v West Indies at Port of Spain, 1st test, 1984/85
LAST TEST:	New Zealand v Sri Lanka at Dunedin, 2nd test, 1994/95
ODI DEBUT:	New Zealand v West Indies at Port of Spain, 2nd ODI, 1984/85
LAST ODI:	New Zealand v Sri Lanka at Auckland, 3rd ODI, 1994/95

Test career, 1984/85–1994/95 (19 y 154 d to 29 y 147 d)

BATTING AND FIELDING

MAT	I	NO	R	HS	AVE	100	50	CT	ST
56	99	8	2465	107*	27.08	3	18	32	0

BOWLING

O	M	R	W	AVE	BBI	5W	10W	SR	ECON
42.4	3	161	1	161.00	1-38	0	0	256.0	3.77

One-day internationals, 1984/85–1994/95

BATTING AND FIELDING

MAT	I	NO	R	HS	AVE	SR	100	50	CT	ST
121	115	9	3143	108	29.65	64.30	2	18	41	0

BOWLING

O	M	R	W	AVE	BBI	4W	5W	SR	ECON
64.5	0	323	10	32.30	2-39	0	0	38.9	4.98

First-class career, 1982/83–1999/2000

BATTING AND FIELDING

MAT	I	NO	R	HS	AVE	100	50	CT	ST
220	383	33	13,974	317	39.92	35	67	180	0

BOWLING

R	W	AVE	BBI	5W	10W
1012	22	46.00	5-72	1	0

List A limited overs, 1982/83–1999/2000

BATTING AND FIELDING

MAT	I	NO	R	HS	AVE	100	50	CT	ST
248	238	20	6888	130*	31.59	6	44	91	0

BOWLING

O	R	W	AVE	BBI	4W	5W	SR	ECON
143.4	703	21	33.47	3-26	0	0	41.0	4.89

Tests as captain

MAT	R	HS	BAT AV.	100	50	W	BBI	BOWL AV.	5W	CT	ST
18	903	86	27.36	0	8	-	-	-	-	6	0

Only test v Pak in NZ, 1992/93 at Hamilton, lost by 33 runs — 14, 9, c3
2nd test v Aus in Aus, 1993/94 at Hobart, lost by an innings and 122 runs — 17, 55
3rd test v Aus in Aus, 1993/94 at Brisbane, lost by an innings and 96 runs — 36, 86
1st test v Pak in NZ, 1993/94 at Auckland, lost by 5 wickets — 14, 18
2nd test v Pak in NZ, 1993/94 at Wellington, lost by an innings and 12 runs — 7, 63
3rd test v Pak in NZ, 1993/94 at Christchurch, won by 5 wickets — 7, 13
Only test v Ind in NZ, 1993/94 at Hamilton, drawn — 63, 59
1st test v Eng in Eng, 1994 at Nottingham, lost by an innings and 90 runs — 25, 14
2nd test v Eng in Eng, 1994 at Lord's, drawn — 37, 0
3rd test v Eng in Eng, 1994 at Manchester, drawn — 7, 13
1st test v SA in SA, 1994/95 at Johannesburg, won by 137 runs — 68, 0
2nd test v SA in SA, 1994/95 at Durban, lost by 8 wkts — 0, 6
3rd test v SA in SA, 1994/95 at Cape Town, lost by 7 wkts — 56, 26 c1
1st test v WI in NZ, 1994/95 at Christchurch, drawn — 11, 16* not out
2nd test v WI in NZ, 1994/95 at Wellington, lost by an innings and 322 runs — 22, 5
Only test v SA in NZ, 1994/95 at Auckland, lost by 93 runs — 28, 56 c1
1st test v SL in NZ, 1994/95 at Napier, lost by 241 runs — 32, 20 c1
2nd test v SL in NZ, 1994/95 at Dunedin, drawn — KR — abs. hurt.

23. Lee Kenneth Germon
Right-hand bat, wicket-keeper

BORN:	4 November 1968, Christchurch
TEAMS:	Canterbury, Otago, New Zealand
TEST DEBUT:	New Zealand v India at Bangalore, 1st test, 1995/96
LATEST TEST:	New Zealand v England at Wellington, 2nd test, 1996/97
ODI DEBUT:	New Zealand v Sri Lanka at Bloemfontein, Mandela Trophy, 1994/95
LATEST ODI:	New Zealand v England at Wellington, 5th ODI, 1996/97

Test career, 1995/96–1996/97 (26 y 348 d to 28 y 98 d)

BATTING AND FIELDING

MAT	I	NO	R	HS	AVE	100	50	CT	ST
12	21	3	382	55	21.22	0	1	27	2

BOWLING

O	M	R	W	AVE	BBI	5W	10W	SR	ECON
-	-	-	-	-	-	-	-	-	-

One-day internationals, 1994/95–1996/97

BATTING AND FIELDING

MAT	I	NO	R	HS	AVE	SR	100	50	CT	ST
37	31	5	519	89	19.96	66.28	0	3	21	9

BOWLING

O	M	R	W	AVE	BBI	4W	5W	SR	ECON
-	-	-	-	-	-	-	-	-	-

First-class career, 1987/88–2001/02

BATTING AND FIELDING

MAT	I	NO	R	HS	AVE	100	50	CT	ST
103	142	35	3123	160*	29.18	4	10	258	26

BOWLING

R	W	AVE	BBI	5W	10W
12	1	12.00	1-12	0	0

List A limited overs, 1987/88–2001/02

BATTING AND FIELDING

MAT	I	NO	R	HS	AVE	100	50	CT	ST
136	105	23	1586	89	19.34	0	7	119	28

BOWLING

O	R	W	AVE	BBI	4W	5W	SR	ECON
1	0	8	-	-	0	0	-	8.00

Tests as captain

MAT	R	HS	BAT AV.	100	50	W	BBI	BOWL AV.	5W	CT	ST
12	382	55	21.22	0	1	-	-	-	-	27	2

1st test v Ind in Ind, 1995/96 at Bangalore, lost by 8 wickets	48, 41 c1
2nd test v Ind in Ind, 1995/96 at Chennai, drawn	DNB
3rd test v Ind in Ind, 1995/96 at Cuttack, drawn	2 c1 st1 (no second inns)
Only test v Pak in NZ, 1995/96 at Christchurch, lost by 161 runs	21,12 c6
1st test v Zim in NZ, 1995/96 at Hamilton, drawn	24, 22* c5
2nd test v Zim in NZ, 1995/96 at Auckland, drawn	25, 1* c3
1st test v WI in WI, 1995/96 at Bridgetown, lost by 10 wickets	0, 23 c3
2nd test v WI in WI, 1995/96 at St John's, drawn	49, 0* c2
1st test v Pak in Pak, 1996/97 at Lahore, won by 44 runs	0, 11 c3
2nd test v Pak in Pak, 1996/97 at Rawalpindi, lost by an innings and 13 runs	55, 0
1st test v Eng in NZ, 1996/97 at Auckland, drawn	14, 13 c2
2nd test v Eng in NZ, 1996/97 at Wellington, lost by an innings and 68 runs	10, 11 c1 st1

24. Stephen Paul Fleming
Left-hand bat, right-arm medium bowler

BORN:	1 April 1973, Christchurch
TEAMS:	Canterbury, Wellington, Middlesex, New Zealand
TEST DEBUT:	New Zealand v India at Hamilton, only test, 1993/94
LATEST TEST:	New Zealand v West Indies at St Georges, 2nd Test, 2002
ODI DEBUT:	New Zealand v India at Napier, 1st ODI, 1993/94
LATEST ODI:	New Zealand v West Indies at Kingston, 5th ODI, 2002

Test career, 1993/94–2002 (Debut 20 y 352 d)

BATTING AND FIELDING

MAT	I	NO	R	HS	AVE	100	50	CT	ST
71	123	7	4217	174*	36.35	4	33	107	0

BOWLING

O	M	R	W	AVE	BBI	5W	10W	SR	ECON
-	-	-	-	-	-	-	-	-	-

One-day internationals, 1993/94–2002

BATTING AND FIELDING

MAT	I	NO	R	HS	AVE	SR	100	50	CT	ST
180	173	15	4881	116*	30.89	69.54	3	32	81	0

BOWLING

O	M	R	W	AVE	BBI	4W	5W	SR	ECON
4.5	0	28	1	28.00	1-8	0	0	29.0	5.79

First-class career, 1991/92–2002

BATTING AND FIELDING

MAT	I	NO	R	HS	AVE	100	50	CT	ST
151	250	22	9438	174*	41.39	19	59	197	0

BOWLING

R	W	AVE	BBI	5W	10W
129	0	-	-	0	0

List A limited overs, 1992/93–2002

BATTING AND FIELDING

MAT	I	NO	R	HS	AVE	100	50	CT	ST
280	265	27	7777	120*	32.67	7	52	130	0

BOWLING

O	R	W	AVE	BBI	4W	5W	SR	ECON
5.5	31	2	15.50	1-3	0	0	17.5	5.31

Tests as captain

MAT	R	HS	BAT AV.	100	50	W	BBI	BOWL AV.	5W	CT	ST
47	2753	174*	36.22	3	23	-	-	-	-	80	-

3rd test v Eng in NZ, 1996/97 at Christchurch, lost by 4 wickets	62, 11 c2
1st test v SL in NZ, 1996/97 at Dunedin, won by an innings and 36 runs	51 c1
2nd test v SL in NZ, 1996/97 at Hamilton, won by 120 runs	2, 59
1st test v Zim in Zim, 1997/98 at Harare, drawn	52, 27 c7
2nd test v Zim in Zim, 1997/98 at Bulawayo, drawn	27, 75 c3
1st test v Aus in Aus, 1997/98 at Brisbane, lost by 186 runs	91, 0 c6
2nd test v Aus in Aus, 1997/98 at Perth, lost by an innings and 70 runs	10, 4 c3
3rd test v Aus in Aus, 1997/98 at Hobart, drawn	0, 0
1st test v Zim in NZ, 1997/98 at Wellington, won by 10 wickets	36 c1
2nd test v Zim in NZ, 1997/98 at Auckland, won by an innings and 13 runs	19 c3
1st test v SL in SL, 1997/98 at Colombo, won by 167 runs	78, 174*
2nd test v SL in SL, 1997/98 at Galle, lost by an innings and 16 runs	14, 10
3rd test v SL in SL, 1997/98 at Colombo, lost by 164 runs	78, 3 c2
1st test v Ind in NZ, 1998/99 at Dunedin, abandoned without a ball being bowled	
2nd test v Ind in NZ, 1998/99 at Wellington, won by 4 wickets	42, 17 c5
3rd test v Ind in NZ, 1998/99 at Hamilton, drawn	0, 18 c3
1st test v Eng in Eng, 1999 at Birmingham, lost by 7 wickets	27, 25 c1
2nd test v Eng in Eng, 1999 at Lord's, won by 9 wickets	1, 5* c3
3rd test v Eng in Eng, 1999 at Manchester, drawn	38, c2
4th test v Eng in Eng, 1999 at the Oval, won by 83 runs	66*, 4 c4
1st test v Ind in Ind, 1999/2000 at Chandigarh, drawn	43, 77 c1
2nd test v Ind in Ind, 1999/2000 at Kanpur, lost by 8 wickets	2, 31 c2
3rd test v Ind in Ind, 1999/2000 at Ahmedabad, drawn	48, 64*
1st test v WI in NZ, 1999/2000 at Hamilton, won by 9 wickets	66 c1
2nd test v WI in NZ, 1999/2000 at Wellington, won by an innings and 105 runs	67 c1
1st test v Aus in NZ, 1999/2000 at Auckland, lost by 62 runs	21, 8 c2
2nd test v Aus in NZ, 1999/2000 at Wellington, lost by 6 wickets	16, 60 c1
3rd test v Aus in NZ, 1999/2000 at Hamilton, lost by 6 wickets	30, 2
1st test v Zim in Zim, 2000/01 at Bulawayo, won by 7 wickets	11, 12
2nd test v Zim in Zim, 2000/01 at Harare, won by 7 wickets	9 c2
1st test v SA in SA, 2000/01 at Bloemfontein, lost by 5 wickets	57, 99
2nd test v SA in SA, 2000/01 at Port Elizabeth, lost by 7 wickets	14, 18
3rd test v SA in SA, 2000/01 at Johannesburg, drawn	14
Only test v Zim in NZ, 2000/01 at Wellington, drawn	22, 55
1st test v Pak in NZ, 2000/01 at Auckland, lost by 299 runs	86, 5 c2
2nd test v Pak in NZ, 2000/01 at Christchurch, drawn	32
3rd test v Pak in NZ, 2000/01 at Hamilton, won by an innings and 185 runs	51*
1st test v Aus in Aus, 2001/02 at Brisbane, drawn	0, 57
2nd test v Aus in Aus, 2001/02 at Hobart, drawn	71
3rd test v Aus in Aus, 2001/02 at Perth, drawn	105, 4 c1
1st test v Bang in NZ, 2001/02 at Hamilton, won by an innings and 52 runs	4, c1
2nd test v Bang in NZ, 2001/02 at Wellington, won by an innings and 74 runs	61, c1
1st test v Eng in NZ, 2001/02 at Christchurch, lost by 98 runs	12, 48 c1
2nd test v Eng in NZ, 2001/02 at Wellington, drawn	3, 11 c1
3rd test v Eng in NZ, 2001/02 at Auckland, won by 78 runs	1, 1 c2
1st test v Pak in Pak, 2002 at Lahore, lost by an innings and 324 runs	2, 66 c2
1st test v WI in WI, 2002 at Bridgetown, won by 204 runs	130, 34 c3
2nd test v WI in WI, 2002 at St Georges, drawn	6, 5 c1

25. Dion Joseph Nash
Right-hand bat, right-arm fast medium bowler

BORN:	20 November 1971, Auckland
TEAMS:	Auckland, Northern Districts, Otago, Middlesex, New Zealand
TEST DEBUT:	New Zealand v Zimbabwe at Harare, 2nd test, 1992/93
LAST TEST:	New Zealand v Australia at Brisbane, 1st test, 2001/02
ODI DEBUT:	New Zealand v Zimbabwe at Bulawayo, 1st ODI, 1992/93
LAST ODI:	New Zealand v South Africa at Melbourne, VB Series, 2001/02

Test career, 1992/93–2001/02 (20 y 353 d to 29 y 357 d)

BATTING AND FIELDING

MAT	I	NO	R	HS	AVE	100	50	CT	ST
32	45	14	729	89*	23.51	0	4	13	0

BOWLING

O	M	R	W	AVE	BBI	5W	10W	SR	ECON
1032.4	312	2649	93	28.48	6-27	3	1	66.6	2.56

One-day internationals, 1992/93–2001/02

BATTING AND FIELDING

MAT	I	NO	R	HS	AVE	SR	100	50	CT	ST
81	53	13	624	42	15.60	66.38	0	0	25	0

BOWLING

O	M	R	W	AVE	BBI	4W	5W	SR	ECON
569.2	37	2622	64	40.96	4-38	1	0	53.3	4.60

First-class career, 1990/91–2001/02

BATTING AND FIELDING

MAT	I	NO	R	HS	AVE	100	50	CT	ST
120	168	37	3555	135*	27.13	5	16	46	0

BOWLING

R	W	AVE	BBI	5W	10W
7165	255	28.09	7-39	10	1

List A limited overs, 1991/92–2001/02

BATTING AND FIELDING

MAT	I	NO	R	HS	AVE	100	50	CT	ST
162	119	23	2002	88	20.85	0	6	50	0

BOWLING

O	R	W	AVE	BBI	4W	5W	SR	ECON
1088.4	4683	143	32.74	5-44	2	1	45.6	4.30

Tests as captain

MAT	R	HS	BAT AV.	100	50	W	BBI	BOWL AV.	5W	CT	ST
3	44	27	11.00	0	0	2	2-76	109.50	0	1	0

Statistics

1st test v SA in NZ, 1998/99 at Auckland, drawn   1, 0/97
2nd test v SA in NZ, 1998/99 at Christchurch, drawn   14, 0/46
3rd test v SA in NZ, 1998/99 at Wellington, lost by 8 wickets   2, 27 2/76

BIBLIOGRAPHY

Bailey, P., P. Thorne and P. Wynne Thomas, *Who's Who of Cricketers*. Newnes, Rushden, UK, 1984.

Booth, P., *Bert Sutcliffe's Book for Boys*. Whitcombe and Tombs, Christchurch, 1961.

Brearley, M., *The Art of Captaincy*. Hodder and Stoughton, London, 1985.

Brittenden, R.T., *Great Days of New Zealand Cricket*. Reed, Wellington, 1958.

——, *New Zealand Cricketers*. Reed, Wellington, 1961.

——, *Red Leather, Silver Fern*. Reed, Wellington, 1965.

——, *Scoreboard 69*. Reed, Wellington, 1965.

——, *The Finest Years*. Reed, Wellington, 1977.

—— and R. Hadlee, *Hadlee*. Reed, Wellington, 1981.

—— and D. Cameron, *Test Series 82*. Reed, Wellington, 1982.

——, *Big Names in New Zealand Cricket*. Moa, Auckland, 1983.

Brookes, C., *English Cricket*. Weidenfield and Nicolson, London, 1978.

Cairns, L., *Give It a Heave*. Moa, Auckland, 1984.

Cameron, D., *Caribbean Crusade*. Hodder and Stoughton, Auckland, 1972.

——, *Memorable Moments in New Zealand Sport*. Moa, Auckland, 1979.

——, *Someone Had to Do It*. HarperSports, Auckland, 1998.

Canynge Caple, S., *England v New Zealand 1902–49*. Barcliff, Falmouth, 1949.

——, *The All Blacks at Cricket 1860–1958*. Littlebury and Co., Worcester, UK, 1958.

Carman, A.H., *New Zealand International Cricket 1894–1974*. Sporting Publications, Wellington, 1975.

Chappell, G., *The 100th Summer*. Garry Sparke, Toorak, Australia, 1977.

Coney, J., *Playing Mantis*. Moa, Auckland, 1986.

——, J. Parker and B. Waddle, *The Wonderful Days of Summer*. Moa Beckett, Auckland, 1993.

Cotter, G., *England versus New Zealand*. Crowood Press, Marlborough, UK, 1990.

Crowe, D. and A., *The Crowe Style*. Moa, Auckland, 1987.

Crowe, M., *Out on a Limb*. Reed, Auckland, 1995.

Devlin, P., *Victorious 80s*. Moa, Auckland, 1987.

Fane, F.F., *Cricket Centenary*. F.F. Fane, Napier, 1955.

Fleming, S. and N. Astle, *Cricketing Safari*. Hodder Moa Beckett, Auckland, 2001.

Gooch, G., *Captaincy*. Stanley Paul, London, 1992.

Greatbatch, M., *Boundary Hunter*. Hodder Moa Beckett, Auckland, 1996.

Hadlee, R., *At the Double*. Hutchinson, Auckland, 1985.

———, *Hadlee Hits Out*. Lansdowne Press, Auckland, 1989.

———, *Rhythm and Swing*. Moa, Auckland, 1989.

Hadlee, W., *Innings of a Lifetime*. David Bateman, Auckland, 1993.

Hammond, W., *Cricket: My Destiny*. Stanley Paul, London, 1946.

Hintz, O.S., *The New Zealanders in England*. J.M. Dent, London, 1931.

Howarth, G., *Stirred but Not Shaken*. Hodder Moa Beckett, Auckland, 1998.

Hutchins, G., *The Howarth Years*. John McIndoe, Dunedin, 1985.

Kynaston, D., *Archie's Last Stand*. Queen Anne Press, London, 1984.

Lawrence, E., *100 Somerset Cricket Greats*. Tempus, Stroud, UK, 2001.

Lemmon, D., *Percy Chapman, A Biography*. Queen Anne, London, 1985.

———, *The Crisis of Captaincy, Servant and Master in English Cricket*. Christopher Helm, London, 1988.

———, *Guinness Book of Test Captains*. Guinness, London, 1992.

McConnell, L. and I. Smith, *The Shell New Zealand Cricket Encyclopaedia*. Moa Beckett, Auckland, 1993.

Mitchell, A., *Cricket Companions*. Werner Laurie, London, 1950.

Morrison, D., *Mad As I Wanna Be*. Hodder Moa Beckett, Auckland, 1997.

Mosey, D., *Wisden Book of Captains on Tour*. Stanley Paul, London, 1990.

Neely, D., *Men in White*. Moa, Auckland, 1986.

Pollard, J., *Six and Out*. Reed, Sydney, 1964.

Pringle, C., *Save the Last Ball For Me*. Celebrity Books, Auckland, 1998.

Reese, D., *Was It All Cricket?* George Allen and Unwin, London, 1948.

Reese, T.W., *New Zealand Cricket 1841–1914*. Simpson and Williams, Christchurch, 1927.

Reid, J., *Sword of Willow*. Reed, Wellington, 1962.

———, *A Million Miles of Cricket*. Reed, Wellington, 1966.

Robinson, R., *On Top Down Under*. Cassell, Melbourne, 1975.

Roebuck, P., *From Sammy to Jimmy*. Partridge, London, 1985.

Romanos, J., *A Century of Great New Zealand Cricketers*. David Bateman, Auckland, 1993.

———, *Martin Crowe: Tormented Genius*. Hodder Moa Beckett, Auckland, 1995.

———, *Merv Wallace*. Joel, Wellington, 2000.

————, *John Reid*. Hodder Moa Beckett, Auckland, 2000.

Rutherford, Ken, *Ken Rutherford's Book of Cricket*. Daphne Brasell Associates Press, Wellington, 1992.

————, *A Hell of a Way to Make a Living*. Hodder Moa Beckett, Auckland, 1995.

Ryan, G., *When the Game Was Played By Decent Chaps*. Canterbury University Press, Christchurch, 1996.

Smith, I., *Just a Drummer in the Band*. Moa, Auckland, 1991.

Smith, N., *Kiwis Declare*. Random House New Zealand, Auckland, 1994.

Sutcliffe, B., *Between Overs*. Whitcombe and Tombs, Christchurch, 1963.

Thomson, A.A., *The Great Captains*. Stanley Paul, London, 1965.

Turnbull, M. and M. Allom, *The Book of the Two Maurices*. E. Allom and Co., London, 1930.

NEW ZEALAND TEST CRICKET CAPTAINS

Index

NEW ZEALAND TEST CRICKET CAPTAINS

NOTES